Daisy's Diaries

By Graham Ham

Table of Contents

Prologue

1. The Start of an Obsession
2. The Landmark Challenge – and into the Fens
3. Back to the Drawing Board
4. Diversion to Le Mans
5. Practising on Rabbits
6. Heading West
7. Fire in the Shires!
8. Northern Landmarks and Punctured in Durham
9. Mountains, Rain and Perilous Descents!
10. The World Strikes Back!
11. Wales, Sheep and More Trouble with Landmarks
12. The Final Frontier

Epilogue

Photographs.

Prologue

The air is heavy with neglect. Not the deliberate, uncaring neglect that comes from laziness, but the aura of neglect that radiates from any object that has endured years of inactivity. Peering into the darkness, I can make out the forlorn shape of a once proud but now long forgotten machine, wiling away the time under the ever settling dust. It's bright edges have become dull and lifeless, once slick oil has turned to thick unforgiving toffee, shiny surfaces, once so proudly displayed, fade slowly under the oppressive carpet of grime and time….. which has passed slowly for nearly a decade.

This could be any half forgotten garage or shed in the country, but it happens to be two hundred yards from my house and this small dark corner of the world is now flooded, once again, with light. The full sad picture, suddenly exposed, can be seen clearly. But a decade of spider webs and grime cannot hide the lines of the thoroughbred that has rested here, patiently, awaiting a new dawn……

A new owner…..

A new lease of life!

But I digress. This moment is a year away yet, and although it is in many ways the real start of the story, I need to fill in a few of the events that lead up to it. Set the scene so to speak, as there's a story to be told, a story that continues and with luck and good health, it will continue long into the future.

This book is not just about saving an old motorcycle from oblivion, its resurrection, or even its subsequent travels. It's far more than that. It's a book about life challenges, life choices, bucking the trend, breaking the mould, learning some harsh lessons and proving some points.

In short, it's about actually living a little!

1. The Start of an Obsession

Amongst other things, but almost certainly above them, I am a motorcyclist. It has always been so, ever since I was old enough to ride on the back of my father's BSA. And from that moment I couldn't wait to 'come of age' so that I could buy my own machine. A string of ever bigger machines followed, as did a taste for adventure. It's in my blood despite life getting in the way, as life does. In fact, it's still, even now, a wrench to think back to the day, in the early 80's, when I parted company with Ruby, the 1955 Triumph Speed Twin that had seen me through courtship, early working life and the arrival of the first of our children. It was time for a car, and finances didn't allow for both, so Ruby had to go!

That bike was almost one of the family. After all, we'd done so much with her, over the years, and it's fair to say that both Diane, my wife, and I were more than a little emotional as we watched the new owner take her away after delivering the Renault 14 car which we had swapped her for. I made a solemn promise there and then - once we had got through the lean years, established our family and achieved financial stability – a Triumph Speed Twin would once again become part of our lives. It would be a 1955 model just like Ruby, and next time she would be for keeps!

And so life went on. I got over the misery of Ruby's parting, and as is the way of things, the promise was forgotten amidst the hustle and bustle that followed. Another child came; two careers were built and lost; I started a business, which after a hairy first few years, grew most satisfactorily; the enlarged family meant a bigger house, bigger car and the goldfish, dogs and hamsters soon followed. The kids grew, as did the business, the mortgage and the bills. Inevitably, the goalposts moved with them and there were always a hundred and one things to keep my mind occupied and my wallet straining.

And so nearly twenty years passed until, in March 2000, everything changed. I was becoming increasingly unhappy with life, which is strange in a way, because in theory I had everything a man can reasonably hope for. But there was a price to pay, and as each week passed I was less certain that I wanted to pay it. The business had pretty much taken over most of my waking hours, and a goodly portion of the others too. It had expanded steadily, re-branded, changed direction, re-structured and finally merged with another in Ireland. I found myself totally immersed in a company that I didn't recognise any more, employing people I didn't know, supplying customers I'd never heard of. I was constantly worrying about seemingly impossible cashflows, marketing strategies, employment laws and everything in between. I never seemed to be home, but when I was my mind seemed to always be churning over events elsewhere.

It all came to a head at that month's board meeting, during which I was asked to give judgements on strategies I couldn't get interested in, so therefore hadn't read, and budgets I didn't understand (and therefore hadn't read either) and I realised with a blinding flash that it was all destroying me. Clearly I couldn't continue – the fun had all gone from life and it was time for a change. I resigned the following morning. I would, I decided, become 'self employed', doing what I chose to do, when I chose to do it and hang the consequences. Friends and family reacted in various ways to this bombshell, but the prevailing opinion was clearly 'barking mad'. I didn't care. I was free and intended to make the most of things.

A busy few months saw me settled happily into this new life style. Working from home when I chose, getting out and about when it suited and generally not thinking about anything in advance. Things were looking up. I still had a vague lack of personal direction however and this gnawed away at me in the background. Then it happened. I was browsing the Internet, looking for hotels in Wiltshire in order to attend a family get together. There on the second page of search results was a link entitled 'For Sale, Wiltshire. 1955 Triumph…' The rest was not displayed, but something, somewhere, stirred in my mind '1955 Triumph' being the obvious trigger of a long forgotten promise. I followed the link and YES!… it's a Triumph Speed Twin!. It's for sale and it's a 1955 bike, just like Ruby. I couldn't believe my eyes as I looked at the photograph and remembered the trusty old machine. It was immediately apparent to me that I was going to own this one, today if at all possible, tomorrow at the very latest. No doubts at all. I quickly printed the advert off, and clutching my prize, I slunk down to the kitchen and casually slid the thing into Diane's vision. She looked at it, looked at me, looked back at it and raised an eyebrow in an expression, which said 'is there any point trying to dissuade you?'

That was all the spousal approval I needed, and I hurried back upstairs feeling an almost childish excitement building in me. I reached for the 'phone, all thoughts of the family get together forgotten, called the number, sweating with anticipation as I asked the dreadful question …"Have you still got the Speed Twin?" He did. "Is it still for sale?" It was. I heard a voice croak "I'll buy it!".The owner seemed confused at such an outright approval of the deal and began, or so it seemed, to try to persuade me that I might not want it. "It's not in good fettle you know, you'll be wanting to have a look first" and when this didn't dissuade me "It's not original, that's why it's this price. You'll have to do a lot to it" I patiently fended off his concerns - no, I didn't want to see it first, no I didn't care about the bits that weren't original, no I don't care about matching numbers, no I'm NOT a bloody tyre kicker! Eventually, arrangements and directions were agreed, and early next morning I climbed into the family Espace, freshly stripped of seats, for a long drive down to Wiltshire. I hadn't felt like this for years. I had hardly slept the previous night and now the two and a half hour drive seemed impossibly long to my anticipation fevered brain.

After what seemed an ice age I arrived at the correct address and it was immediately plain why the owner had pressed me on details – what I gazed at was in a sorry state indeed. She was tatty. She was oily. She was a 'bitsa' and the owner seemed keen to point out the wrong tank, forks and front wheel. She was quite simply the most wondrous sight to my otherwise sensible but temporarily crazed, rose tinted eyes. Nodding politely as the owner rattled off the catalogue of things wrong, I didn't actually listen to any of it. She was about to be mine, and that, really, was that! I hastily concluded the deal, handing over a pile of the green stuff to the bemused man (clearly he had expected to haggle), checked the log book (I'm not *totally* stupid) and in short order loaded my prize into the Espace via the scaffold plank I had brought with me in an unusual fit of sensible forward thinking and then left quickly, just in case matey changed his mind

On the way home, I christened her 'Winnie' for reasons which I cannot adequately explain, and therefore won't. All old machines should have a name, otherwise they won't know it's them that you're shouting at when they break down miles from home. Having named her, I thought I'd better get more important things sorted, and stopping in a lay-by, I 'phoned home and issued a request to my bemused other half. "Get onto the insurers", says I, "get me insured!, "here's the model and registration number – no, stuff the cost, just please make sure there's a cover note in force within two hours!" That done, I focused on the next task and peeled off into the nearest town, searching for leathers, helmet and gloves. It's a Harley dealership I find, which means it's expensive. I don't care, I'm on a mission. "Give me that jacket, that helmet, those gloves – thanks and bye bye!" I rapidly made my exit, clutching these new prizes and leaving a bemused salesman with a fistful of the folding stuff shaking his head. Setting off homewards once again, my mind turned over the other issues, MOT? Tax? Stuff it, those can wait - I simply have to, and will, ride her today!

Another age passed as I drove home. I kept glancing in the rear view mirror to catch a glimpse of Winnie in the back, and, grinning like an idiot, I wiled away the time trying to remember what Ruby had looked like and planning what I'll need to do in order to return Winnie to her true looks. Back at home I couldn't wait to unload her and have my first critical inspection. The family duly gathered in the drive with a mixture of amused expressions as I carefully reversed her down the plank. The looks on their faces as exhibit A, sad, tatty and oily, emerged were a picture - clearly dad had lost his senses and shouldn't be allowed to get excitable or handle sharp objects. Ignoring this I quickly donned my new riding apparel, and with a triumphant grin at the assembled doubters, took my first but long awaited ride. Down the road I went, wobbling slightly, until I reached the first bend and applied the brakes. The front forks, it transpired, were too short. This became evident as the front mudguard jammed against the frame, doing something disastrous to the gyroscopic balance, whilst locking the front wheel in an unnatural relationship to the back. The hair raising experience of carrying straight on when we should be leaning majestically and skilfully into, and thus round, the bend, was not one that I'd ever care to repeat.

A very scary experience, was that, and very nearly an extremely painful one. Certainly a crushing blow to my immediate plans involving riding without a care into the sunset, collecting flies in my teeth due to the impossibly wide grin that would certainly be fixed to my face. Returning to the house, carefully, the disappointment screaming inside my head was made worse by the obvious amusement of the family. I could feel a tingling flush of embarrassment and shame creeping up my cheeks as, with heads shaking and grins spreading my wife and daughter returned to the house. My son completed the misery by sauntering over and saying "So are you going to get a new one now then?" Before long, I am left alone with my misery, and I began to survey the problem. Over the next few days, telephone calls were made to the first supplier I could find on the Internet, measurements were made and the problems were quickly identified, as I discussed the machine with a person of far superior knowledge. We spent a fair amount of time comparing descriptions and measurements. And it soon became apparent that the front forks, wheel, mudguard and tank were all from a later machine. The problem with that was that although the parts were theoritcally from the same model, believed to be a 1958 version, there had been huge design changes in those few short years. The engines had undergone a complete metamorphosis, and amongst other things the overall design ended up physically smaller. Considerably so, in fact. We surmised that at some point a previous owner had succumbed to a meeting with Mr. Sorry-Mate-I-Didn't-See-You, and in his subsequent attempt to fix things had made the common mistake of confusing the two models.

That initial setback didn't deter me at all. I set to work over the following weeks, scrabbling together all the bits whilst rediscovering some of the long forgotten joys of owning a classic motorcycle. It all came back, the fun of auto-jumbling, the search for those elusive bits and bobs, the thrill of the find, and all along parting with large piles of the green stuff like confetti. Along the way, the family were exacting enormous entertainment from my predicament, but I was determined to sort things and tried to take their scepticism in my stride. The new front end was duly cobbled into place, and the great day arrived in June when I ventured forth once more, on a vastly improved machine. How on earth had I given this up for so long? How had I come to forget the sheer joy of blasting along on a big twin, throaty roar in my ears, wind in my face, oil on my shoes…! Oil on my shoes? Bugger! More jumbles then, more bits, a re-bore while I'm at it, more of the green-stuff heading for new owners. Oh blimey, a new carburettor as well, and then the petrol tank sprang a leak. Ah … the joys of classic motorcycling! Seven months, and the wrong end of £1,200 later, including the forks and tyres, she's right. Oh yes she is! Even the family had stopped giggling into their dinner, and were queuing up for a ride on the back! I settled down to a daily routine, and we started to clock up the miles, do Winnie and I. But I wasn't to know that this was just the beginning of what would become a far greater passion in my life and I had no inkling of the quirky event that waited, literally just around the corner.

A regularly used classic bike (or car, for that matter) attracts quite a bit of attention, and I was getting used to strangers accosting me on a regular basis to regale me with their own tales from distant times and places. But I wasn't quite prepared for the chap who turned up in June 2001, because he had noticed Winnie on her daily rounds and was about to place me in a real quandary! On returning home one day from work I found this particular person in my porch, peering through my letterbox. I approached with caution and from a safe distance enquired as to whether I might assist him. The poor man nearly jumped out of his skin, but, recovering magnificently, he pointed at Winnie and asked "Is that yours then?" Ah, another one of these. "Yes" says I, relaxing a little since he didn't appear to be holding an axe, "Why?" "Well" he says, "Do you want another one? Only I live just down the road, and I've got one just like this. It's years since I've ridden it, but I'm sure you would soon get it running, and you'd make a good owner for the old girl!" I ran his statement around in my mind for a few seconds. I blinked and looked away. I looked back – he's still there – so he must be real. Resisting the temptation to pinch myself, I recovered my wits and responded in a clear, off-hand, don't really care sort of way…. "Wah?" I squawked.

It's a bit surreal this, I thought as I walked down the road, all of three hundred yards to his garage. We're back where we came in at the beginning of this story as he opens his garage door and light floods in to reveal a 1948 Speed Twin, differing from Ruby and Winnie in that it was made in the last year before Triumph's famous nacelle became standard. This one sports a separate headlamp, a quaint instrument panel in the tank and no conventional suspension. Instead I was delighted to see that most infamous of Edward Turner's less celebrated designs – the Mk1 Sprung Hub. The bike seemed, to my less than expert eye, to be all original and complete and the owner was telling me all about it, but I wasn't really listening. I caught bits, like "last run nine years ago" and "too old to ride" but it's just background noise because I was absolutely and hopelessly Smitten (note the capital 'S'). Despite the layers of grime she is, I was thinking, the prettiest thing I'd ever set eyes on. I determined there and then that she would be mine. He named his price and I agreed, I think, without even listening. She'd been waiting patiently in the dark all that time (for that day – for me!) and I was going to pay whatever this dear man wants. We concluded the deal and I left with a promise to return in short order with the agreed sum. But as I walked the three hundred yards home an urgent and worrying thought niggled at me - the fact that after Winnie and her fettling costs, I had absolutely promised Diane that no more money would go on bikes until I had furnished her with a new bathroom. The funds for which currently nestled in the building society and represented all available capital. I knew that if I asked first, the answer would be the wrong one but I equally understood that Fate had delivered to me this opportunity and who could argue with Fate? It was immediately clear to me that the best thing to do would be to buy the bike, say nothing, sneak the new arrival up the drive, park it just so and then go indoors and wait for an opportune moment to look meaningfully out of the window and pronounce something like "Isn't she pretty!?" whilst adopting some form of pathetic "don't be cruel to me I'm a helpless fluffy animal" type of expression. I felt absolutely sure that Diane couldn't fail to agree and that common sense would prevail.

I won't go into the messy details here, but many years on I am still paying the price for that rash leap of faith! Anyway, Daisy came into my life. Daisy? Well it's appropriate, as it's a good name for a cow, and there are many design features that were popular in 1948 that make riding such a beast an entirely bovinesque experience. I was delighted to discover that after a good few attempts, she cleaned up just fine and that underneath the patina of neglect was a very tidy machine indeed. Her engine however, was in poor condition. Not so bad that she didn't run, and there was no possibility of any further expenditure, so I set about fettling her as best I could and then started using her. Daisy oozed character and charm, and if I was smitten when I first saw her I quite simply fell in love once I started using her!

Here's the thing then. With my life-style fundamentally changed, I had time on my hands to set about enjoying myself a bit and the acquisition of a pair of Speed Twins was a big step towards that ideal. Although I was materially less wealthy, the stress was gone, I had found that 'missing bit' and quite simply, life had never been so good. And with my old interest in the classic scene rekindled, I began visiting an increasing number of shows and auto-jumbles, swapping yarns with fellow enthusiasts, making new friends and generally feeling very happy that all the effort had been worthwhile. Next I re-joined the Triumph Owners' Club, decided that I would be an active member and, in short order I signed up for a number of rallies and gatherings. This attracted the immediate attention of both Chris and Chloe, my children, as it would involve camping. It did not attract any interest at all from Diane, however. She loathes camping with a fierce determination normally reserved for wasps, ants and politicians. Camping indeed – and on that note, when was the last time I had been camping? Not for many years, that was for sure. Little was I to know that one of these events would sow the seeds of an irresistible challenge that would lead me and the kids in pursuit of high adventure and discovery with the old Triumph, and for those who know me, confirm for them beyond any doubt that I had truly lost any remaining marbles.that may have still been rattling about between the ears!

The real story begins here

2. The Landmark Challenge – and into the Fens

"Are you really, really sure about this?" That was Diane, some time after my impromptu announcement that I intended to 'do' the Triumph Owners' Club's Landmark Challenge. On Daisy in fact, and not only do it, but hopefully land the Individual Gold Award. And yes … I *was* sure about it. In fact I have never been so sure of anything and had thought of almost nothing else since being captivated by the large colourful display in the Triumph Owners' marquee at a Northampton show. This display had explained the challenge, told the story of the previous year's winner, accompanied by numerous photographs, and dared any and all to 'have a go' . Something stirred deep inside me as I gazed in awe at that heroic adventurer posing with his machine at a variety of exotic, historic and far-flung destinations. I had ridden Daisy up to this event in response to a plea from the club for owners of 'older' machines to bring them for display. Being 1948, she was in fact the oldest machine on show and they had accordingly given her pride of place in the marquee, parked beneath the Landmark display.

It was here that a fellow owner helped to make up my mind about mounting an assault on the challenge. He'd interrupted my daydreaming with a comment that provoked the bulldog spirit in me.

"You wouldn't be wanting to do that on your old nail." I turned to study the source of this declaration and noted the broad grin of a friendly but clearly mischievous fellow clubman.

"Oh, you don't reckon?" said I, the competitive demon in me prodded into wakefulness..

"Nah. Not practical mate. Even if the bike survived it, I doubt *you* would eh?"

I look at Daisy, then at my provocateur who, as a small audience began to form, felt he needed to embellish his reasoning.

"Well, I mean, it's 1948 innit? No suspension, ancient electrics, cruising speed of what?…60 mph if you're lucky? It'd take you a year! You'd have to be mad to try it!" His audience seemed to agree with him, throwing a few ribald comments in for good measure. This all happened in a good natured way, but it was clear they all believed it. Nobody would be mad enough to attempt such a challenge on such an old-fashioned machine, surely. Riding home from that event, I found myself fighting an irrational urge to prove them all wrong. Why couldn't I do it? People have scaled Everest, explored just about every nook and cranny on Earth and, when we get right down to it, even landed on the moon! This is just a paltry collection of 50 Ordnance Survey map references, each with a cryptic clue to identify the Landmark residing there, and you have a riding season, January up to December each year, to solve and visit them, collecting photographic evidence of your visits as you go. Sure, Daisy is a very old machine, and there would be a few dramas, but it couldn't be that hard surely?

The challenge works likes this; There are a range of awards ranging from bronze to gold, depending on how many of the 50 Landmarks you manage. Then there is the overall Individual Gold, a spangly great trophy by all accounts, and one which I am steadily convincing myself will be mine, goes to the oldest machine that completes all 50. That'll be Daisy then, I decided, and I wasted no time once home digging out the published list of the current year's challenge before retiring to my computer to spend the evening feeding map references into the thing. It was then that the scale of the challenge began to sink in.

Take a large map of the United Kingdom. The largest you can find. Spread it out on the floor. Take 50 coloured map pins, cup them between both hands and then stand over your map and throw the pins up into the air letting them cascade down. What you're now looking at is a good representation of the Landmark Challenge. Note the random pattern, and particularly note that no remote corner is left without a pin. The size of the task became apparent but being a man of firm resolve, I pressed on with the planning by attempting to carve up the map into manageable portions which could be picked off in individual sorties. Next I had to decide whether to try and identify the Landmarks in advance, or whether to just wing it on the day each time and hope something obvious presented itself. Two evenings of research on the good old Internet had most of them identified, with only a few that were not clear. They ranged from interesting historical sites such as standing stones or castles, through windmills, viaducts and interesting bridges to stadiums, famous sites such as theatres and a smattering of various museums or public interest sites thrown in.

So the task was now clear, and after a bit of discussion with the family, we reckoned that if I'm to do something this stupid, it really should be for charity and once you've said that to a few people, particularly in the local pub, there's *no* turning back. Within a month helpful associates have chosen the John Jackson Youth Scholarship for me, they've agreed and are eager to publicize it. Before I knew what was happening the charity have arranged (with the help of aforementioned associates) to come down in order to meet me, take photo's and tell me all about their work. The Scholarship scheme, named after that famous Jazz musician, is run and supported by a bunch of professional musicians with the aim of assisting underprivileged youngsters with a possible flair for the art to develop their skills. They do this by providing both financial support and, of course, their own skills, running a series of residential workshops through the year as well as festival activities and personal support. Pretty soon I've got lots of sponsors queuing up – again thanks to those mischievous associates, and that's that - I've *got* to do it now.

Back to actually planning my assault on the challenge then, I'd carved up the map in order to attack it in chunks, and a plan had emerged that would see me picking off everything roughly south of Birmingham over a number of weekends, some of which would need to be of the long variety, and the rest would require a more extended effort. Now that I was my own master in life, I could take any number of days out of what would have been work, which would give me ample time to do the Northern, Welsh and Scottish bits. It was also clear that I needed to be half sensible and choose a more central geographic location from which each foray would commence and finish, due to the mildly inconvenient fact that I live in the furthest south east corner of Kent. There were two fairly straightforward reasons for this and I make no apology! First, there is only one real road out of the far southeast corner of England, which during this particular summer was undergoing major, major road works. No fun at all using a modern conveyance, but on a machine this old and due to the nature, length and disposition of the project, it would be madness. There would be nowhere to go should disaster strike! Second, it actually takes an hour and a half just to reach South London from this corner, where I would then be presented, for my pleasure and enjoyment, with the M25 motorway. The alternatives to that dread road are unthinkable – endless urban sprawl, traffic lights and junctions. I simply couldn't allow enough time off to do that each time and I had no inclination whatsoever to take Daisy round the M25. After some deliberation then, I chose Cambridge as my starting point for all forays that would take us North of the Thames.

With all the necessary preparation done then, and with the first months of the year already gone, it was decision time. We'd make a start by attacking the East first – Cambridge, Suffolk, Norfolk and Lincolnshire. There were a total of six Landmarks in these fair counties and the choice of East as the first full weekend sortie was not without reason. For all my blind faith, Daisy was truly untested in terms of reliability, durability and general fettle. I also had the niggling worry that she had, after all, spent nine years standing in that dark garage and the potential for problems with bearings, magneto windings and the like was far from certain. So this was an easy option designed to find out the stark truth, for better or for worse. From our chosen start point at Cambridge, an anti-clockwise route had been plotted that should see the six Landmarks found and recorded and have us arrive back at the start point again some three hundred miles later - whilst never actually taking us more than sixty miles away from it in real terms. That meant that any disastrous occurrences would allow us to get recovered in a timely fashion.

The days ticked past, but I had one further task to complete. A crucial task, too, because in typically cavalier fashion I had thrown myself into the few rallies attended thus far with a minimum of actual thought or preparation, and I had learnt very quickly that camping without suitable equipment is not fun. I had bought the cheapest tent I could find, and hadn't bothered with any supporting infrastructure such as panniers, cooking and eating utensils, kettle, stove or indeed a light. I had reasoned that just as in my youth, rallies were organised events and as such would supply all the necessary, surely? Wrong. Even if that was true, the Landmark was a very different bag of onions entirely and therefore it was vital that before setting off, a pilgrimage to the local outdoor activities store would be absolutely necessary.

Off I went then, armed with a list of the required (or so I thought) items. The kindly proprietor took pity on me and was good enough to spend nearly an hour putting me right on a number of things. He even took pains to go out and check Daisy over before making recommendations. I returned some hours later with a full set of the necessary paraphernalia, which the kids and I then set about trying to fit together in the garden. They were keen to test out this fabulous array of explorer's tackle, so spent the night out there, pronouncing everything in order the next day. We then spent a goodly amount of time working out out how to fit it all on Daisy and still have room for one of the youngsters to fit on too, and after trying out a number of scenarios, with only a mild bout of buffoonery, we settled on a configuration that looked like it might stay on after the first ten miles. New throw-over panniers were sourced to finish off the whole thing, and I declared Daisy to be finally ready for the great adventures ahead. The East, here we come!

Unloading Daisy and camping gear from the back of the Espace, at a convenient lay-by on the A428 west of Cambridge I had a sense of great adventure about to commence out there on the open road. Although this was to be a mere taster for the far greater distances that would be traversed later on in the year, I was fairly confident that if we can get through this weekend without mishaps then the rest would just be more of the same but for longer, surely, albeit with different scenery. And another heartening fact is that I'm not alone as I thought I would be. Both of the young Ham brood have enthusiastically signed up for the challenge in turns and I have Chris, my son, riding shotgun on this first foray. He has no idea what he's getting himself into, but the exuberance of youth has left him keenly ready for anything.

It was four o'clock on that Saturday afternoon and after loading Daisy up with our new gear, we were off. Unfortunately the weather hadn't responded kindly to the great occasion as it was grey and overcast as far as the eye can see, with a fine drizzle drifting across the landscape. The first Landmark was only a few miles from our start point, and was something I'd never had experience of before - a military cemetery. It was a strangely sobering, unsettling experience and I felt slightly uncomfortable taking photographs of Daisy at the entrance. We went inside, and I promise you there can be very, very few things quite like a field full of white crosses to focus the mind. Our mood became somewhat contemplative as we moved off into afternoon traffic.

We now had to ride through Cambridge in order to head East into Suffolk. We'd spent a good while in the cemetary, so it was approaching rush hour which proved to be no fun at all. I had already learned that Daisy hates stop-start traffic and it wasn't long before she got hot, bothered and overheated. I struggled to keep her running at each of a seemingly endless string of red traffic lights and finally lost the unequal struggle as she stopped with a huff on the ring road somewhere in the northwest suburbs. Heat was radiating off her engine fiercely, and she had a smell about her that can be mistaken for nothing else – she was cooking!

Fine, I had been there many times before with various ancient bikes of my youth, and I knew the drill, which simply entailed waiting for the poor old thing to cool down. Twenty minutes would be about normal, so we parked her up and watched the choking traffic rumble on by whilst we listened to Daisy making 'tinc, tinc' noises as she cooled down. Finally she was ready and started without fuss and we got back underway, managing to free ourselves from the nightmare Cambridge circular without further incident, heading East towards Newmarket. As we picked up the A14 our spirits lifted as the drizzle eased, with even a hint of brightnes beginning to show. This was more like it.

Newmarket came and went as we continued on into the evening and we found ourselves getting dry in the wind. The countryside was beginning to open-up too as we crossed into Suffolk, heading for Bury St. Edmunds and with the rain giving way to broken cloud, through which the sun made an occasional glorious appearance, we began to enjoy the ride. Daisy seemed absolutely content to rumble along at a steady sixty mph, with her deep burbling exhaust note like music in my ears. I turned to look over my shoulder at Chris, and the big grin he displayed said it all. However it wasn't too long before Daisy's 1940's seating arrangements made their presence well and truly felt, and after an hour we both needed to take a break. We stopped in a lay-by in order to rest the nether regions and do a map check and we both agreed that life really couldn't get much better than this as the last of the clouds finally cleared to the West and a glorious late afternoon sun bathed us in it's warmth.

Motorcyclists are nothing if not a communal breed, sharing a comradely spirit and it was gratifying that within minutes of our stopping a chap on a big shiny BMW pulled in to ask what the problem was and whether there was anything he could do to help. This happens to me a lot as I amble my way through life on Daisy, and even at this early stage of our association I was getting used to such encounters. Explanations followed, and as we described our mission I could see that he clearly thought we were as certifiably mad as a tin of frogs, but was too polite to say so. He didn't run away though, so directions were checked and after another incredulous look at Daisy off he goes, followed by us a few minutes later. After a while we left the A14 where it begins to head south and took the A1120 at Stowmarket. This is where we really began to enjoy things as the road became much smaller, much twistier heading off east again into the sticks. By now, evening was drawing in and I reckoned we still had about fifteen to twenty miles to cover before we'd reach the next Landmark. The sun was sinking steadily and I already knew that Daisy's not blessed with particularly stunning lighting abilities, so we needed to get a wiggle-on. The road was fantastic though, and as it twisted and turned into the hazy Suffolk countryside a light mist began to hang around the fields. I was reminded just how utterly captivating the English countryside can be, and the urge to just stop and stare across the fields was hard to resist. But resist I did, allbeit I let the speed drop a bit.

We were looking for an old post mill, according to my detective work earlier on, and we were getting pressed for time because we also needed to find somewhere to camp. We pulled up for a map check, and it dawned on me that I really should have planned the camping, rather than trust to luck that I'd simply find somewhere just when needed. I also realised with a feeling of desperation that my economy comedy map, being a largescale thing covering half of Britain, didn't actually show the little roads we were now heading into. Just how stupid a mistake that was came home in spades as we realised that we were looking for a fairly small Landmark in roughly 100 square miles of blank paper! Placing the mark on the map at home had seemed all too straightforward at the time. We had no idea of the reality that a myriad of little country roads all heading for uncharted places would bring. What to do?

Chris expressed an opinion that we should just camp in the nearest field, as he was tired and hungry, I agreed with that sentiment, but after trundling around for another twenty minutes, we hadn't found anywhere suitable. By now, we were thoroughly lost and, as the light was going fast, we both began to feel a bit desperate. Suddenly, rounding a hedge lined bend, we stumbled across the post mill, almost by accident. This was a huge relief because I could at least tell where on the blank bit of map we now were. We quickly got our photograph and set off to continue our earnest search for camping. As the last light faded I turned the ancient lightswitch on Daisy's tank panel but the resulting orange glow from her headlamp failed to help much. And oh my, when it gets dark in the country it gets really, properly *dark*! We've spent our lives as townies, have Chris and I, and we don't really get proper dark in our towns these days. It was a shock to find the real stuff, up close and personal. In fact, things were getting fairly desperate when, as if by divine intervention, we spied a B&B sign emerging from the gloom, and I decided that I'd be more than happy to forego camping, and shell out the readies if they had a vacancy. What luck we had too, because at the end of the lane we found a big country inn, and yes they did indeed have a vacancy.

The room turned out to be a delightful bed-sitter situated in what were clearly the stables in by-gone years when this very inn served as a vital safe haven for the stagecoach of an evening. With no further ado we booked in and the landlord insisted that Daisy be bedded down for the night in his garage. That done, we looked forward to a few beers (coke for Chris), some good old country home cooking and a comfortable bed. The locals were very friendly, and wanted to know what we were up to on such an old bike, this far from civilization. As the tale was told we found ourselves at the centre of a small gathering and by closing time we felt as if we'd known these people for a lifetime. But bed time beckoned. We had a full day the next day, and this one had been quite a challenge in itself.

We were up bright and early the next morning, and bright was indeed the word because it was gloriously sunny. After a hearty breakfast we were pleasantly surprised when the landlord insisted on only charging half his normal fee because, he informed us, he rather liked the story we'd told him about our challenge the previous evening. What a nice man, and the gesture left us both feeling remarkably content with the world as we set off again, heading north. I knew we were heading north because I had about my person a small but rather splendid plastic compass, which I had got from a Christmas cracker that year! But even armed with that technological marvel, there was trouble ahead and we soon became hopelessly lost in the tiny back roads that simply don't show on my map.

The compass is almost useless, because most of the roads refuse to behave themselves and take us north as we require, but instead they snake around the landscape changing direction every hundred yards or so, or so it seemed. They persistently head off anywhere but north. It was at this point that Daisy, clearly sensing our vulnerability, suddenly decided to start mucking about. We pressed on with an intermittent misfire jarring what would otherwise have been a splendid ride, and as the miles passe it got steadily worse as the morning wore on. After about an hour of this, I couldn't believe that I still hadn't managed locate us on the map, which doesn't even contain any reference to the numerous villages that we've passed through, but this train of thought was summarily halted when Daisy decided she'd had enough for the time being, thank you, and promptly stopped dead with an impressive backfire. We coasted to a stop.

Dismounting, a slightly panicked Chris urgently grilled me about what was that bang, what has happened, what we can do about it and how do we get home? Very good questions indeed, I considered, as I ditched the riding gear and crouched down to start the process familiar to most classic motorcyclists at one point or another - the application of skill, luck or miracle, to coax life back into the old girl. So there we were, at a rather early stage on the first of our forays in pursuit of the Landmark Challenge Individual Gold Award. We'd managed two landmarks only, and put less than one hundred miles under our wheels. To add to our misery it started raining again, we were cold, we were lost somewhere in Suffolk with a map that may as well detail Mars, and we no longer have a working motorcycle. I began poking and prodding around under Daisy's tank, but after a while Chris remembered that we have breakdown cover and suggested, rather persistently, that calling those fine people would be the only sensible option. "Certainly not" I say, being very reluctant to surrender so quickly, although it was already dawning on me that we were an awfully long way from home.

Determined to show young Chris that where there is a will there is a way, I continued prodding optimistically at the BTH magneto in the vain hope of finding the problem. The usual drill then suggested itself and I took the spark plugs out, rested one of them on the engine where I could see it, and set about checking to see if the magneto was alive. Kick, kick, kick. - turning over the engine I could see that there were good healthy sparks so pausing only to give each plug a good clean I put them back in. Trying to start her again produced an unexpected result. Kick, kick, kick, BANG! An impressive, rifle-shot of a backfire issued forth and I had to stop myself laughing out loud as Chris jumped about three feet in the air and ran for it. He was not used to this sort of thing at all, and told me in no uncertain terms what he thought about it - from his new, safer position fifty yards up the road! In his view it's all over. We should call recovery, and go home. Trying to calm the lad, I suggested that whilst the situation is not good, certainly, I was confident there would be a simple explanation. Chris did not look at all convinced, but held his peace and sat down on the grassy bank as I continued to search for the answer.

That sort of backfire really isn't good it is true, especially if you notice, as Chris had, the impressively long finger of flame that had issued forth from the silencers and had been the cause of his rapid retreat down the lane. I started to worry that she had done something fatal, like shredded the magneto pinion, which is a feeble fibre thing , or that at the very least it has slipped on its taper, which would of course completely throw the ignition timing. Worse still is the thought that a valve might have stuck open. My mind ticked busily with imagined horrors, but I knew a logical approach was required if I was going to solve the mystery. I decided to try the cylinders one at a time, simply by disonnecting a plug and kicking, and soon discovered that the left hand one was in fact fine and running evenly. The right one caused the backfire – every single time.

At this point, having observed more displays of thunder and flame Chris had clearly decided that Daisy may spontaneously combust at any minute and retreated even further down the road, with his fingers jammed firmly in his ears. His face told me that he was not at all impressed with this suddenly nerve racking game, and that we should jolly well stop playing silly buggers and call the nice breakdown man. Undeterred, I began searching for the cause of the right hand cylinder's pyrotechnics, checking the valve clearances first, and finding all to be in order. That's good, and as I worked, I managed to convince Chris that having one cylinder running smoothly is good news, as it means that nothing fundamental is broken. All we have to do, I explained confidently, is find out what's causing the problem with the other one. Daisy is a simple soul in that respect and with no modern elecrtical gubbins like coil, rectifier or even a battery in the circuit, there are only so many things it could be!

This is of course so much bunk, but I started by pulling the points on the magneto to bits, checking, cleaning and re-assembling. Next I pulled the HT leads off, checked the contacts then connections and cleaned everything, put it all back and got ready to try her again. Chris, who had slowly crept back to watch, took his cue and all but sprinted away down the road, fingers back in ears! He needn't have worried because she was absolutely fine this time round, starting smoothly and running evenly. We don't know exactly what the cause of the mystery backfire was, but now she was thump-thump-thumping away in a steady and even tickover. Chris returned slowly, tensed and looking ready to bolt at the first sign of danger. It took me a while to convinve him that Daisy was not about to explode spectacularly, and was quite safe, but eventually and reluctantly he agreed that he'd get back on so we could get underway again. We had lost nearly forty minutes mucking about there, and with a lot to still get done that day there was a sense of urcency about things now.

We consulted the map. We don't know why we did this, other than a vague hope that it had undergone a metamorphosis in the last half an hour, and turned into something useful. Alas it hadn't. What was evident, however, was that the amount of distance covered so far woefully inadequate. If we were to have any chance of meeting our target of six Landmarks that weekend we would need to press on and ride Daisy that much harder. Given that she was showing signs of curmudgenly reluctance thus far, this was a worry But things soon began to look up. We miraculously managed, after only mild clownery in the navigation department, to blunder into the A144, which actually existed on my novelty map. Turning north, I got Daisy settled down to a steady 65 mph, with no sign at all of her earlier problems, and pretty soon we were passing through Bungay and heading for Norwich on a lovely rustic 'B' road of the sort that probably made up the main roads back in Daisy's younger days. Riding a classic motorcycle on such a road is an experience guaranteed to warm the soul, the two being perfectly suited to one another. Unfortunately it seemed like no time at all before we were forced onto dual carriageway around Norwich itself and on into Norfolk in order to reach the coast and the next Landmark.

The Holt Steam Railway is what we were looking for, and according to our research back home it connects the little town of Holt to the holiday resort of Cromer, along the Northern coastline. We found it with ease, and it's a popular attraction judging by the packed car park and picnic area that greeted us on arrival. Daisy obviously felt that it was time to wake Chris up again as we pulled in, by letting off another loud backfire just as we stopped. This time though, it was not just Chris she upset, as all hell broke loose around us.The rifle-shot from Daisy set off a cacophony of car alarms right across the car park, followed by what appeared to be a whole concert party of babies, suddenly wailing their hearts out, jerked unceremoniously as they were from their slumbers! I felt the red flush of embarrassment creeping up my neck and cheeks as seemingly the entire population of Holt turned to stare in hostile demeanour at these hoodlums who had barged in here in their leather jackets and destroyed the peaceful tranquillity with their nasty, noisy motorbike. We quickly took our photograph then scuttled into the shop, bought some coke and crisps, and as quickly as possible pushed Daisy out to the road, with the stares continuing to bore into us like lasers. Once out of view, we both saw the funny side and had a good chuckle as we ate and drank. I was Nervous about the backfire however, and started Daisy just to be sure that the problems of earlier had not reappeared. I grinned to myself in relief as she bursted into life, turned to Chris to reassure him that all's fine, only to see him down the road again, with his back to me, fingers firmly in his ears!

Three landmarks down then, and it was time to turn West. Before long we had picked up the A148 heading across Norfolk without further incident, once again we were on perfect roads for Daisy, and the sun had come out too. Things were clearly looking up, but we were increasingly against the clock with something like one hundred and fifty miles still to do and three Landmarks to find. We hadn't stopped much in last few hours so we were feeling it. We finally did stop at King's Lynn for a late lunch, a country pub that used to be a water mill served the purpose nicely, and after a pleasant hour watching ducks and dragonflies busy themselves along the banks of the adjoining stream, we were off again towards the Wash and our next landmark, which I believed to be the Sutton bridge, an old iron thing that spans the border between Norfolk and Lincolnshire. Arriving there Daisy displayed the same bad manners as earlier, letting off a ripping backfire that extracted a "Woaaagh" from Chris and made me jump too. We got the photograph taken, but our attempts to get underway again quickly failed. Daisy had other ideas, apparently. After several minutes of trying, the best she managed was a loud spit through the carburettor as the kick-start rebounded violently against its stop. A classic 'kick-back' every time. Chris had effected his by now familiar retreat and I decided to give it a rest for ten minutes or so, not least because my kicking leg was so much jelly after the exertions.

As we sat in the lay-by we could see the intense heat radiating from Daisy's engine in the harsh sunshine and Chris began his litany of doubt, checking that I've still got the breakdown number. Oh he of little faith! It then dawned on me that we actually had the makings of a brew in Chris's rucksack, a fine idea we both agreed, and pretty soon we had a bubbling kettle hissing away on the little primus stove as we waited for Daisy to cool off in the Saharan sun. It was a full thirty minutes before She would play again and enable us to set off West into the fine summer backdrop of Lincolnshire. We really needed investigate this overheating back at home, preferably before our next foray, but at that moment we still had two more Landmarks to get, one of which was away to the North nestling amid the Fens. Time was running away from us but strangely such worries dissolved into insignificance because it would have been hard not to enjoy the ride that was unfolding.

It had turned into a scorching afternoon, the roads we'd chosen were fantastic, as was the countryside we were riding through and Daisy had settled down again nicely out on the open road. Landmark number five, a tropical forest of all things, was knocked off in short order and after only the shortest of stops for the photograph, Daisy obliged with minimal mucking about, and we were away for the final one of this foray some twenty five miles to the North of us. Our comedy map was actually of some use here, as it showed some very clear routes up to where we needed to be. We chose a 'B' road which seemed to take us most of the way and this turned out to be the pick of day, as with the sun off to our left bathing us in glorious late afternoon warmth we picked our way along an alternately wooded, river hugging road which was virtually dead straight, but undulated lazily like a shallow roller coaster as far as the eye could see. We truly couldn't believe how picturesque this road turned out to be, and suddenly it didn't matter about time anymore, or anything else for that matter. It turned out that this wonderful road took us to within five miles of the air museum that is the last landmark, and with that done, we headed back south the way we came, into the stunning beauty of a wonderful sunset, blazing across the fields to our right.

Daisy however, had begun to show signs of further problems. She was getting upset at low revs, with the symptoms particularly showing up at junctions where we have to slow right down or stop. Whatever problem she'd been having these past few days was clearly getting rapidly worse, and I found myself willing her not to let us down with only sixty odd miles to go. I eased back on the throttle, to cruise along at fifty, and conducted a conference with Chris over my shoulder. We agreed that we dare not stop now, however many aches developed in the nether regions, for fear that Daisy would call it a day and spoil our achievement. We simply had to press on ever Southwards and hope She kept going. Finally, we approached Cambridge once again and by then both of us were reduced to desperate fidgeting in an attempt to ease the increasing pains in both legs and backside, and at least to move it around a bit. When we finally arrived back at the car, which mercifully still had all of its wheels and indeed windows, it was pushing eight in the evening.With the last of the day's light fading, I refleced that we probably could not have ridden even another five miles, such were the aches and pains. Nor would Daisy, it seemed, because as we pulled into our lay-by, she refused to tick over at all, finally succumbing to whatever gremlins had infested her with a loud spit and an amusing 'pop'. As for us, we were tired, aching and my backside had gone on strike but we congratulated ourselves on the fact that we'd done the first

six Landmarks and were therefore officially on our way to lifting that trophy!

3. Back to the Drawing Board

Sitting at home the following weekend, I performed a mental post-mortem on the first of our landmark forays. It was abundantly clear that I had made several large errors of judgement. First and foremost was the pressing issue of Daisy. She had not let us down on that first trip out, certainly, but those niggling worries I had harboured about her general mechanical state were looking like far more of a reality. Her final few miles had been a struggle, and the way she had stopped when finally arriving back in the lay-by at the end of the tour was distinctly unsettling. I chided myself for being so foolish - what had I honestly expected after nine years of dormancy? I had been rash to expect any different, and an urgent investigation to ascertain the extent of the deterioration was called for before any further jollies could be considered.

Secondly, I had learned that my usual approach to adventure, a mixture of maximum impatience with minimum preparation, was possibly not the right approach to the landmark. If I was to succeed on the much longer wanderings to come, in pursuit of the other forty-four remaining landmarks I would be an idiot not to actually investigate the positions of such vital things as campsites. It simply hadn't struck me as being an issue, but once out there in the wilds it had become startlingly apparent that campsites are not around every other corner when you need one. The landmark, obviously, is a very different situation to say, attending a rally, where you are heading for a single gathering place and on arrival, expect the organisers to have thought of such things as where to throw the tents up. This self-critical train of thought also led to a sharp reminder about maps. Maps, when you are lost in the bush, so to speak, are a fundamentally vital bit of kit. Possessing a map which, for example, fails to show eighty percent of the roads or villages that one is actually travelling on or through, is at best ill advised and actually, in the cold light of day pretty damn stupid. I know this now as I find myself thinking back to that post mill. We had been lucky to have actually stumbled across the thing at all. Equally, Daisy's shenanigans in Norfolk and Suffolk had focused my attention on the very real need for more than just a plug spanner and a penknife, shoved hastily in pockets almost as an afterthought. What, I demanded of myself, would I have done if something more serious had occurred – if a vital oil banjo, for example, had actually worked loose and began spouting the stuff all over the place? I would have been utterly ill prepared to deal with that or worse, given that I had neglected to take even a most basic selection of spanners.

None of these fine and sensible thoughts had occurred to me at all, back when I was in the grip of the rabid enthusiasm and blind optimism that had led me to take up the challenge. But apparently, a good experience is that which leaves one intact to fight another day, better informed, better prepared and indeed better organised. The first foray was therefore clearly a good experience, I decided, and after all was I not right now applying the lessons learned in my planning and preparation for the next sortie? Also on the plus side, we had six landmarks in the bag and had in theory proved that the thing, if broken down into bits, can be done with relative ease. We have also made some new friends out there in the boonies and most importantly we have enjoyed ourselves. Finally I also considered that this type of adventuring could not possibly be anything other than valuable life experience for the young Ham brood, of a sort which they would definitely not get from almost any other activity. Chris had certainly had his moments of doubt, particularly when Daisy was at her most troublesome, but he had perked up considerably coming home in the car. Things always look remarkably different once the immediate threat that they bring with them is past, and Chris had managed to turn most of the mishaps into talking points rather than negative memories. We had laughed at our luck in finding the mill, agreed that the chap running the big pub B&B was a jolly decent fellow, laughed even harder at the memory of the Holt car park and picnic area, where Daisy had left such an impression and finally, we had agreed that far from being at all discouraged by her antics, we could actually discuss with pride her achievement in making it back in one piece, still running, despite clearly having an engine that is well past it's sell-by date.

All in all then, we were not at all put off and from the safe surroundings of home we set about enthusiastically listing the things we need to do before the next foray. I say 'we' because the kids, and even Diane, are now getting fully into the spirit of the challenge, and we are all involved in task of working out a way forward. The biggest of these is to urgently make an attempt to sort out Daisy herself. The following day, being a Sunday, I was free to make a start. But where exactly does one start when there is no clear idea of what's actually wrong? There are many obvious things that can cause problems with a machine of this age, especially when the history is unclear, but there are only so many things that can give the overheating and general misbehaving that had dogged us on our first trip. These mostly revolve around the peripheral parts such as magneto, carburettor or top end (pistons, bore, valves and cylinder head) and so those were the things that received my immediate focus. The problem, of course, is that once you begin to delve into an ancient engine, it's a bit like lifting the lid from Pandora's box – there are any number of horrors waiting to jump out at you!

As I unbolted the carburettor, it was apparent that the studs that hold it on had not been disturbed for many, many years and this led me to thinking about Daisy's past life. What *did* I actually know about her? When, for example, was the last time someone had undone those self same nuts, and what exactly had been done? How long had this collection of parts that made up her engine unit actually been together? Could it even be possible that they were all, in fact, the original components that left the factory as a working motorcycle way back in 1948? There was no way of knowing, of course, but I found the thought rather appealing and not a little romantic. As the carburettor came free these thoughts were reinforced after only the briefest inspection: it was absolutelyworn out and actually had a crack in it, underneath where the flange meets the manifold of the cylinder head. I marveled that Daisy had managed to run at all, let alone in traffic and heat, but at least this quickly gave an answer to those niggling problems because a cracked manifold can only lead to a weak mixture, which in turn leads to heat and of course aids the vaporization problems that make a hot engine almost impossible to start.

That got me thinking hard, though. If the carburettor was that worn, I reasoned, then the engine itself must be in equally poor shape, so I carried right on with the spanners and set about lifting off the cylinder head to have a peek at the general condition of valves, bore and pistons. It is truly fortuitous that I did so, because what I found in there was truly shocking. The head itself was also cracked, again in a place between the cylinders that is almost impossible to see with the thing in place. All of the valves were badly worn and badly burnt, but what really shocked, and indeed, fascinated me was the state of the actual piston crown surfaces. Take a telescope on a clear summer evening, and wait for the moon to rise. Focus in on the thing, and imagine it being a different colour, not dissimilar to say, a piston crown. What you are looking at is a fairly good representation of Daisy's right hand piston, which indeed looked as if a passing meteor shower had come a bit too close and left a number of it's constituent parts embedded therein for eternity. On closer inspection, there also appeared to be a fair sized chunk missing from the top edge of the piston. These discoveries did absolutely nothing to convince me that the rest of the engine would be able to endure the adventures I have planned. With a feeling of resignation, I accept that the rest would have to come apart in order to investigate further.

The thought of stripping an engine is often too much for many owners, but it's actually not at all difficult. Meccano for adults is probably a good way of thinking about it, and I was not at all afraid to wield the spanners further in my quest for mechanical surety. The barrels came off next, revealing further woes when the majority of the piston rings, freed from their entrapment, fell apart with a disdainful clinketty-clink and decorated the workshop floor. Except, that is, the top ring on the right piston. This one appeared to have burnt itself into its groove, and looked like an un-mined coal seam running round the top of the piston. It was here that the piece of crown had also disappeared, leaving an ugly scar that joined the coal seam. This would explain the moonscape piston then, and I imagined that piece, together with several bits of compression ring, bouncing around the combustion chamber causing merry havoc. I began to wonder with no small sense of awe how Daisy had actually run at all, let alone conveyed Chris and myself all round Suffolk, Norfolk and Lincolnshire, but at the same time I had to admit to a growing respect for a design that could continue on after such a clear disintegration of what I have always thought of as vital parts.

Having got this far then and finding nothing good, the inevitable question was whether the internals were any better. Removing the pistons, I tenderly tested the big ends by grasping the con rods firmly and easing up and down to feel for play. What I found was not what I expected surprisingly, for there was no big-end wear that I could detect, but something far more sinister became apparent. The whole crankshaft assembly was moving from side to side instead. I sat and fiddled with this new discovery, fascinated at the sheer amount of lateral movement I was able to effect, whilst contemplating it's meaning. What it meant is that the engine has to come out altogether in order to split the crankcases and sort out the obviously totally worn-out main bearings. This led to another jolting revelation, which is a far scarier one than the mechanical challenges facing me – cost. Clearly none of this is going to come free, and having already spent the bathroom fund once on Daisy, how on earth am I to break the news to Diane that the same Daisy would require yet more of our hard earned funds before she could take to the highways again? It was fairly obvious to me that this would be a very tricky situation indeed, and my mind began working on the best way to introduce the subject in such a way that the conclusion would be favourable.

That evening, I retired to the local hostelry and tried out various approaches in my head, but none of them seemed likely to obtain the result required. In fact, the more I thought about the whole thing, it seemed increasingly likely that far from receiving any kind of spousal support, I would, in contrast, face a harsh inquisition during which I would be

asked to explain just how I had come to exchange a sizeable slice of our worldly wealth for a barely disguised pile of scrap. I had to admit that there was no ready answer to this, or at least, not one that doesn't invite a swift dink round the ear with the frying pan. To add to my mental woes, there was also the almost unbearable shame that would inevitably come from failure. The charity would be less than brimming with gratitude at my consummate lack of success. The sponsors will have to be told why they can hold onto their money and all those associates who had so enthusiastically pushed me headlong into backing up my mouth with action, will be contemptuous to say the least. And finally, that smug git that had started all this, back in the TOMCC tent that day would be proved right. It was all unthinkable, and if I could not find a way to get Daisy back into action, pretty damn soon, I felt that the only option would be to quietly emigrate, or do a Reggie Perrin and simply disappear.

With nothing better to do, I continued with the dismantling, whilst continuing to try and think of ways or ruses to acquire the necessary funds to put things right. It struck me that at least a proportion of the required bits could be 'borrowed' from my other machine, Winnie, but even this had it's difficulties as she was now in the possession of my father. With the arrival of Winnie and then Daisy, my father had found his own interest in classic motorcycles re-kindled. I was besotted with Daisy by then, and anyway I can't ride both at once, so it seemed sensible to allow him to indulge his renewed desires. It would surely be churlish in the least to ask for her back, merely to rob parts in order to indulge my own pleasures. There was also the age difference between the two machines, some eight years, during which a number of significant design changes had been introduced meaning that I could only really use top end components such as barrels, pistons and valves on Daisy anyway. As I thought it through, it became obvious that Winnie only represented a partial answer at best and could only really be considered as a last resort. I put that desperate kind of thinking to the back of my mind for the time being. In the mean time, I dismantled Daisy's entire engine and there was no getting away from the fact that it would need just about everything fixed or renewed. Bearings, bushes, a rebore, new pistons, cylinder head, valves, carburettor ... the list seemed to be endless and the cost would be truly frightening. The weeks were sliding past as well. Things were starting to look fairly dim on the landmark front!

Another week galloped past, with no clear inspiration, and I began to face up to the reality that it was game over for this year, after only a paltry few miles and a handful of landmarks. I had just decided that I would have to come clean with everyone when I suddenly hit upon a wizard ruse. It was cheeky, and it was a bit outrageous, but these facts only served to convince me that it was therefore, a particularly fine ruse indeed. I would go and see my old colleague, Steve Williams, with whom I had founded the company from which I had recently resigned, and see if I could persuade him to stump up some company funds in order to assist Daisy back onto the road to glory. This, I felt had a fairly good chance of succeeding, due to the fact that he was the 'associate' who had organised the initial contact with the charity I was allegedly in the process of supporting, and was in fact very involved with the trustees! I was sure he would not want to see things come to such a pitiful halt so early in the challenge, and would no doubt feel almost duty bound to offer assistance. I went down to my old offices the next day, casually like, and soon found myself sipping a coffee in the boardroom where, until only recently, I was numbered amongst those that wielded executive power. It felt rather strange to say the least, but I was there on a mission and wasn't about to let anything deflect me.

You don't work as closely with someone as I had with Steve, for twelve years, without getting to know them quite well, and vice versa. Steve quickly decided that I was there, in his words, 'on the scrounge' and just as quickly guessed that all was not well on the Daisy front.

"Crashed it then, have you?"

"No I bloody haven't!" I shot back, "but, well, now you mention it, there has been a teensy bit of a set-back..."

I don't get the chance to explain, as Steve was well ahead of me.

"So it's blown up then, and now you're here on the scrounge, like I said."

Before I could conjure up any clever responses to that he continued "How much?"

Suddenly, it seemed, this was going awfully well, and experience has taught me that there's no point in being shy in such circumstances. I pulled a number out of the air, to see what sort of response might be forthcoming. I could not quite bring myself to maintain eye contact as I did this, choosing instead to stare over Steve's shoulder whilst adopting a nonchalant air.

"Shouldn't be more than a grand" I heard myself mutter "which of course I haven't got on account of being unemployed."

This I know is dodgy territory. Steve was one of the people firmly in the camp that thought I was stark-staring mad to resign my position. He had felt a little betrayed as well, I guess and we had stayed well clear of the subject ever since on the few occasions we had met up. I did not expect any kind of sympathetic response, and I wasn't disappointed.

"An unemployed twat, is what you mean, and you've got some bloody neck coming out with that argument, if you don't mind me saying."

Ah, not going so awfully well then. But then his next statement just as quickly cut off this thought.

"Eight hundred quid is all I'll put up, although Christ knows why I should. And this is a one-off, in return for which you will owe me a massive favour, which I *will* call in at some point. Oh and you'd bloody well better win this thing if I do!"

And that was that. Eight hundred pounds, just like that! Problem solved. I was free to go out and get it all sorted! I thanked Steve profusely for his generousity, although I knew he'd get value out of me somehow as a result. That was in the future, however, and therefore irrelevant. I hurried back home from the meeting to begin the search for parts. It was vital to get things underway as soon as possible, due to the obvious challenge involved in finding all the required bits for an engine made way back in 1948. I was sure that this would prove interesting at the very least, but a solid morning's furtive research (courtesy of various offerings in a well known newsagent's) provided me with a number of possibilities which, I was sure, would at least get the ball rolling. I made the telephone calls and began to tot up the damage as bit by bit I found suppliers for what I needed. It was hard work. Several calls led to the taking down of further numbers, which themselves led to yet more numbers until, by the end of the afternoon, my desk was awash with hastily scribbled details of various specialist engineers, bearing stockists, carburettor outlets and general parts dealers. The remainder of the day flew by.

That evening I took stock of my progress. The re-bore, with new pistons to match, was no problem. All I had to do was take the barrels and old pistons up to Essex, an hour and a half's drive, where an old style engineer had promised to work his magic. Bearings and crankshaft fettling would also be easy, with an engineering supplier in Dover able to deliver the required expertise and parts. Gaskets, seals and perfunctory bits and pieces as may be necessary were all available mail order from Devon. Things were looking up but I still had two very clear problems, for which none of the calls had provided an answer. The carburettor on Daisy, although a thing of beautiful antiquity, was not an easy thing to replace or get fixed. Known as the pre-monobloc, production came to a halt in the early fifties with the introduction of the much improved monobloc version that superseded it. As the name suggests, the later carburettor is a one-piece design, incorporating all of the necessary gubbins into one casting. Daisy's has a rather quaint separate float-bowl, which stands upright and proud to the side of the carburettor body and is attached by a flange and banjo at the bottom. The resulting assembled appendage is delightful to look at and probably remarkably inefficient, but it is an essential part of the character of the machine. I therefore declined the numerous suggestions to just 'throw it away and fit the later one' although I had to quietly accept that it might come to this given the time frame I was working to. The second challenge was sourcing a replacement for the old cast iron cylinder head. These are quite common, when you don't actually need one of the things. Go to any auto jumble if you want the proof, happy in the knowledge that of all the things you may wish to find, a Triumph cylinder head isn't one of them. I guarantee that packs of the things will

follow you round the place, peeping from every other box. Of course, if you were to attend the same jumble, wanting nothing else but a Triumph cylinder head, they will have magically disappeared. Strange but true.

I decided to get the engineering works under way, and whilst waiting for those jobs to be completed, I would resume the search for the more elusive parts. A further week dragged past and despite collecting an ever-increasing list of numbers where 'I might get lucky', I hadn't so far. I was beginning to feel enormously frustrated, but I consoled myself with the thought that having received the cheque from Steve during the week, at least I would be able to take the barrels to Essex and the crankshaft to Dover this weekend. In the event, a chance conversation rendered all such plans unnecessary.It happened on the Friday evening in, of course, the pub. I was drowning my sorrows, as one does at such times, in the company of a fellow Triumph owner. I described to him the challenges of the week just past and was moaning that it was going to take weeks or even months before I would find the correct parts to finish Daisy, and that by then I would have no time left for the landmark challenge. Failure would have to be conceded and I would have to give the engine money back whilst bathing in a spotlight of shame. Or something like that. I probably even affected a nasal whine as I bent his ear, but far from tipping his beer over my head and telling me to snap out of it, he did something far more dramatic.

"I know where there's a complete engine for your bike, recently rebuilt and ready to run" he said. He had of course let me ramble on, enjoying my misery, before telling me this but he wasn't joking it turns out. He told me where I could find the treasure and the following day I made the call and sure enough, I was able to secure the apparently reconditioned lump, complete with magneto and dynamo. There was a catch however. If I wanted the thing, I'd have to collect it from Manchester, which is a good five hour drive each way, but this seemed a small inconvenience compared to the alternative of a soul-destroying search for individual parts. I was left with only the carburettor to find then, but it seemed that luck was now firmly on my side as I continued to make calls to my list of potential saviours. I hit gold dust when I spoke to a company who not only agreed that they could help, but unveiled the fact that they actually had genuine, brand new Amal pre-monobloc carburettors, still in the original box and wrappings. Did they have the right one for Daisy? They did, and yes I could, if I was prepared to hand over a hundred and sixty five quid. Ouch! That was a shock to say the least, representing rather more than I had left over in the Daisy fund after the engine acquisition, which had set me back nearly all of the eight hundred pounds donated. But there was nothing else for it, and I agreed to buy one there and then, reasoning that I would only get a minor beating about the ears, if I took care to pick my moment to come clean with Diane.

It was only a matter of days before I was happily settled back in the garage, with my new treasures, ready to put it all together and launch Daisy once more on the trail of adventure. Chris was keen to help, too, and with the two of us at it the engine slotted in with almost no clownery at all. Only minor blood loss to my fingers resulted, but we pressed on getting primary drive, clutch and casings refitted in short order and finally, it was time to take the superb shiny new carburettor reverentially from it's wrappings. A thing of beauty indeed, but it's got a serious purpose so on it went. By the end of the weekend, she was ready and it was gratifying to here her burst into life after only a couple of kicks. She sounded wonderful. Crisp and eager. A test ride round the block saw me grinning like an idiot – she was perfect. Better than perfect, but more to the point, She was ready for the landmark challenge once more.

Over the next week, running about locally with a refurbished Daisy bedding in, I started thinking that the fitting of an engine of unknown provenance is a bit risky in the cold light of day. After all, it may have looked shiny and new but I had no real idea how well, or not, the engine had been built. Had the builder used good quality components? Were the tolerances and the fit of things like bushes and bearings properly checked and adhered to? How much of the thing has actually been reconditioned? Of course, in my haste to find a solution, I had utterly failed to ask all of these pressing questions or request evidence of components fitted or cost. Neither had I actually checked things over before chucking the thing into Daisy's waiting frame. We would find out soon enough, and it was high time that we got back on the landmark trail again, so it was back to the maps in order to choose some 'safe distance' forays that could be taken at a leisurely pace whilst everything beddded in. Unfortunately, there were not that many landmarks particularly close, and the list of 'local' sites was only four long.

One of these was very close, the South Foreland lighthouse down here on the south coast, near Dover. Being just twenty miles each way with plenty of green lane routes to choose from it seemed an ideal starter for the 'new' engine. Setting off one afternoon, in lovely weather, it was fantastic to be back on the open road, even after only a short break. We meandered across the Sandwich marshes heading vaguely west, Daisy purring along as I gently coaxed her on through winding lanes and pretty little villages. But it wasn't long before I was jerked back to reality, receiving an almighty shock as suddenly I caught a strong whiff of burning oil. I looked down past my leg to see the black stuff everywhere. Bucket loads it seemed, absolutely covering Daisy's timing side, my shoe, my leg and all over her exhausts. Pulling up rapidly in a blind panic, I get off and surveyed the mess, as acrid oil-smoke boiled up from under the tank engulfing me in a sulphurous cloud. Anyone used to riding or working with classic machinery will know that a small amount of hot oil can look like a gallon once it escapes the confines of the engine and spreads. What I was looking at here however, was not a small amount of oil. It covered every surface of the timing side, had coated the gearbox, smothered the oil tank and toolbox, and was boiling away on most of the exhaust system. The stuff was dripping in great glops from the underside of her petrol tank, before cascading in an almost surreal waterfall effect down her engine fins where it added to the general mess underneath.

What on earth had happened? Nothing good clearly, and I had that awful sinking feeling as I crouched down to take a closer look under the tank. It was difficult to see anything amidst the carnage of all that oil, but it didn't seem as though anything had a large hole in it. There are only two other possibilities I could immediately think of, those being that there was a leak in the oil feed to the rocker boxes or the oil feed to the oil pressure gauge, mounted rather cutely in the tank itself, in a panel which also holds ammeter, light switch and a rather neat lead-light. As it was clear that most of the oil was indeed cascading down from that tank recess, I groaned inwardly at the thought of attempting to get the panel off, with it's nightmare of wiring lurking inside the diamond shaped hollow that it covers. And that thought led to my next problem. I had failed to learn from earlier escapades, and still only had a paltry few tools stuffed in various pockets about my person. None of these was the little eight-millimetre socket required to remove the panel securing bolt. Cursing my own stupidity once again I sat heavily on the grass verge and glory be! I could suddenly see the problem clear as day, right there in front of my eyes.

Daisy has a rather quaint copper pipe, feeding off a banjo down on the timing chest and connecting to the oil pressure gauge. Under the dynamo it goes, before running round in a gentle curve, following the dynamo's contour, and finally straight up in front of the push rod tube, where, just before the tank recess, it joins onto a flexible rubber pipe. This joint is firmly held together with a stout hose-clip. Or rather, in this particular instance, it was *not* firmly held together with a hose-clip. The pipe was waving about in the air, connected to nothing at all, pointing straight up under the tank, and has

clearly been pumping the black stuff merrily into the air at some forty pounds per square inch.I shuffled closer and peered up between the exhausts, and there was the rubber hose, dangling innocently and uselessly. I grasped hold of the thing, and realised with deep shame that the whole mess is a self induced event, resulting from sloppy workmanship on my part – the hose-clip was not tightened when I put it all back together leading to the inevitable result that it has blown off under the pressure. I was able to reconnect it with no problems, and scrabbled about in my pockets for a screwdriver with which to do up the clip. The rest of the journey was completed to the accompaniment of a constant, thick and acrid smoke, which boiled up and engulfed me at every stop. I was also attracting amazed stares from onlookers who clearly viewed what they see with deep distaste or, in some cases, outright amusement.

Back at home, I set about the tiresome task of cleaning up the mess, whichwas actually almost impossible with the bike in one piece. The stuff had worked its way into every nook, cranny and crevice and every ride for a week afterwards was rewarded with yet more of it creeping from unknown hiding places to drip or dribble onto engine, exhausts or the floor. That fairly short ride had also caused the expected bedding down of new gaskets and the loosening off of nuts and bolts just about everywhere, so a good hour with the sockets and spanners was spent getting everything just so again, once the basic clean up has been completed. I consoled myself with the fact that the mishap had been entirely my own fault, and therefore did not constitute an ongoing problem. Quite the reverse, Daisy was feeling much more settled and responsive to ride, cruising along easily at the 55mph running in speed on almost no throttle at all. She sounded beautiful as we pottered around the local streets on our daily business and was showing far less inclination to get hot and bothered. There was no doubt in mind then. We were ready for the main assault!

4. Diversion to Le Mans

The unexpected telephone call that was to change my plan for the coming month came on the following Tuesday. Long before I had made the decision to start and build a business, I had, like most people, held a steady and settled career job. The last few years of that part of my life had been spent in the role of Port Services Manager at the freight terminal in Ramsgate, but it's never that simple and I had also inherited a few additional 'hats' along the way, one of which was the esteemed post of Liaison Officer to Her Majesty's Customs and Excise. Those stout gentlemen, by necessity, tend to operate at odds with the rest of the Port Community in that their very role requires them to actually interfere with the normal, smooth running of the operation. Their frequent desire, for example, to take the wheels off trucks in order to look for some substance or other tends to be a bit of a disruption, and of course the owners of the truck in question were invariably not impressed. A Liaison Officer's job was to attempt to work out best practice between these parties of opposed interests, smoothing over ruffles here, looking for compromises there, but in general getting kicked from both sides and being used as the communal punch-bag. In any such position though, one tends to meet and become friends with certain of the characters involved and one of these was Dave. We'll simply call him a senior Government employee for the purposes of this story, and during the two years of my tenure in that position we became very firm friends both in and out of the official environment. This was helped along immeasurably by the fact that Dave kept a 'bottom drawer' from which, in times of stress, he would produce a variety of decent whiskies to aid the process of diplomatic negotiation!

That was all in the distant past, but this was Dave on the telephone now. I hadn't seen or spoken with him for well over a year and it was great to hear from him, but it got even better when I heard what he was calling about. He opened the conversation with "Is that right what i've heard then - you're retarded?" booming into my ear. Before I could respond to that, he clarified things somewhat "Sorry *retired*... My mistake!" He hadn't changed then, I thought, as I explained that whilst certainly I was not employed these days, I was keeping myself busy on and off, with my own choice of work. "Always were a skiving bugger" he offered "And that's why I'm calling – have you ever been to Le Mans?" A pause, whilst I tried to catch up with the sudden change of tack. I explained that no, I never have been there – but why on earth was he calling to ask such a strange question? As usual with Dave the answer wasn't a straight one, instead he answered with another question "Do you remember Tim?" and now I was completely lost. He did go on to explain, after I asked what on earth he was jabbering on about, that he had got into the habit of going to Le Mans for the 24 hour endurance race that the circuit is famous for hosting. He had been making the pilgrimage every year for the past seven or so, with his sons, a few friends and Tim, one of his colleagues from the Service. I had met and dealt with Tim on many occasions, and had got on well with him I recalled, but what did all this have to do with me exactly? I asked the obvious question and Dave explained that due to unforeseen circumstances, two of the group booked this year have had to drop out, and therefore he, Dave, was in possession of two very hard to come by tickets for the whole event, with camping, going cheap. "Would you be up for it?" he asked. I was taken aback a bit at this point. Why on earth did my name come to mind? I've never had any interest in racing, and certainly even less interest in *car* racing. Why ask me?

I asked the question, and after a short pause the booming reply clarified things "You're missing the point old mate!" he declared. "It's not about the bloody *racing*, it's about the camping, the beer, the eating and partying! I can't think of a better bloke to ask!" he added. I said nothing, so he continued "You *do* realise that there's a big classic scene down there, don't you? You'd be in your element." I still said nothing, but Dave is, if nothing else, tenacious and knows which buttons to press "Hey! Why don't you trailer that old thing of yours down there? It would be a hoot!" He carried on for a while, passionately describing the thing in such a way that I had to admit it sounded like fun. But I don't know… I'd have to think about it and give him a call back. In fact, he'd convinced me, but I'm wondering how on earth I would broach the subject of yet another non-earning fun-jaunt, which again doesn't involve my long-suffering wife. Diane had been awfully good, and unbelievably understanding so far, as she watched me dump a career and then drift into this almost nomadic and quite possibly menopausal hobby at the expense of much of our leisure time together. But I suspected that there would be limits to her patience and it's very obvious to me that suggesting I should be allowed to flit off for a week's boozing in France could well be the trigger that invites an almighty explosion, especially in the middle of the already time-consuming Landmark challenge. No, I'd definitely need to think about this, but I promised Dave that I'd call him back soon. "Better be bloody soon matey," he said "We leave on the evening sailing next Tuesday!"

As I replaced the receiver, it was clear that I wouldn't be going. Given some time to work up to it with Diane, I *might have* been able to construct a persuasive argument. Or at least work out a good bribe that from my perspective would see the correct spousal response. But next week? Absolutely no chance. I'd be a suicidal fool to even suggest such a thing and I decided that I might as well just ring Dave straight back and tell him the truth. I would be declared a lightweight, no doubt, but I would explain about the landmark and hide behind that for a reasonable excuse. I was reaching for the telephone again when Chris, who unbeknown to me had heard the whole conversation, or at least my end of it, piped up. "Are we going to go Dad?" I stopped and turned to face him. "What's this 'we' business" I asked "and you're not supposed to eavesdrop on other people's telephone calls!" I added, exasperated as I realised that this is what he'd done.

"I didn't deliberately" he protested his innocence "I was in the hall cleaning my shoes – like you told me to! Its not my fault you shout down the 'phone!" I backed off, having no intention of being embroiled in a petty argument with a teenager right now, thank you.

"We can't go unfortunately." I explained "Your mother would go ballistic if I even suggested it, and you've got school anyway!" He didn't respond, but there was a huge look of disappointment on his face and with that, I wandered off to the kitchen to search the 'fridge for beer. I know how wheedling and persuasive both kids can be when they really want something, and I could see Chris was scheming some kind of logical argument which I had no intention of getting sucked into. I completely forget to telephone Dave. I ran a bath shortly after, and when I had floated around soaking for about an hour, I returned downstairs to where the family were watching television. But as soon as I enter Chris piped up with "Mum says it's OK for you to go, but that I'll have to get permission from school" I stared at him for a split second, and then cast a fearful look at Diane, only to be met with a face that in all but actual words is saying "This is going to cost you – dearly". And it didn't take long to discover what scheming had been going on in the last hour, as the girls presented the details of a deal that would see Chris and I in Le Mans next week, whilst they, at my expense apparently, went to London for a show, a hotel stay and of course, shopping in Oxford Street on the Saturday. I tried to do the mental arithmetic, but gave up at the thought of mother and daughter let loose in London, armed with funds. I concentrated instead on the thought of father and son set loose in France, armed with a tent and an old motorcycle. I quickly agreed to the blackmail and retired to make the call to Dave accepting his kind offer. I told him that I was going to ride Daisy to Le Mans and not trailer her as he had suggested. He expresses an opinion that I was, in fact, barking mad, but I explained that there are two very good reasons for my decision. One, the weather forecast was good and the ride would be fantastic. Two, I don't posses a trailer or for that matter, even have a tow-bar on the car!

I met up with Dave on the Monday, in order to hand over our camping gear, spare clothes and other paraphernalia, which he had offered to take down for us in his car. He had Tim with him, and we retired for several pints in the local pub, where the pair regaled me with tales from previous Le Mans expeditions. We parted company that afternoon having agreed that Dave, his two boys and Tim would be the advanced party, leaving on Tuesday evening and driving down overnight and that we'd make our own way down and meet up with them on the Wednesday. If all goes to plan Chris and I will get an early ferry and be at the site late afternoon. Packing Daisy is much easier now that the bulky gear has gone on ahead, and I chose to use the space for some more sensible precautions against the unknown. A full set of tools, plug spanner, spare inner tube, some gasket goo, spare bulbs and some spare chain links. This was more than I'd ever had the space to carry before, and confidence was high for a successful trip come what may.

Wednesday morning, six o'clock, and it was raining. In fact, it was throwing stair-rods down outside and I'd been caught out yet again in the planning department because we still don't posses any sensible waterproof riding gear. Our total protective kit still consisted of a pair of thin nylon water resistant trousers each and little else. We both put on extra layers under our jackets, and I packed a pair of spare gloves into Daisy's tank bag, knowing from experience that my first pair would get saturated after a while. With that we ventured out into the thoroughly grey and miserable morning and set off towards Folkestone and the Channel Tunnel. Once out on the open roads, we were subjected to a buffeting wind which whisked the ragged black clouds across our heads and threw the rain harshly at us in great sweeping waves. By the time we had covered the thirty or so miles to Cheriton, we were not only thoroughly soaked through but uncomfortably cold. When we pulled up under the harsh bright lighting at the check-in for our crossing, I could see that my entire body surface was glistening and shiny with water. My teeth began chattering as I attempted to converse with the patient stewardess, and I mentally shriveled when I inserted my hand into the damp clammy pocket of my jacket to retrieve the tickets. There is nothing quite so distasteful as a waterlogged leather jacket, I thought, but that thought soon changed as I tried to insert my hand back into the equally waterlogged glove. I gave up, stuffed the thing into my teeth, and headed off towards the terminal building which looked warm and inviting, but most importantly, dry.

Pulling up as close as possible to the main entrance, I killed Daisy's engine and braced myself for the horrible moment when I'd have to get off. Anyone who has been soaked over a fair distance, due to inadequate precautions, will know exactly what I mean. I had settled into a fixed slouch, where most of my joints had got at least half rigid and whatever moisture had seeped through the leather and nylon (and there was quite a lot) had at least been warmed marginally with body heat. In short, I had settled into a cocoon of semi optimised misery and the awful moment of actually moving and standing up would, I knew, shatter all that and allow a myriad of new and cold leaks to work their horrors on me. The act of dismounting and walking would cause the soaked jacket to transmit the most unpleasant clammy sensations. I was also waiting for the inevitable grumps from Chris, who was doubtless wishing he had stayed home in bed, and would probably start suggesting that we give up any minute now. As we walked into the blissful warmth, my spirit was further dragged down by the squelching and squishing coming from my shoes, which, it is now plainly obvious, are full of water. I cursed myself yet again that I still had not got round to buying any boots. Chris was at least luckier in that department as we had recently picked up some ex-para boots for him at an Army & Navy store, but none were to be had in my size. I squished my way miserably to the nearest table, sat down, removed the things and poured about a pint of water into a large indoor tub, complete with small tree, nearby.

Chris was having no such problems, and it appeared that he was not remotely bothered by the conditions. He even offered to go and get coffee for us both, and as he cheerfully headed off to the cafeteria I pondered the fact that I will probably never get the hang of teenagers. Or was it possible that the experiences he had been having on these adventures was paying dividends, and he's far more prepared to go with the flow? I didn't know the answer, but it was a pleasing thought and I began to feel my mood lighten as I went through the motions of removing all the wet gear and hanging it around the place in a vain attempt to at least dry it a little bit. Chris returned with two large steaming styrofoam cups and as we sat and drank I surreptitiously removed my socks, one at a time, and set about wringing them out in the tub. Chris was appalled by this apparent delinquent behaviour, and told me to stop as I was embarrassing him!

Twenty minutes later our train was announced and we were called for loading, which meant climbing back into all the clammy damp gear again. A truly distasteful experience, but there was nothing for it so on it all went, and out we go into the waterfall once more. We had to stop at Passport Control, whilst I scrabbled about in the tank bag looking for the things, then we were through and being flagged over at the security checkpoint. They wanted me to pull into a side-lane for a check. I just wanted to get on the bloody train and get out of that damp gear, but there was no point arguing, and over we went to the checkpoint where we were subjected to a sweep with some kind of device that I presume was 'sniffing' for explosives or some such. Finally we were allowed forward, but as we headed up and over to the loading platforms the sky opened once again and we were caught in a fierce cloudburst that soaked us more thoroughly than anything had so far that morning.

On the train at last, we had a whole compartment to ourselves. The Eurotunnel or 'Le Shuttle' trains are a fascinating design and the operation is actually very smooth. Unlike ferries, travellers stay in their car in large airy compartments and although it is possible to get out and wander around, there is nothing really to see. There are no facilities other than airline style toilets. If, like us, you are travelling with a motorcycle, you literally just park in the compartment and sit on the floor! On this occasion, we took the opportunity to drape various wet and soggy clothing over just about anything that would hold it, and the venting system was at least blowing warm air onto it all. I chatted to Chris about the appalling weather, and we both fervently hoped that France will offer an improvement. The thought of more of the same made me shudder, because we I knew we had some three hundred and twenty miles to cover the other side and here we were after only thirty, thoroughly soaked, bedraggled and not very warm. Daisy was also looking rather bedraggled, and as the water dripped off her to form an expanding puddle, decorated with a psychedelic rainbow of colours, I thought that she won't cut much of a dash in Le Mans. She was spattered with mud and road dirt, and had that smudgy brown/grey residue smeared over most exposed surfaces –in short, she looked a mess. I cheered myself slightly with the thought that at least the camping gear and spare clothes went ahead in a dry car.

The black square that is the window suddenly flashed into daylight once more and within minutes the PA system announced arrival in Calais, urging all drivers to return to their vehicles. For us this meant climbing back into that damp gear once again and I steeled myself for what was about to come. But once you're wet you're wet, and we were soon seriously wet. I don't really mind being wet, as such, but being wet and cold is just pants. I was wet and cold right then, as we sat under a bridge and watched the maelstrom of wind and rain that we had just escaped. This had not been helped by the lorries that had been continuouslysweeping past at some 70mph, engulfing us in repeated blasts of air, spray and dirt. We had managed no more than fifty miles and it had been nothing short of torture. I hadn't even managed to maintain a decent speed, due to my open faced helmet, which allows the hammering rain to batter my face and make my vision seriously deficient. And this was hard rain too, each drop stinging like a needle point as it hit. Thankfully, French roads have wide hard shoulders, in which I was able to position Daisy, well out of the way of those barrelling trucks, in an effort to survive at the 40mph we were being forced to ride at. That was the fourth bridge we'd sheltered under and Chris was getting fractious about the number of stops we were making, but I was just not prepared to carry on in that downpour and I explained to him that it would be bloody dangerous to try. I fetl sorry for the lad though, as I reflected that this great adventure was turning into a miserable and, for him, boring endurance. We climbed up the sloping concrete foundation and sat high up to get out of the spray from those trucks, and I almost laughed as I looked at Chris. He had a little river running off his helmet, onto his nose, where the water gathered in dripped before falling. He was ignoring this and sat there, hunched, looking out at the rubbish we've been riding through. Suddenly, Chris voices his feelings, "This is crap!" I couldn't agree more and I wanted to go home, I decided, but I wasn't going to be the one to suggest it, hoping that Chris would. Should he have voiced any such thoughts I would readily have agreed.

He wasn't about to suggest any such thing though. Instead he offered a different approach "Can't we find a services, and then we can wait until it stops," he said. "At least we can get food then" he adds. This seemed like as good a plan as any, and we climbed down to Daisy, mounted up once more, and headed out into weather. The services were a good twenty miles further on, it turned out, and when we finally got there I was on the edge of losing the will to live. We pulled into the place and rode right up to the entrance of the cafeteria, where there was a cover, lurched to a stop and almost collapsed in a heap right there. I had never been wetter or colder in my entire life. I put Daisy on the stand, and marveled at the cloud of steam coming off her. She looked a complete state, and an observer could be forgiven for thinking that we'd just ridden her through a series of increasingly muddy fields. I couldn't be bothered to worry about that though, I was just desperate to get inside and warm up. Chris had beaten me to it and had already disappeared into the place, and I followed *toute-suite*.

Inside, we looked at each other as an alarming puddle spread around our feet. Chris struggled out of his jacket, pulled off his helmet gave his head a good scratch and exclaimed "Thank God for that!" before heading straight over to the food counter where he critically began to inspect the offerings. I got my own gear off more slowly – my jacket seemed to weigh three times it's normal amount, the gloves felt like a pair of sodden turfs and my shoes were full of water again. My shirt and fleece had both succumbed to leakage and were damp all around the chest and arms. The nylon trousers had given up any attempt at resisting the rain some time ago and my jeans now sported a big dark patch around crotch and knees. I stood there feeling relieved, at least, to be rid of it all and I turned to survey the food counter. Chris was coming back from his inspection and as I turned he clocked that big dark stain and bursts out laughing as he exclaimed "Dad! – You've peed yourself!"

"Yes...very bloody funny" I muttered, not a little amazed at his continued good spirits. "It's all right for you, you're sheltered behind me," I added "I'm getting the full force of all the weather!"

"Yeah right!" came the sarcastic response. He then pointed at the counter area, made the simple statement "food" and smiled happily. We went to get a tray, and in short order we were sitting with large sausages, large coffees and giggling like a couple of schoolgirls at the state we'd got ourselves into. There's nothing like food and warmth to restore some semblance of spirit, but we were soon talking about what we should do next. Chris still hadn't even begun to look like he was ready to quit and in that way of blind optimism he occasionally shows, he assured me that it's just a matter of waiting. I failed to see the logic of this but one thing I did agree with him about, is that we were not going to go out in that rubbish again, and in the meantime I decided to teach the lad a trick or two in the survival department.

"Get your gloves and jacket," said I "and follow me". For an instant, I think Chris believed that I had lost my senses and was about to go back out. Instead, I headed for the gents toilet, carrying my jacket, gloves and shoes. Inside, I saw what I was hoping for, but first I laid my sodden stuff out on the washbasins, and attempted wring it all out in the sink before grabbing a handful of paper towels, which I proceeded to stuff up sleeves, in shoes and inside gloves.

"What are you doing?" enquired Chris.

"Trust me, and do the same" I said, reaching for his gloves and stuffing them with towels.

"What for?" he's wasn't convinced at all "I'm not doing that – it's stupid" he added.

I can't be bothered to argue and simply leave it, saying, "OK, suit yourself, but just watch and you'll learn something and probably be much drier!"

As he slouched by the basins, looking as cynical as only a fourteen year old can, I reflected that it may seem to him that I've lost my marbles. Clearly all that water has addled my brain, but as I squeezed and squished the arms of my jacket and my gloves, then pulled the saturated towels out and re-charged with fresh ones, he began to see the merit of my actions. Of course, being a teenager, he wasn't about to admit anything, but he did grab a handful of the things and begin shoving them in his own jacket. He managed to convey a clear message - 'I'm only doing this to humour you' and I smiled to myself in that way that only a parent of teenagers understands. After three refills I was feeling a bit guilty for wasting the towels, but needs must when the devil drives and I went for one final stuffing. Then it was time for the warm-air hand dryers, and I demonstrated to Chris how to thread the sleeve end over the thing and allow the hot drying air-rush to do it's stuff. It was tedious this, but quite effective, with even Chris quickly seeing the merits of the operation and doing the same on another dryer. We were there for over half an hour, swapping sleeves, gloves and shoes until everything was at least only damp rather than sopping wet, as it was when we started. Miraculously, when we finally exited, we saw through the windows that it had actually stopped raining. On the minus side, we were now being scrutinized by the counter attendant, who was clearly wondering what on earth we'd been up to in the Gents for nearly forty minutes and had equally clearly convinced himself of an answer that definitely didn't meet with his approval. I wondered whether the gendarmes might show up before we leave!

Eventually, we went outside and had a look around at the sky. It was definitely brightening and the rain had stopped for sure so we decided to make a go of it, helped by the fact that I was not about to go and face the attendant, with his withering glare and ask for more coffee. We got ourselves togged up again, only wincing slightly at the horrible sensation of warm, damp clothing, which I know from experience, will rapidly become cold clammy clothing once outside and we exited under the continued suspicious glare of the Frenchman inside. Helmet on, only shuddering slightly as the wet earpieces slid damply over my ears and the clammy strap tightened round my neck. Gloves on, ditto the horrible sensation, climb onto Daisy and attempt to fire her up. Nothing happens. Another kick, then another and another. Nothing. Not even a pop. I leaned under the tank and tickled her up again, flooding the remote float well and truly. Ease her over compression and then a big heave on the kick-start. Still nothing, not a sausage. I immediately reached an all time low for the day and slumped in the seat to stare into oblivion. "Don't do this to me Daisy, not here, not now!" I was thinking, and Chris, bang on cue, mutters "Oh great!"

I dismounted, removed helmet and gloves, scrabbled about in the tank bag for a plug spanner, and proceeded to remove a plug for inspection and a spark test. It is soaked with petrol, indicating that Daisy has succumbed to the Prince of Darkness' famous weakness in the wet. Attaching the plug to it's HT lead, I asked Chris to hold it against the cylinder while I kick, but he's gathered a small knowledge of the workings of such things and quickly backed away muttering "No way". We bickered for a few seconds, but he was adamant and I couldn't be bothered, so I did it the hard way, holding the thing myself whilst trying to kick and squint down to see if there's a spark. I already knew the answer I suppose, but confirmation followed. Not a sausage. Bugger. Squatting down on the cold wet concrete was horrible, but there was no choice, as I struggled to get at the magneto. Everything under there was coated with filth, so I revisited the tank bag for some Kleenex, tried to wipe the worst of it away, and then removed both HT connectors from the Magneto body. These were full of water but that's easy to sort out by making little twisted sausages from Kleenex, shoving them into the pick-up and wiggling them around. I held my lighter under each one, being careful not to melt the things, until I was happy that they are good and dry. I gave the same treatment to the HT lead ends themselves, before reassembling it all and trying the kick-starter once more.

Daisy was still sulking, and producing no hint of the healthy blue spark I was expecting. I cursed virulently, looked at Chris, shruged, and headed back down behind the engine. This time I removed, after a Herculean struggle, the screw on end-cap behind which live the points. It's possible I reasoned, that water has got into this part of the magneto, and a set of damp or wet points would easily cause a lack of sparking action. As the cap came off, I was amazed as something like an eggcup full of water poured out and dribbled down my hand. Clearly this would cause the problem, but I can't think how it got into the cavity which is, after all, a sealed unit to all intents and purposes. I spent a good five minutes dabbing the Kleenex in there and by then Chris was looking over my shoulder wanting to know what's going on. I explained about the water in everything and how that effects the electrical connections, causing the lack of sparks. But having dried things as best I could, I try again only to discover that after several hefty kicks I am no further forward. There are still no sparks. Crouching once more, I muttered about the difficulty of getting the points and their assembly dry and Chris asked why I didn't do the same trick with the lighter. I explained that the ancient carburettor, with its leaky float chamber which has been freshly flooded, is directly above the magneto, dripping petrol. It would be pretty dodgy holding a naked flame under that, I suggested, and he got the point. What we can do though, I suddenly realised, is take the end plate and points off and take them inside to the hand dryer which would surely do the trick. A few minutes later I had them off, but as we headed back inside, it occured to me that the French gentleman, already highly suspicious of our earlier long absence in the gents, must now be absolutely convinced of wrongdoing. He watches us both disappear back into them once more. I avoid eye contact, and hurry into the place, eager to get this done and get out again as quickly as possible, but it took nearly ten minutes under the dryer before all the bits seemed thoroughly dry. Finally, we scuttled back out again, under the continuing steely glare, and I had to resist the urge to stop and try and explain. It would only confirm the man's suspicions I'm sure. At last I had everything re-fitted, and once again straddled Daisy. The underside of my foot was already painful, with the beginnings of a mighty blister I thought, from the earlier kicking, and I winced as I heaved the thing once more. Not only did Daisy spark, but she also started on the one cylinder that still has its plug in place. Hurrah! What a relief .

Every cloud has a silver lining. We had lost another half an hour, but by the time I'd finished mucking about and we were ready to go, the weather had improved further. It hadn't rained for nearly half an hour, the tarmac was beginning to dry up and there were even breaks beginning to show up amongst the clouds in the otherwise grey leaden sky. With Daisy now ticking over sweetly beneath us, like a cheap Japanese watch, I looked over my shoulder and hail Chris. "Ready then?" I ask. "I was ready an hour ago" he quips, but there's a grudging half smile there so I took that as a positive and let out the clutch. We threaded our way through the service area and out onto the road once more, heading for Rouen first, taking the long coastal dual-carriageway that connects Calais, Boulogne and Le Havre and this turns out to be a sore test for Daisy as the road undulates like a roller coaster between a number of fairly severe inclines. Down into the dips we would build up a head of steam before turning up at the bottom and facing the long steep climb up the other side of each, testing Daisy to the full and causing me to work the gearbox several times in order to keep the poor old girl moving without strain. And so it went for miles, until eventually Rouen was behind us and we got onto the smaller road that takes us across country to Alencon, then Le Mans. There was evidence of a new motorway under construction, but this existing road was far more suitable for Daisy's abilities, sweeping along between sleepy little towns alternating with woodland or heath, with bright yellow gorse bushes bordering the tarmac. The air had got steadily warmer as we continued south, and the sky was becoming increasinglylighter, with more and more breaks through which patches of blue sky were showing. We stopped in a lay-by and looked back along the incredibly straight stretch of road and could see the dark clouds, almost black, that we had left behind us.In the other direction, the one we were heading towards, a vast blue sky stretched to the horizon. A cricket chose that moment to strike up a tune, off to our left, and there was no traffic in sight at all. The road stretched ahead, empty, and the only sound wass a light wind in the trees to accompany the cricket. After the rubbish start to this trip, it was serene in the extreme!

Eventually reaching Alencon, we avoided the new motorway to Le Mans, this section of which had freshly opened, and took the smaller route through some delightful little villages as it meandered south. We had something like thirty miles left and I stopped after a while to make a telephone call to Dave. He seemed surprised that we were so late, and I was shocked on checking my watch to find that the time really had been tramping on.It was nearly 7.30 in the evening, and I told Dave that we'll give him the full story on arrival, over a few beers. He gave me directions to what he refered to as 'the pub', which was apparently opposite our campsite, and armed with that we got under way for the last leg of our journey. We were soon on the outskirts of the town, which is a fairly sizeable place, and picked up the ring road following signs to the red camping zone, our base for the week. Although it was early in the week, it was obvious that there was already a fairly large number of visitors there from the UK, judging by the number of GB-plated cars we encountered. And what cars – MGs, Bentleys, TVRs, Aston Martin and Porsches, you name it there was an abundance of them. The race set was here in force, sporting their own road versions of iconic racing legends. Daisy was attracting a lot of appreciation as we continued round the ring road and we got honked, tooted and waved at numerous times before we found the red sign off to our right and turned off. The the roads here were very, very busy, with the whole area around the racetrack and the camping zones completely grid-locked. There were Gendarmes at every junction, doing their best to keep things moving, but they were fighting a losing battle I reckoned. It was even difficult to filter through the mayhem with Daisy, and before long she was getting hot, bothered and temperamental. Fifteen minutes later however, we finally found the junction across from which was the entrance to our campsite. I turned turn left as Dave had instructed, and there at last was the big pub.

The road leads down a long slope to the main stadium and circuit, but half way along is this large bar. It has a sizeable forecourt sloping sharply down to the road, and is itself built on a platform with a large veranda. The net effect is to give patrons a very good vantage point, looking down on the main drag to the circuit and across to the sprawling campsite opposite. The place was absolutely heaving with happy souls enjoying what had become a warm, sunny evening, and as we rode down the hill to the forecourt, pulling up on the apron, a loud cheer went up from the veranda. We threaded slowly up through the crowd, in an attempt to park Daisy somewhere close, and I suddenly became aware that we'd picked up a following of about four happily drunken admirers. Another one decided to assist us, and pushed ahead yelling "mind y' backs!" and using his arms like a snowplough. We stopped under the veranda, the crowd pushed in around us, and before I had even turned off Daisy's overheated engine, someone was pushing a pint of beer at me! Several more were patting me on the back, Chris was receiving the same welcome and we were both overwhelmed by the sheer bonhomie and almost Mardi Gras atmosphere. Helpful hands reached out to steady Daisy as Chris and I dismounted amongst the jostling crowd, and by the time I had managed to remove helmet and gloves and get her on the stand, I was the proud owner of two pints of beer, with several more on offer. Marvellous!

We dumped the helmets in a flower bed just by the pub entrance, stretched, and both found ourselves fending off a barrage of questions "What is it?" "How old is she?", "Have you ridden her all the way?", "Which ferry did you catch", "What? All the way from Calais?", "Wanna beer?" And in the middle of all that, Chris was standing nine-feet tall with pride, enthusiastically regaling his new friends with stories of our recent trials and troubles. He'd got a beer too, I noticed – I'd better keep an eye on him. Over the hubbub I heard my name being called and looked around to see Dave and the rest of our party up on the veranda. Excusing myself from my new found mates, I made my way through the crowd towards the steps, but Chris was having far too much fun telling stories to follow me at the moment and I went up to meet Dave on my own. There was more beer waiting at their table and I realised I'd have to watch myself as well as Chris, although there was no more riding to be done today what with the entrance to our campsite being directly opposite. I gratefully accepted the offered chair that they'd kept for me, and finally sat down to soak up the surprisingly warm evening sunshine and atmosphere. Tim and Dave, gave me a run down on the layout and what's in store for the week.

This whole area, the campsite and the pub, are at the centre of what has become, unofficially, the British sector of race week. The Brit contingent to the Le Mans 24 hour race is usually about 80,000 although they tend to be spread across a number of large campsites around the central stadium. The one we were staying in was fairly small and is actually a cattle market for the rest of the year. That means you can camp under the tin roofed stalls, which I imagine normally are filled with next week's dinner. Crowds of Brits, in party mood, gather here at the pub to watch the steady arrival of various owner's clubs and tasty machinery. And this is one of the real attractions of Le Mans week – it has a huge classic following, albeit the four wheeled variety, and Dave's enthusiasm was infectious as he rattled off the marques to look out for. You have, he told me, the AC Cobras, the vintage Bentleys, MGBs, Jaguars (E, S and even C types in abundance he said), Ferraris, Morgans and everything in between. "Oh, and you get the odd crappy old bike turning up as well." That was Tim's contribution. This reminded me to check on Chris, and I stood to peer over the balcony to see him still holding court. He seemed to have acquired another beer, and was earnestly discussing some finer point of Daisy's design with a man who seemed to be fascinated with the sprung hub. They were both crouched down and peering at the back wheel, and I wondered just what Chris was telling the guy. But he seemed happy, so I decided to leave him to it.

When I got back to our table, more beer had appeared. I realised that this could turn into a bit of a session but before that happened I needed to get Daisy parked up, and more to the point, get something to eat. Dave agreed. He despatched his boys Dan and Mitch to go and get the food started – "They're doing us a Spag Bol" he declared. The beers were consumed whilst we idly chatted about the week ahead and eventually we all got up to go across to the camp. Pushing back through the crowd, I found Chris still burbling away, helped I'm sure by two pints of ale he's not used to. I tell him it's dinner time. and as we retrieved our gear, Dave set off across the road and we got set to follow. The crowd gave us space to turn round ready to leave. I thought about pushing Daisy across to our camp, but the track up to the campsite was on a steep incline. We'd ride. Daisy started first kick, and as her deep bark echoed across the area, another huge cheer went up from the veranda. I looked up and there was a crowd of happy alcoholic grins looking back at me. I nearly fell off laughing as we slowly pulled off the forecourt, because the crowd had burst into and impromptu, whistled rendition of the theme tune to 'The Great Escape' the film in which Steve McQueen made at least one bit of his escape bid on a pre-unit Triumph. (disguised to look like a German machine) It was British 'off the cuff' humour at it's best and I had a suspicion that this would happen to us numerous times if we visit this bar through the week!

Up at camp, we settled down to enjoying the huge tub of Spaghetti the lads had produced and then just sat outside the tents watching the last of the sun's rays dying on the Western horizon. Chris had been sensible and moved onto coke but Dave, Tim and Myself, renewing our friendship after more than a year's gap, indulged a bit too much. At some point in the evening, Dave's chair collapsed under him, a result of leaning back too far, and he promptly went over backwards into the little half-tent serving as food and beer store, demolishing the entire thing. The lads, who had been watching us, collapsed into laughter and Dave seemed to find his new position just as comfortable as his chair was, and carried on regardless. All around us, across the site, a mighty party was in full swing, with music, laughter and the odd firework going off, but the long day caught up with us and we retired, some of us distinctly unsteadily, to bed.

There was nothing major to do until Friday evening when the real events linked to the racing were due to begin, starting with practice and qualifying. The party atmosphere was certain to continue building steadily, and Chris and I decided to spend Thursday and Friday exploring all the roads around Le Mans and the surrounding villages. We started by following the others through the lanes to the local town of Arnage, (the place after which the recent Bentley model was named), where we got ourselves on the outside of breakfast. The sun had come out with force that morning, and even at 8.30 it was already hot. The others told me that it was likely to get much hotter through the day, but right then, sitting at a table under large umbrellas, waiting for the French version of bacon and eggs, it was almost ideal. We were seated at a pavement cafe right by the main road (it was actually quaint and picturesque) through the village, and passing us was a constant stream of very extravagant cars which excited Dave, Tim and the lads no end. For me there were also some fantastic classics mixed in with them, and I even spied an old motorcycle. By nine o'clock the pavement cafés along the entire street were absolutely packed with people and there was nowhere left to sit. One got the impression that the huge crowd of people were there for a reason, and it wasn't long before I understood what that was.

It's customary it seems, when driving through the villages in race week, to stop by any of the crowded pavement cafés and sit, revving your engine until the mob responds and a count down begins. If you want to get a loud cheer from the boisterous patrons, you need to produce a display of 'smoking tyres' at the end of the count. The more smoke, the louder the praise and applause. It was fascinating to sit there and just watch this spectacle going on, and I marveled that the local people simply got on with their daily lives, completely ignoring it all. I guessed that they must be used to it, and certainly they must welcome the annual boost to the local economy. The tolerance of public behaviour that would be deemed completely unacceptable anywhere else, was underlined by the attitude of the Gendarmes. The whole thing appeared to be a bit of a game – the tyre smoking would happen seemingly spontaneously, but I couldn't help but notice that it happened at whichever café was furthest from the Gendarmes, who, in turn were moving around the whole time. Occasionally one would appear from nowhere and catch someone in the act, but a wagging finger and a cynical raised eyebrow would be the only reprimand to most. The message was clear then- Have a bit of fun, but keep it sensible because we *are* watching!

Our group split up after breakfast, with Chris and I deciding to take a ride round the surrounding area using the roads that form part of the circuit where possible. These would be closed for the racing but were open until the evening when practice was due to start. By race day, it would be necessary to go out into the surrounding lanes to get around at all, and cutting across country would be the only way to get to some of the viewing areas, such as the Arnage bend, or the Mulsanne straight. This morning recce would come in handy later on! By lunch time we had worked out how to get around, and had marked various short cuts and routes that could be used when it all gets shut off, on a map of the circuit and surrounding roads supplied by Dave. By then, the heat was intense to say the least and we returned to the camp site , met up with the others once more, and agreed that lunch in Arnage would be the thing to do. Traffic was getting pretty nasty though and it seemed that half the circuit and most of the surrounding roads were in total gridlock. All folk heading for the outlying villages with the same plan as us. Chris and I could filter past the long queues and so pressed on ahead in an attempt to secure a table at one of the pavement café's. We were lucky, finding and claiming what we needed as the village rapidly filled to bursting point. The others took nearly half an hour to join us, but then we all sat there in the glorious weather and watched a repeat performance of the endless line of tasty machinery filing past. There was a noticeably larger Gendarme attendance by then, however, and that kept the grandstanding to a minimum.

After lunch, it was back to the site, and time to park Daisy up for the day. We spent the afternoon wandering around, visiting the circuit, the Le Mans museum and finally the big pub, before meeting up once again with the others and heading back to enjoy an evening in the sun and a large barbecue. From our position above the surrounding area, we could look down on the airfield that was adjacent to the circuit, watching an endless line of private jets and helicopters shuttling the corporate VIPs in and out. The evening was finished off by a walk down to the circuit, where a funfair was in full swing, a number of bars attempted desperately to serve the throng, shops buzzed and a plethora of little stalls sold various offerings to eat, if one dared. A final visit to the pub on the way home rounded the day off nicely and then it was bedtime.

It was wise, apparently, to get a good night's sleep when one can earlier in the week, because precious little would be had from now on as the huge gathering swings fully into party mood. Bizarrely, there were a group of Danes camped next to us who, as a way of getting themselves into the right frame of mind for the big race, had a tape of racing cars variously accelerating at full chat, or crashing through gears at some hairpin or other. They played this at full volume continuously and it made sleeping almost impossible. After a while it was grating seriously on the nerves, but thankfully someone else felt the same and a harsh verbal altercation eventually took place, after which the Danes, protesting loudly, turned the thing off. Further attempts to sleep were only occasionally disrupted by the odd firework or burst of noise or laughter from one or other of the group camps nearby. There was no denying however, that a great atmosphere was building, and as I drifted off I wondered what tomorrow, which I'd been assured is when the *real* party begins, will be like.

Friday dawned, and we were awoken by a loud murmuring nearby. As I slowly became conscious, Chris stirred too, and we both lay listening to a seemingly one-sided conversation that was clearly not English, or French. It was Dutch, I thought, as I turned over and tried to get back to sleep, but the monotonous monologue continued. Chris muttered something about wishing they'd shut up and somebody else obviously agreed because a very belligerent English voice yelled out.

"Oi! It's bloody six o'clock! Some of us are trying to sleep so will you shut up about your sodding tulips!"

Chris spontaneously started giggling, which started me off, and we both listened hard to see what would come next. But the Dutchman had got the message and with no more entertainment, we dozed off again in the early light and don't come round again until nearly ten o'clock. We stumbled blearily out into the bright sunshine, to find most of the others in the act of brewing up the morning tea. I shuffled off to the ablutions block to freshen up before breakfast, which apparently was best had at a little café about half a mile up the road, towards the town. Dave, Tim and the boys decided to walk up as there would be no place to park, they said. Chris and I were going to have a ride down past the circuit and around the campsites first, and agreed to meet up with them all at the café. The airfield was already busy, we noticed, as was the general area at the entrance to the stadium and track. Traffic was murderous at the junction there, with many a Gendarme attempting to keep things moving, but once past it we could stretch Daisy's legs down the long straight road, past the campsites on the right and down to the end of the enclosed part of the track. As we continued to thread our way along we could tell from the building atmosphere that this was going to be a great fun day.

We were still in the British sector and It was clear from the now packed fields that most of the visitors had arrived, set up camp and were killing time till the race in that peculiarly British way – by consuming vast amounts of ale! Already they were lining the roads, sitting on the grassy banks or fences watching all the tasty cars go by. Daisy attracted a number of cheers or shouted compliments, and at regular intervals Chris, who had never before experienced such a gathering, would lean over my shoulder to exclaim his amazement at the scenes. We headed round in a large circle, back towards our own site and that appointment with breakfast, arriving just in time to see the others filing in. There was no menu. Breakfast was a large bowl of coffee, bread, butter and fried eggs. That was it. If you don't like coffee and eggs you're out of luck. We do like those things, and as we ate, Chris enthusiastically told the gathering about the scenes down towards the track. "That's nothing," he is told by those who have been before "They're just waking up at the moment. Wait until later, when they've had a shed-load of beer. You will be amazed at what goes on!"

We discussed the day's plans, and Chris and I were told that whatever we decided to do, we must make sure that we got back to the camp-site by eight o'clock. We were to be taken, Tim announced "to a restaurant the likes of which you will never see anywhere else in the entire world!" That sounded amazing, but they wouldn't tell us any more. Knowing Dave as I do, I thought the place must be pretty out of the ordinary. Great! something to look forward to then, but for now it was back to the site for a while, freshen up and then off around the area again to see what transpired. We had booked a lunch table at Arnage again, and as Chris and I got ready to leave, we all agreed to meet up there later.

Now then, it's a tradition in Le Mans, that on the Friday during race week, various parts of the roads around the circuit become unofficial 'checkpoints'. Unofficial because they are manned, not by French Gendarmes as you might expect, but drunken Englishmen. When passing one of these 'checkpoints' you will be stopped and asked to provide 'smoking

tyres' up the road for the entertainment of the crowd lining both sides of the road for about 200 yards. It doesn't matter what you're driving or riding, but the more extravagant your wheels, the more insistent the crowd are that you must please. If you decline, your attention is drawn once again to that long line of happily drunken spectators and you may now notice, possibly for the first time, that they are armed with big plastic water cannons! You can expect loud derision and a thoroughly good soaking if you try to escape without making the effort. Occasionally a few Gendarmes will show themselves, just to make sure that things are not getting out of hand, and it was a piece of pantomime second to none. It was great fun to watch, as Chris and I discovered when we pulled in at the big pub for a couple of cokes.

Picture this then; There were two chaps 'manning' this particular checkpoint. The pub forecourt was absolutely packed, as was the road that runs down past it. People were lining the thing on both sides, there were a lot of water cannons on display, and *everything was* getting stopped. Those that thought they were safe from the water, smug behind wound up windows, and therefore able to ignore the challenge laid down, found that they really should have locked their doors. More than one local French family, and indeed incidental visitor, declined to put on the required show, and suddenly found all four doors opened and half a dozen water canons spoiling their day! The best part for us was seeing the occasional unknowing *poseur* in their open topped TVRs or Ferraris, clearly caught out and more than a bit rattled as they tried to decide between abuse of their expensive tyres or having their pride and joy (and themselves) thoroughly soaked inside and out! Some simply tried to push their way through without stopping. Oh Dear!

While we watched the fun and games Daisy was attracting more than a little attention, and Chris, the duty hero, gladly talked with any who wished to know more. My attention was distracted however, as down at the checkpoint a motorcyclist on a modern street-fighter style machine had been stopped. As the crowd cheer, jeer and cajole, this chap removed helmet and gloves, handed them to the guy that had stopped him, and settled down in the saddle once more. They want a show? Here was their man. He gave his throttle a number of almighty blips, held the front brake firm, revved hard and dumped the clutch. Smoke boiled from the rear tyre as the wheel span madly. He stopped suddenly and studied the crowd. The crowd roared a cheer and egged him on. He sat back, cupped his ear up towards the pub, as if to say 'What?' He got a louder roar, and, with a couple more blips and a quick check to make sure the way was clear, he was off popping a wheelie right up through the cheering crowd. He got huge applause as he came down at the end and stopped. He turned facing down the hill now, and cupped his ear again. Another huge roar, and down he came, slowly, grinning at the crowd. He stood up on his pegs as he came, and as he got to the pub, he hit the front brake hard, bringing his rear wheel up to head height – a 'stoppie'. He hung there, rear wheel waving around in the air, and then working the crowd for all they're worth, he proceeded to bounce up and down on his front wheel, like a pogo stick. Up and down he went, pulling these and various other stunts to ever more enthusiastic applause.

Chris was mesmerized by the display, quite forgetting his own audience, and particularly when this guy did his grand finale. He donned his helmet and gloves once more, took a bow to the crowd and waved. The crowd was going wild, but he cupped his ear again and got a much louder roar than any that had come before. He sat and blipped but then shuffled up to sit on his tank, pulled hard on his front brake again, wound up his throttle until his engine screamed and dumped the clutch again. His rear tyre span even more wildly than before, on the tarmac, and rapidly started to burn furiously, a huge plume of smoke was soon billowing from it as his front forks depressed to their maximum. He stayed on the spot, seemingly forever, engine revving madly and wheel spinning wildly. The smoke now obscured most of the audience and just as I was wondering in amazement whether he had any rubber left at all, he was off, to a wild standing ovation from the highly appreciative crowd. Smoke hung thickly in the air, and a buzz ran through the crowd on the forecourt. They were having a seriously good time.

Next up is a Citroen 2CV, and the crowd went wild as the driver grinned at all and sundry and attempted to give it the rev treatment. Dumping the clutch, the 2CV bounded like a Kangaroo on its springy suspension and promptly stalled. Another wild cheer, but the guy stayed dry as he sheepishly started his engine again and slunk sedately up the road. It went on all afternoon until, deciding to move on and see what was going on elsewhere, Chris and I found ourselves stopped at the checkpoint. But luckily the bare chested drunkard peered through his alcoholic haze took in the antique look, the tank top instruments, the sprung hub, exposed battery holder and mercifully realised that here is a machine that would simply be a waste of time trying to wheel-spin or wheelie. He let us off with a theatrical "Nah!" to the crowd, and a signal from him seemed to excuse us the water ordeal. We got a cheer anyway, as we headed up the corridor of water canon, not a drop was aimed our way and I was a bit staggered and ridiculously flattered that instead, another drunken, whistled rendition of 'The Great Escape' went up all around us. Although this had happened earlier, I hadn't realised that Chris doesn't get the joke, but that second time he had clicked that was aimed at us and I found myself having to explain about Steve McQueen and the film.

We headed on down to the bottom fields by the track again, and as we were filtering through all the traffic I was amazed, and indeed heartened, to be buzzed by a little moped. Chris was horrified, but I was laughing, as this little machine and it's rider pulled up alongside to offer us that universal 'give it some' gesture of the throttle hand. Chris's horror came from the simple fact that the rider was not wearing a single stitch of clothing! We accelerated away, leaving the streaker to entertain the crowds, but the muttering from Chris suggested that he had actually just been a bit shocked by the close encounter. I was still chuckling as we did a long circuit that took us round to our lunchtime rendezvous, where we found Dave, Tim and the crew relaxing in the early afternoon sun. Having stayed clear of the stuff all morning, I grabbed a beer, and we settled down to swap stories from our morning's meandering, whilst the street show continued unabated. Dave then told us of the treat we are to experience later. The Mulsanne straight, he told us, is one of the public sections in normal life, but the fastest, longest straight in the race. It has, he told me, a lovely little Chinese Restaurant half way down it which, although cordoned off for the race, can be accessed via some back lanes and a couple of fields. The owners have an arrangement with the local farmer, and we were booked for a meal there this evening. Dave went on to explain that the very fast straight goes past the restaurant literally five feet outside the windows, and went on to promise us a meal the like of which we have never experienced before.

He wasn't kidding. Getting to the place was entertaining in the least, and this restaurant must be one of the best kept secrets in Le Mans. You simply wouldn't find the thing unless somebody in the know had showed you, which is how Dave had discovered it several years ago. Bumping across the field behind it, we parked at the rear and could now see that the normal entrance from the road has been blocked by crash barriers. It was possible to look over these, just, and see up the road to the bend at the top. With the exception of the restaurant front it looked for all the world like a section of Silverstone or some other such pure racing track. The practice sessions were due to start in a while, and our table, right by the windows at the front, was ready. We ordered a right old mixture to share amongst us all, and as the starter dishes arrived, we heard the first car going down through the gears rapidly as it approached the bend at the top, before accelerating hard up through them again as it screamed down the straight. The noise built rapidly to a crescendo as the thing howled past us, less than twenty feet the other side of the windows, which vibrated. "Woooaah!" exclaimed Chris, shocked at the ear splitting din. Several cars later, it was interesting to note just how different they sounded, and Dave, Tim and the others had fun trying to guess what each car was by it's engine sound.

Dave certainly wasn't wrong when he'd told us this would be a meal like no other we have ever experienced, but even so, nothing had prepared me for what came next. We heard a gaggle of rapidly decelerating engines approach the bend, sounding like angry wasps in the distance, and I could count about four, I thought, as they came round to the straight and hit the pedal. There was obviously a fight for position going on there and as the cars hurtled past the restaurant on their way down the straight, they were bunched neck and neck. The noise was indescribable, but what was more startling was that not only did the windows vibrate this time, but the table we were sitting at was shaking, all the cutlery was rattling and I watched in fascination as ripples spread across my beer! Another bunch tore past shortly after, with the same effect, and when I looked up, Chris had his fingers jammed in his ears, and a startled look on his face. Small particles of dust were by now dropping from the overhead lighting, and I couldn't help but think of the marvellous dining room scene from the film 'Carry on up the Khyber' where the British Embassy staff stoically work their way through four courses as the room disintegrates around them from the battle raging outside. It was impossible to actually hold a conversation by then, as the full compliment of cars was on the track, relentlessly hammering past time and time again. Quite an experience, and certainly one which it would be hard to repeat anywhere else.

After the meal, ears and nerves shot, we walked to the last of the sun's rays dying over the western horizon;.The plan was to carry on round the back roads to some of the marshalled viewing points scattered around the circuit. The Arnage corner is, I was told, a great place to go, but as we threaded our way towards it the roads became gridlocked with like minded souls attempting the same. Eventually we got there, parked in an adjacent field and walked up the large bank overlooking the bend and its approach, and there we spent half an hour watching the cars, lights blazing, gears crashing, exhausts screaming and spitting fire. Wonderful, if a tad heavy on the eardrums. Back at the campsite there was an almighty party going on, and the pub across the road was absolutely heaving. The Gendarmes had brought the daytime activities on the road to a halt, and were now keeping a steady presence to ensure that things stayed that way. Our group wandered across for a few beers before settling back at camp to just relax and listen to the cacophony of noise all around us.

Chris and Mitch (Dave's son) went off down to the circuit, where they wandered around various vantage points and watched the last practice sessions until midnight. As they came back, a while after the end, the first of what was to be an ongoing barrage of fireworks went off somewhere in the middle of the site. This seemed to be a signal, and before long there were rockets flaring all around us.Detonations abounded and we sat transfixed, listening to the debris landing on the roofs of the cattle sheds with a continuous pinging noise. And so eventually we headed off to bed, leaving the younger lads to sit about chatting and enjoying the experience to the full. They were allowed a beer each to be going on with. Most of us didn't get much sleep, but it was fine just lying there listening to the mayhem going on outside. Race day dawned with a blazing sun and clear blue skies. The heat was such that I abandoned any attempt at personal protection and had resorted to riding around in shorts and sandals. I took extra care out there. For Dave and the rest, racing buffs that they are, the day was spent entirely at the circuit but Chris and I planned to continue sampling the villages and roads all around Le Mans.

We decided to start with a breakfast of croissants and coffee in Arnage, and although it's only two miles away, the roads were so congested that it took nearly twenty minutes to get there. Daisy was overheating pretty badly under those conditions and I could feel the intense heat radiating off her engine and cooking my bare legs. The village was as busy as ever, although once again the street show had been suppressed by a visible police presence all along the main street. We sat in the early morning sun, talking about the highlights of the previous evening. Chris burbled on about the restaurant and the all-night firework party, admitting that he hadn't gone to bed until after three in the morning. But we were delightfully sidetracked by the arrival of the Bentley Owners' Club – complete with no less than six of the big 6 litre classics. They parked in lines on both sides of the road and I couldn't resist placing Daisy in front to get some photographs of this rare sight.

After breakfast, the traffic was that bad we decided it was time to lay Daisy up for the day and head on foot down to the circuit. They had a Classic race underway, which preceded the main event. It was something else to watch, as the cars were lined up along the side of the track with the drivers on the opposite side. When the starting gun fired the drivers ran to their cars and had to start them before pulling out and away. It was a real treat to watch those old bygone racers giving it their all around this famous circuit, and one of the drivers taking part that year was Stirling Moss. We took a wander around the track, with it's myriad of corporate stands, food stalls, beer tents and the posh exhibition-style offerings by most of the big names that were actually racing. Audi, Bentley, MG, Ferrari and Porsche all had large representations and we spent a fair while browsing the displays. The main event started at four pm, and, courtesy of Dave we had grandstand tickets to watch the start. The place was crammed full, and from our high seats we looked down on a sea of bright banners depicting support for the carriers' favoured teams. It was like cup final day at Wembley.

The tension built as the cars finally formed up and headed off behind the pace car for the warm up lap. They were gone for a while, but a buzz suddenly went up through the crowd as, in the distance, we saw them approaching once more, still at sedate speed. Just before they reached grandstand once more, the pace car peeled off up the pit lane and the racers floored their accelerators to come screaming past for the first lap of this long twenty-four hour endurance race.

The noise from both cars and crowd was absolutely eardrum splitting but soon they were all past and a strange quiet settled on the place. We stayed for the first few laps, but then we set off for a bimble around the circuit to various vantage points, where we'd maybe stop and watch a few cars hurtle past. As it got dark, we found that the thing to do was sit on the grass banks by one of the chicanes, and watch the cars come screaming down the straight, lights blazing, exhausts spitting, crashing down through the gears and hitting the anchors hard. The disks on the brakes glowed bright red in the dark, and as the cars accelerated away again, spitting flame, the noise was indescribable! Then it was over to the funfair in the middle of the stadium area where we went up the big wheel for a panoramic view of the whole circuit. It paused at the very top, and it was great to just sit there looking down at the heaving crowds, the cars hurtling round in a blaze of light from their multiple rally spots. Finally the thing brought us slowly down to earth and we wandered from there up to the pub. It was about midnight by that time, and us old un's agreed that it wass almost certainly time to partake of a final few pints of giggle-juice before bed. The lads wandered off again, to pursue their own enjoyment back down at the circuit, as the rest of us wandered back to the thriving campsite.

We awoke to the heartening news that the British Bentleys were out in front, and Dave insisted that we must join him for what he says is a traditional wander around the campsite to find the biggest beer-bottle-pyramid. These have slowly taken shape over the week as each group consumed their stock and placed the empties in an ever expanding construction by their tents. We reckoned the Morgan owners have it this year, having built a truly impressive wall of empty bottles stretching some ten feet long by more than six feet tall. Then it was time for a final breakfast in Arnage, before returning via some circuitous country roads to break camp for the long haul home. We agreed to meet up with Dave later in the week to retrieve our gear and then, pausing only to wave spirited goodbyes in response to the numerous farewells yelled at us we threaded our way through the site.

And that was that. We were on the road once more, heading out towards Alencon, and it wasn't long before the tide of Brits going home began to start passing us. That was another memorable thing about our Le Mans week – the procession home up the long straight roads between Le Mans and Rouen was conducted in something like carnival atmosphere. The local French population came out in force to line the roads, laybys and roundabouts, eager to witness the constant stream of interesting and rare cars, the like of which are probably never seen in such concentration anywhere else. For many it is an anual event for the entire family. They set up picnic tables, deckchairs and barbecues and make it a big occasion. Again, for Chris and myself this was an entirely new and not unrewarding experience. When we saw the first of these family groups, happily ensconced in the middle of one of the roundabouts just outside Le Mans, We were bewildered. "What are they doing?" Chris asked over my shoulder, but no answer was necessary - it became obvious when they all waved at us and called out some encouragement or other. As we progressed further, the gatherings increased in intensity and many of them wave the Union Jack or the flag of Saint George whilst cheering, waving or offering up their glasses (red wine, of course) in a toast. We responded in kind to each, and by the time we reached Alencon my arm was tired from all the waving!

The downside to being a part of that parade however, was the stream of maniacs in the TVRs, Jags, Porsches and everything in between, who felt that they must perform for the crowds and were, it would seem, hell bent on wrapping their kidneys round the nearest tree. The problem was that there was every chance that one of them would take us with them as they frequently passed us at ridiculous speeds, far too close for my liking. Before long though, the Gendarmes were out in force with their radars and we were entertained by the regular sight of the French version of 'you're nicked Sonny Jim!' being played out in numerous lay-bys.

But it was impossible not to feel good about it all: a feeling of bonhomie buoyed the spirits, as the journey, free of the normal emptiness of the miles, fairly shot past. The more modern of our sports car escorts had long since departed to the horizon, but as we progressed steadily north, the older examples began to pass, much more slowly. We were treated to a mixture of the fairly common Morgans, MGBs and older Jags, interspersed with some real treasures such as AC Cobra's, Lagondas and the like. The occupants of these more sedate sportsters, obviously having a bent for the classic era, nearly all slowed down to inspect Daisy, the appropriately ancient bike, and then we found ourselves waving back at these kindred spirits as they tooted, hooted or yelled encouragement as they passed. All in all it was a hell of a pleasant experience and a thoroughly nice way to end what for us had been an enjoyable and certainly a different week.

We maintained a leisurely fifty-five to sixty mph and although it was murderously warm, Daisy took the return trip in her stride, burbling along beneath us with ease. I reflected happily that she had conducted herself flawlessly the whole week, and this suggested that she would do likewise on the rest of the landmark challenge. Some nine hours after leaving we landed back in Blighty without incident, and as we completed the final thirty miles I enthusiastically reminded Chris that that's another eight hundred odd miles behind us, incident free, and that the Scottish leg of the landmark should be no problem at all to such seasoned adventurers! He mumbled something along the lines of me being a bit silly, but I thought I could see he's a bit proud of himself, and I suspect, of Daisy. This was confirmed to me in no uncertain terms, over dinner that evening as Chris, brimming with enthusiasm, recounted to his sister the things that we had done and seen through the week, the crowds, the sights, the highjinks, culminating in an awestruck account of the return trip home. Diane raised her eyes to the ceiling as she looked over at me, the unspoken question, "What on earth have you started here?" clear on her face. We'll put this one down as a success then, I smugly told myself.

Finally then, it was time to extend the range of our forays and it had come to my notice that there was a weekend rally being held within sensible striking distance, at a village near Hastings. There were two Landmarks down thereabouts, which would be fairly easy to knock off with a good day's ride out from the rally campsite but on announcing this fact to the family, I had an immediate problem - Chris and Chloe both want to go! This was going to be tricky, as although it was Chloe's 'turn', this one involves a new experience which neither of them had ever had, a real rally. Chloe's claim to this trip became far more pronounced when she heard that it is in fact the Rabbit Rally, clearly conjuring up visions of the fluffy animals in her mind rather than a field full of old bikes and tents. Salvation and a solution came when I found myself explaining my latest plan at a dinner with my parents that weekend. My father, (universally known as Grandad) decided that he would join us on the other Speed Twin, and do the full camp and landmark thing with us. That solved the problem outright as one of the kids could go on his machine, and it would be a right merry family adventure. Suddenly the plan has taken on a far more enjoyable facet.

Even Grandad seemed to have an extra spring in his step as the great day came closer, bringing with it the need to plan and get organised. It soon became apparent that he was woefully ill equipped for such things as we surveyed his stock of camping necessities. He had a stove. That's it, if you discount the enormous ten-year-old sleeping bag, which with the best will in the world would simply not fit on a motorcycle. We therefore had to take another trip to the camping shop in order to fit him out with the necessary tackle. Here's a thing; everything these days comes in ever smaller, more compact, infinitely better designs. We chose a two-man tent, laughing at the fact that it was smaller, when packed, than his old sleeping bag. We added a bedroll, compact inflatable mattress, sleeping bag, a gas light and a little folding stool – Grandad was nearly seventy, and a few home comforts would be vital if we were to drag him from his crypt and force the great outdoors on him! Next, we had to sort out the loading of Winnie, his machine, in order to make sure that he was comfortable with everything bungeed in place. This was proven by the simple expedient of taking a local ride around the nearby countryside, with all the gear and a willing participant pillion, in the shape Chloe. Grandad declared everything to be good, so we were ready for the next stage of our adventure that coming weekend, and another one hundred and fifty miles would hopefully be put under Daisy's wheels, taking her running in period ever closer to completion ready for the much longer forays that would follow.

5. Practising on Rabbits

The Rabbit Rally is hosted every year by the Triumph Owners' Club, Rother branch, in Sussex, and hopefully this one would be a stroll in the park for the freshly refurbished Daisy. It's only seventy-five miles away from home, along the coast to the West, and our route was to be one of my favourite weekend rides. There was no need for a dawn parade, either, and we could safely leave in the afternoon of the Friday, and still have plenty of time to get there, set up camp and find the bar before the sun set. Chloe was riding pillion on Daisy's little pad this time, whilst Chris mounted up behind Grandad, with the luxury of all the mod cons that the later 1955 machine has to offer by way of suspension at the rear and a large comfortable dual seat. Both kids had full rucksacks, carrying spare clothes and some of the camping paraphernalia we'd be needing.

It was four o'clock, and all was well. It really was a glorious balmy afternoon and we couldn't wait to get out into the green lanes that make up almost the entire route. Out of Ramsgate, through the school traffic, we were soon on the back-roads between the ancient towns of Sandwich and Canterbury. After thirty minutes or so we crossed the old Dover road, and cut across country through the Barham woods where the canopy of trees made a refreshingly cool contrast to the blazing sunshine. We threaded our way through the network of single track roads, duly arriving at the quaint country pub that we had earmarked, in the sleepy little village of Stelling Minnis. We'd had a gentle ride and were still fresh, but a refreshing drink was in order anyway, so we sampled a half pint of Olde Badger's Scrotum or some-such brew, whilst the kids settled for coke and crisps. Heading off again, half a mile later we connected with Ye Olde Roman Road of Stone Street, which is a gloriously humpty, bumpty but fairly straight route that took us down to Lympne, on the edge of the Romney Marshes.

This was classic biking at it's best, with a maze of tiny unmarked roads meandering across the marshes, heavy with the heady scents of the summer countryside, little hamlets, lambs gambolling in the fields, hawks hovering in the sky, small country inns, fantastically old, nestling quietly in chocolate box surroundings…You get the picture – Ye Garden of Olde England at its grandest. Some of the roads here had those very high hedgerows at each side, and as they snaked along with 'S' bend after 'S' bend, we rarely got out of second gear. We cautiously eased our way along waiting to meet the inevitable caravan or tractor that seem to be so carefully placed by the Gods at such times, in the worst possible places, just to test us. No such bad luck presented itself on this occasion however, and our progress remained steady and undisturbed. This was official, unadulterated 'Bimbling' – note the capital 'B'. It was that good!

But enough of that nonsense. We eventually, and not a little reluctantly, found our way out of the marshes, just East of the ancient fishing town of Rye, and after threading our way through the town, past the tidal harbour with it's parking plot so beloved of motorcyclists as a gathering place on those long summer evenings, proceeded in a leisurely fashion westwards, through Winchelsea, with it's rather amusing hairpin-bended hill, up and over, and without further ado, we pulled up after a few more miles at the Rally site. They'd got this well sorted too, the rally being in the field behind a large country Inn (The Robin Hood) just outside the village of Icklesham , which boasts a well appointed beer garden backing onto the camping site. That will be the focus for grub and beer then! We checked in, proceeded to the corner of the field closest to the bar, unloaded Daisy and Winnie, and set about making camp.

The first jarring note of the weekend made itself known at this point, when we noticed that Winnie was displaying a distinctly oily patina, with a liberal coating round the top end of her engine, which was dripping down to make a nice mess of her otherwise shiny chaincase. Investigation showed that she had lost a rocker cap, leaving her right hand exhaust valve free to spray the stuff liberally through the resulting hole. I got out the Kleenex, and cleaned up her dribbles, before throwing up the tents. Grandad was chewing his blanket by now, however, over what to do about the problem with his bike, so we ambled over to the welcome tent to enquire about rocker caps for old Triumphs, and the likelihood of being able to find one hereabouts (after all, this is a Triumph rally, so surely someone will have one in their pocket?). A quick conference reminded us that there is a fine establishment, the Miller emporium, in St Leonard's, Hastings, where all things classic Triumph could be had in exchange for some coin of the realm. It was only ten miles away, so we agreed to make that the first stop next day, before we go landmark hunting for the rest of the day.

The weather had settled down to delivering a glorious evening so, despite the oil problem with Winnie we decided on a leisurely ride down to Winchelsea beach as the sun set, and were absolutely captivated as we watched a near full moon rising magically over the sea. A truly stunning sight, which caused us to loiter for nearly an hour before heading back to camp to spend the rest of the first evening watching late arrivals trickle in, whilst sipping on a glass of the finest mental sledgehammer the Robin Hood's cellars could offer. In due course some lads that I had partied with at a little rally in Belgium appeared and as greetings were exchanged we agreed to share some fluid refreshers later on. By that time the last of the sunlight finally gave way completely, but in the moonlight Chloe was delighted to note the emergence of a plethora of bunnies in the next field, and she set off to stalk them as I reflected that the 'Rabbit Rally' is just that. She spent an age, down on all fours, in the dark, creeping ever-so-slowly towards her targets and managed to get within thirty odd feet eventually, before they decided that's quite enough of that thank you and vamoosed in all directions. She came back flushed with happiness, and settled down to wait eagerly for them to return. She then repeated the whole exercise, all over again.

The evening passed slowly by, but Grandad retired early (poor old thing, combined age of him and Winnie was 120 years!). Chloe found some friends in the beer garden, and with nothing pressing to do I wandered up to the pub where I settled down in the cosy bar to swap yarns and imbibe with the lads, before finally turning in at 11.30 or so feeling very satisfied and content, which was the whole point of these rallies, after all. We were all up by seven thirty and already it was getting hot. As we brewed some tea, the talk turned to the choice of routes to the landmarks we intended to find, and how lucky we were that the day was set to be a classic scorcher. Looking at the rally agenda, we noted that breakfast would not be available until nine, by which time we intended to be out on the road, so we finished the brew and hit that very road. There were two landmarks within a leisurely day's striking distance, but first we had to get down to St Leonard's, to Mr Miller. We got underway shortly after eight, arriving in Hastings too early, so we hunted down a café, where breakfast was duly dispatched. The Miller establishment was open by then, so we presented ourselves there in order to obtain the vital cap. Winnie was soon kitted out with a shiny new one, at a cost of three pounds, but the shop was such a fascinating jackdaw's nest of treasures that it was fully ten thirty or so by the time we finally said goodbye and threaded our way out of Hastings, heading west. The first landmark was about forty five miles away, on the edge of the South Downs behind Brighton. It was lovely geography was this, if you chose wisely, and we had deliberately plotted a 'rural' route that took us across country, including a number of inviting single-track roads, if the map was to be believed.

Riding at leisurely pace it wasn't long before I noticed that Winnie, despite the shiny new rocker cap, was still busily producing a Herculean oil slick all over her engine. I pulled ahead of Grandad, and at the first opportunity we pulled into a lay-by where more Kleenex was brought to bear. It wasn't obvious where the problem was but it needed investigation, so I got Grandad to start and run her whilst I peered under the tank. Aha! It became clear immediately that she was blowing oil out of the rocker box gasket, where it joins the cylinder head, and had fooled us with the missing cap! I explained things to the others, and suggested that we should attempt to sort the problem, so it was out with the spanners, to check all the nuts and bolts that hold the thing down. They all seemed good and solid which suggested closer inspection was called for, and in due course it transpired that the gasket was actually a very poor fit.

I suggested that we undo the bolts, and lift the rocker box in order to attempt to straighten things up, which we did, putting it all back as best we could and setting off again half an hour later fervently hoping it would be better. No such luck, was the answer to that hope. We stopped for lunch at a little country inn, strangely situated *inside* a chalk pit and it was immediately apparent that Winnie, far from being fixed, was settling down to be a royal pain. In fact she'd managed to cover herself with more oil than ever and as she stood in the hot sun, a gentle cloud of oily smoke drifted from under the tank, whilst hot oil dripped down her barrel fins making a nice mess of her chaincase.

Bugger.

Further incensed prodding around revealed that not only had we failed to make the gasket fit better, but a half inch piece had now come out altogether. There was a pesky little gap in the rocker seal, from which hot oil bubbled straight to atmosphere! We don't have any gasket stuff with us, so we adopted one of those desperate bodges that keep you going until proper repairs can be carried out at home – we stuffed Kleenex in the gap, and wedged more of the stuff tightly into the head fins under the rocker box to catch any dribbles. Not ideal, and certainly not pretty, but we hoped that it would do the job. Pausing only to visit the gents, in the vain hope of removing some of the oil which was now ingrained on fingers and palms, we ordered a pub ploughman's each for lunch before setting off on the remaining short stretch to the first landmark, which was one of the few that I had been unable to identify in advance. The clue was simply 'strange noises from the basement in this house' and we were guessing that it was maybe a water mill, an interesting haunted pub, or something of that order. On arriving at the spot marked 'X' nothing seemed to present itself, and in fact the only structure of any sort in view was a bridge over a railway cutting. There was nothing strange about the bridge, certainly nothing that would match the clue. I re-checked the map reference that had been supplied, but this only confirmed that we were supposedly in the right place so we decided to cross over the bridge to ferret about on the other side. And there it was – as we crossed, we could see that the railway disappears into a hill about two hundred yards up the cutting, and there, projecting from the hillside, was a house built over the tunnel entrance!

After getting the photo of this bizarre structure, we checked Winnie over, and decided to change her nappy. The earlier bodge was working but the Kleenex had become saturated. That done we struck out West again for the next landmark, which was about twenty miles across country. Choosing to stick to the tiny back-roads, and with Winnie's incontinence plugged we were really enjoying things in the near perfect weather.

The Roman villa, which nestled amidst the South Downs, was found easily without further incident, but we didn't have time to go in, so we took a short rest, got the photo, changed Winnie's nappy again and finally got the map out to consider a route back to the Rally. On that map, Grandad noticed that we were in fact close to Bignor Hill, a fairly well known National Trust beauty spot, and he suggested that as we're here, we should go up it. Pretty soon we were on a long rough uphill ride through thick woods, twisting and turning, dodging the ruts and holes, until we emerged from the trees on the top of the hill, where the road promptly stopped.

The view was stunning. We pulled up, got off, in order to enjoy the moment, and what happened next will stick in my memory forever. Picture the scene; two classic motorcycles, in perfect weather, parked on the top of the South Downs, surrounded by grandiose views. Before we knew it, Grandad had picked up an admirer (I'm far more experienced, saw him coming, and took evasive action!) and was basking in his audience's admiration, whilst he talked expansively about the bikes. Without warning, Winnie delivered him a shocking blow – her side stand bolt snapped, without warning, and she promptly fell over with a mind-juddering CRASH! I think I might have died laughing, but the immediate concern for the fuel spilling everywhere and the possible damage that the rocky surface might have inflicted galvanised me into action. As it was I still couldn't help but snigger as we scrambled to pick the bike up. I was actually almost in tears, desperately trying not to laugh out loud, but poor Grandad was clearly hugely embarrassed and his audience was no longer quite so full of admiration. You had to be there.I guess, but it's a memory etched on my mind for eternity.

I soon stopped laughing as we surveyed the damage though. The fall had bent her handlebars, crushed the nacelle headlamp trim and had taken a few lumps out of her paintwork on the stony surface. Grandad was all upset, but I settled him down with assurances that this was 'campaign damage' – you have to expect it if you use the thing, and anything that was bent or chipped could, with some effort, be fixed!

After ensuring that everything was as straight as we could make it, we stuffed Winnie's defunct stand into Chloe's back-pack and headed back towards camp, still sticking where possible to back-roads. Unfortunately it soon became apparent that Grandad and Winnie were not keeping up so I stopped to find out what the matter was.He explained that there was a drumming noise coming from the tank that got louder with speed. Investigations soon showed that where she had gone over earlier, she had dislodged the padding in the tank recess. The tank was now vibrating against the frame, and so, at the expense of more time, we loosened off the tank, sorted out the padding and put it all back together. She was fine after that, and we set off again in earnest, looking forward to grub, beer and in Chloe's case, more bunnies.

But the day has one more nasty surprise in store for us yet. As we bowled along a delightful wooded back-road, easing down a gear to sweep round a tight corner, we came face to face with a full grown stag! Huge and majestic it certainly was, but nevertheless standing in the middle of the road! I have no idea to this day how we missed the thing, and my memory is scratchy as to what happened next, but somehow we came to a sliding, panicked halt, diagonally across the road, and the stag was gone. Just like that, off into the trees so fast that I sometimes wonder if I'd dreamed the whole thing. Sadly, Chloe had missed it altogether, being behind Grandad and looking in the wrong direction at the time. Back at the Rally site that evening, it all made for a good yarn, and I promised Winnie a smacked bum when we got home!

The evening got into full swing, and it rapidly became apparent that TOMCC Rother knew how to lay on a good do. Food was available at the pub, beer was despatched in satisfactory quantities, everyone was in good spirits, the band, '90% Proof' eventually got underway, proving to be excellent entertainers. The evening flew by. The weather remained fantastic, and as our hosts fired up the biggest spit roast I've ever seen, at the bottom of the field a full moon rose over the sea once more. Chloe went bunny hunting again and, much later, as the pub closed, another fully equipped (if you like lager or bitter) bar opened up in a marquee in the field. Eventually we all ended up around the midnight bonfire. Absolutely brilliant!

Chloe and Grandad turned in shortly after the fire was lit, both utterly exhausted, but Chris and I stayed watching the the thingburn down, nattering to various people and polishing off the remainder of the beer. The last of us stumbled off to bed at around 3.00 am. Good people, good venue, good food, good beer and well, just a damn good do all round, not to mention the fact that we'd bagged another two landmarks.

Now we were ready for the big ones!

6. Heading West

Daisy had settled down rather nicely, with no further dramas and her new engine had also definitely been run-in. This happy state of affairs meant that we could cast our eyes further a field. The kids had been debating who would do what in terms of sharing the pillion duty, and they'd managed, to my amazement, . To reach a blood-free consensus. Chloe had opted for the two shorter forays to the West country and Wales respectively, while Chris had gone for the long haul north, into Scotland, on what would be at least a week's worth of camping. With a day's holiday looming at her school and Chloe keen as mustard since the Rabbit, we decided to tackle Devon, Cornwall and all points thereabouts next. I had a brother, Colin, able to offer a very well placed overnight stop in Bournemouth, and with that in mind we began to plan our strategy.

A study of our Landmark map revealed that from Ramsgate it was about 175 miles to Colin's house and from there we would have a 600 mile round trip, near as made no difference, encompassing seven landmarks. That was 800 odd miles total which, on a sprung hub I suspected, was going to hurt. Nevertheless an optimistic plan emerged which had us leaving on the Saturday afternoon for Bournemouth, where we then planned to go out for a meal with 'Uncle' Colin. After a hopefully relaxed evening we would set off early on the Sunday and get as far as we could. Monday was going to be the tough one, and wouldsee us hopefully completing a big loop, ending back home in Ramsgate, sometime in the evening. Marvellous. A plan with no downsides I reckoned and Chloe, in her matter of fact way, agreed wholeheartedly.

Saturday arrived, as Saturdays do, and off we went, loaded up for a full weekend of camping and fun, but the weather had decided to do it's best to make us suffer for our small pleasures. It was a fine afternoon - of drizzle, mist and grey stuff. We were absolutely soaked through after an hour and had to stop because I was having real trouble with the mist. It carried on that way, too. I stopped for what seemed like the fifteenth time to wipe the lenses of the sunglasses I wear with the open face helmet, but I couldn't see a thing again after two minutes riding as the glasses yet again collected a fine layer of condensation. Constant wiping with the finger was required to keep even a rudimentary window on the world open. Worse than that my beard, obviously feeling left out, started dribbling a persistent little funnel of water straight down my neck. The beard had seemed like a good idea at the time. I hadn't had one before the bikes came, but the planned miles left me with the idea that the thing would offer some protection in the sun, equally it would keep the wind and any rain from chaffing my face and although it managed all this magnificently, I had not reckoned with it's funnelling effects. In short, this was already a miserable experience, with neither one of us having any fun at all.

Before too long we were stopped under yet another bridge to get out of the misery, and stamping about trying to get the worst of the wet stuff off not to mention get a little circulation going. Despite the conditions Chloe seemed to be in remarkably good spirits. She had enjoyed the benefit of being behind me, certainly, which had kept her largely dry, but I'was sure she couldn't be having much of a good time.

"You alright then?" I enquired, and the smile she flashed back at me as water dripped from her helmet seemed to defy logic.

"Yep!"

Right. OK then. We couldn't stop for long because progress had been inordinately slow and time was increasingly against us as the grey afternoon began to give way to a sullen, murky evening.We already knew that Daisy is blessed with electrical apparatus in keeping with her years, supplied by Lucas, the Prince of Darkness himself, and I was further depressed at the thought of the next stage of our journey, which would, for our comfort and convenience, put us on the Southern section of that blighted carbuncle of a road, the dreaded M25. From Ramsgate to anywhere there's just no way to avoid the damn thing if you want to make even remotely sensible progress, and in the type of weather we were currently enjoying it would be a challenge. This belief was reinforced almost immediately as we headed down the slip road into a vast cloud of road spray, whipped into a frenzy by the endless line of heavy goods vehicles sweeping along at barely diminished speeds in the gloom.

We were buffeted repeatedly as the maelstrom engulfed us from all sides, and the only thing to do was hunker down in a miserable squat, chin pressed as far as possible into chest, peer from under the lip of the helmet whilst I desperately counted off the miles to the blessed exit that would take us Southwest. After half an hour of torture and misery and with huge relief, we peeled off onto the A3 – a much more suitable road for Daisy once past the initial six lane stretch to Guildford. From there, it stretches and winds its way up across the Hog's Back, round the lip of the Devil's Punch Bowl,(a huge prehistoric crater miles across), before dropping down to the coastal plain around Portsmouth and Southampton. We stopped at the first available place for a rest and a general wringing out, during which Chloe continued to display a cheerful disposition entirely out of keeping with the circumstances. That girl was beginning to worry me! Ten minutes later, during which I had tried, but utterly failed, to roll myself a cigarette due to the impossibility of completing the task with damp trembling fingers, we were off again towards our rendezvous with Colin in Bournemouth.

We must have looked a pretty picture, judging by Colin's face on our arrival at his house – our blessed shelter for the night. He's not a motorcyclist and considers such activity to be, at best, a misguided attempt to achieve a second youth (unsuccessfully in his view). As we divested ourselves of sopping wet garments, which we hung over the bath, I could see that nothing about the current scene was changinghis opinion in much of a hurry! But he soon made with the teapot and while he and I caught up with family stuff, careers and generally set the world to rights, Chloe headed off for a long soak, still insanely happy. I suspected that the promise of pizza in town later that evening had more to do with that than anything else. Two hours later, we were ensconced in a rather pleasant Italian restaurant, poring over the large scale map, on which I'd marked the landmarks in felt-tip. Chloe, readily embraced the idea that big roads are bad, small roads are good, and so spent a long time tracing various routes with her fingertip.She bubbled with enthusiasm each time she managed to make a 'complete' connection between two marks without resorting to green or blue roads. Even Colin got the bug, as we pondered various undoubtedly picturesque options, whilst balancing the need to make progress against the desire to enjoy. By the time we left we had a pretty good route plan for the morrow, which would be supervised by Chloe from the rear! Off to bed then, the next day would be a long day's riding it seemed.

An early six thirty start saw us waving goodbye to Colin and heading northwest through the urban sprawl that is Bournemouth. The weather had improved marginally, in that it was only grey and miserable rather than wet, but this happy state of affairs was short lived. We were no more than about 20 miles into the day before things set in like previous day – a miserable mist and drizzle came down to claim the horizon and a chill in the air added it's own particular edge. Luckily, in Colin's warm bathroom, our clothes had largely dried out overnight, but it was fairly clear that this wouldl not last long. The route that we had marked out the previous evening began to puzzle me before long too, as it seemed to meander rather more than was strictly necessary as far as I could see. Stopping on the outskirts of Poole, I questioned Chloe as to her choice.

"We've *got* to go that way Dad, just look at the places we can see!" None the wiser, I asked her to clarify, and pretty soon we were both chuckling like teenagers behind the bike sheds at lunch break, as I followed her finger to 'Puddletown', 'Piddle Hinton' and 'Piddle Trenthide'. All of which reside on the banks of the river 'Piddle' itself. I found Chloe's logic difficult to argue with, and the wide-eyed awe she displayed as she recited the names left me no choice. Clearly this was a facet of the English heritage that just had to be explored for real. We proceeded along the agreed route, and I was buoyed by the sniggering behind me as each of the names went past, in the flesh. Even the weather had lost it's ability to make me miserable as we bowled along, and it seemed like no time at all before we threaded into the little town of Martock, home of the Treasurer's House - our first landmark of the day. It had been easy to decipher the clue in advance, 'Home of the Money Man' and the place itself was easy to find. We got our photograph and studied the map once more, me suspiciously, Chloe with enthusiasm, but it seemed that good sense had prevailed for the next stage and she had chosen the A303 and A30 to convey us westwards from there towards Exeter, where we'd turn south to the next landmark at Torquay.

We took stock and checked the time – it was eight fifteen, and after an hour and three quarters we had covered some 50 miles, which wasn't too bad considering the conditions and the detour for the landmark. Daisy was going beautifully, and I pondered once again how, in contrast to her passengers, she liked these wet damp conditions, in which she seemed to keep relatively cool and unflustered. The mist and drizzle had not set in as badly as the previous day though, and when all's said and done we were having a good time. We threaded our way back out of Martock, and onto the A303. This was a good road, officially. It snaked it's way west towards Ilminster, where a lazy turn to the South West would deliver us to Honiton just inside the Devonshire border. Honiton of course, is the home of Tri-Supply, where all parts Triumph from the 40's to the 80's can be had in exchange for any number of beer tokens. Nestling in the countryside is the authentic farmhouse and converted barn known simply as 'Meriden' (after the famous Triumph factory, of course), and if you don't have an interest in things Triumph that's fine too, for Oliver Barnes, the proprietor, runs a fine B&B as well. We weren't stopping there, more's the pity, as we still had a goodly number of miles and a bunch of landmarks to get under our belts before sunset. We pressed on towards Exeter.

The next landmark, according to our precision mapping (ahem), was situated down on the coast, in Torquay. We had already identified it as the Babbacombe model village. To get there, we had to circumnavigate Exeter, and this involved another motorway stretch before we could take a coastal route due south. Daisy was running so well that I took the opportunity to catch up a bit in the time stakes by winding on the throttle. The burble became a throaty growl as I watched the needle tick up.. 65, 70, 75. Just as it pushed to 80, the ancient mechanism had clearly had enough and suddenly I was watching with wonder as the thing started jumping around wildly between 10 and 110. It was impossible to tell what our maintained speed was, but Daisy's exhaust note told me that she was stretching her legs in a most satisfactory fashion, and the vibration through the bars and footrests added to the thrill. I glanced over my shoulder as the M5 rejoined the A38, and yelled a "You OK?" to Chloe. The answer was lost in the wind, but the grin said it all - we were definitely having fun.

I completely failed to spot the speed camera. Two weeks later, the Devonshire Constabulary would send me the nice little demand for funds, probably to help finance more of the damn things, but I couldn't help wondering what the officer who vets the catch of the day would think as he gazed upon the sight of a 1948 motor bicycle, loaded to the gunnels and two up, shattering his dual carriageway speed limit.

Ooops!

Oblivious to this soon to be presented opportunity to become poorer, we saw Newton Abbot appear on the signs, and we peeled off onto the A380 with an associated wind down on the hurtle-juice. Once below 70 again, the speedo needle stopped its wild gyration and settled at a steady 65. Newton Abbot passed by and we were soon threading our way into Torquay, where we got hopelessly lost. My large-scale map was useless there, so we resorted to stopping and asking directions - always a mistake in my experience, as there is nothing like local knowledge to send you miles in the wrong direction. Torquay was no exception to this unwritten rule of the Universe, and it was a full 30 minutes before we found the model village. It was time for a rest, a map check and a little drying out, so we head for the cafeteria clutching the map and settled down in a corner seat with mugs of tea and pastries. We were damp, but not overly so, and as we spread out the map to review our next stage Chloe remarked that it was only 10:15, with nearly half of the day's planned mileage done, so Daisy had done very well to get this far by now, hadn't she? I explained to her that although this was certainly true, and we'd actually covered about a hundred miles so far, we'd done it on mainly clear straight roads. The afternoon route that picks its way along the coast was going to be much slower going.

We looked at what was in store for us, continuing on south from our current location, we had a landmark right down near Start Point to get next, which we thought to be a military memorial of some kind. From there we would turn West once again, along the coast towards Plymouth where we'd bear north and inland again for a rendezvous with some standing stones on the Bodmin Moor. Then we had a final long leg through St Austell and on to the Lizard, right down there in Cornwall. As we chatted away, I told Chloe about standing stones, describing as best I could the mystery that surrounds such things, then we also touched on 'The Beast of Bodmin' and the stories claiming the existence of a large Panther type creature that apparently roams the Moors. Her eyes were wide with wonder as she traced her finger across the map to the area in question, and after a quick study she was eager to get at it once more. Refreshed and rested, we continued on our way South. According to my map there were only a very few roads down to this part of Devonshire, and the road that we were on should have led us straight to a coastal stretch with our landmark half way along it. What I hadn't noticed from the map was the large sea inlet at the mouth of the river Dart, and particularly the absence of any roads crossing it. I was certainly unaware that this is a feature of the Devonshire coastal region, and realised, too late, that one has the choice of a long detour inland, or one waits for the little ferries that ply a leisurely trade across the inlets. Like most travellers heading West, I had always used the main routes further inland, so that this particular regional feature had been lost on me. Landmarking certainly broadens the knowledge somewhat, but it was clear there and then that it also has the ability to play havoc with any planned schedule!

There were other issues too. The roads were getting much smaller and twistier, meaning that progress was very ponderous indeed and if there were many more obstacles such as the ferries, it was clear that we would lose an awful lot of time – time we didn't have. The particular ferry causing concern at that moment certainly wasn't going to hurry up on our account, and we watched impatiently as it slowly came towards us. It was a little platform pulled along on chains running across the seabed evidently. As we waited, I earnestly began to review the route options, whilst explaining to Chloe that we might have misjudged things somewhat and would do well to get inland again as soon as possible after the next landmark in order to pick up better roads and less obstacles. Chloe didn't agree. She was, she informed me, thoroughly enjoying herself, and didn't I think this was wonderful, quaint and pretty? Isn't this, she said accusingly, exactly why we came and, not to put too fine a point on things, the whole point of doing the landmark challenge? I countered by explaining that whilst all that was certainly true, we had many miles to get through this weekend, still had five landmarks to find, the weather was awful, and we had to be home by Monday evening because Chloe had school on the Tuesday! I showed her the map, showed her how pitifully few miles we'd managed since Torquay, tapped my watch to focus her on the time – which was steadily ticking by, pointed at the ferry, and finally suggested she see things my way.

I never win arguments with She Who Must Be Obeyed at home, and shouldn't have expected much more success with the junior version. I retreated, somewhat shocked, under the withering accusation that I sounded like 'an Old Fart' while Chloe turned her attention back to the map, humming happily to herself as she deliberately traced a route that stayed firmly near the coast. Right, so be it then, I thought as I pushed Daisy onto the now waiting ferry. We would run out of time, and not get all the landmarks, the challenge would be lost, because I certainly won't find time to come all the way back. But I had to concede that Chloe had a point and that this was what it was all about. I surrendered, and joined her at the map, still mentally chewing my blanket but resigned to the fact that I'd just have to take it all as it comes. As the ferry docked and we headed off, I was still smarting from the simple put down that Chloe had flipped my way. Old fart indeed! But all such thoughts were soon distant when, ten minutes later, we threaded our way through the outskirts of Dartmouth looking for our route south and back to the coast.

Map trouble soon arose yet again, and somehow we missed the A379, the road that should have led to our next landmark.Instead, we ended up on a myriad of roads which seem to cut across country in a completely random fashion and all of them were damp, small and twisty. There were almost no signs on any of the junctions and the few that there were pointed to places that didn't show up anywhere on our novelty map. We attempted to follow the compass instead, but that proved to be an impossible task with the 'S' bended roads we were on, and all the time the leaden grey sky enveloped us in a thick, wet, miserable blanket. We were soaked again in no time and with the overhanging trees dumping what seemed to be buckets full of water on us at every opportunity it was becoming a truly depressing experience. I began to fret once again about the fact that there were still a lot of miles to cover that day, that time was galloping by and that all our gear was thoroughly soaked through, as were we. In desperation I pulled up at some God-forsaken crossroads in the middle of nowhere, confirmed beyond any doubt that we were properly lost and tried in vain to make sense of the map whilst sheltering under some trees. It had, I noted, got considerably colder too and I looked over at Chloe, bedraggled, wet and miserable. She had that bright shiny sheen that is the hallmark of severe wetness, and had an almost comedy look about her in the oversized waterproof trousers that she was wearing. As I watched, little rivers of water ran off her helmet, dripping from the edges and I realized that this was hopeless.

"Want to go home?" I said, feeling justified in my own cowardice because it's for the good of the young 'un. I had clearly underestimated the resilience of youth however, and was somewhat surprised when she squared her shoulders, gave me one of those looks that had led to the "old fart" put-down of earlier, and responded; "Don't be silly Dad! We've only just started and we haven't camped yet!" with that, she demanded a look at the map and I felt strangely belittled as she busily traced her finger around on the by now damp paper. Only just started? That's what she had just said. I felt like I'd been on the road for a week, and was so damp that I couldn't help but shiver as I stood there.These thoughts were cut short however, as Chloe found a bit on the map that might be where we are, or so she told me. I couldn't quite work out how she had come to this conclusion, but all resistance had now deserted me. The only thing I could do, I decided, was continue to strike out South at every opportunity and hope that before too long we found the coast road. It was a full hour later that we finally did find the thing, the only road in the area, it seemed, which actually appeared on my map. The compass had been an absolute saviour in the end and it also appeared that luck had begun to favour us at last because within five minutes we were pulling up at the next landmark. It was indeed a military memorial, and a memorable one to boot. A Sherman tank mounted on a plinth, no less - but more to the point there was a big, inviting, warm-looking pub opposite the thing. As I took the photograph, the rain began to ease off, giving way to a grey mist that cloaked everything and left visibility not much better than a hundred meters in any direction. But that could wait. The pub had my entire attention by then and I noted that the time was now just after one o'clock, therefore it would seem absolutely sensible to go and investigate the lunch menu. Chloe agreed with that wholeheartedly and the two of us traipsed across the road without further ado.

There's something about a good traditional rural pub that lifts the spirits, and restores one's sense of well-being, especially in that sort of weather,. That one was no exception, with it's ancient, but cosy bar fronting a small dining area and a large fireplace, stacked with logs and roaring a welcome to all that enter. I ordered a pint of Sussex Ale and a Coke for Chloe, before heading to the table nearest to that fire. We began the ritual that will be familiar to so many motorcyclists, peeling off the sodden jacket, working the waterproof trousers down over equally sopping shoes, full of water, hanging gloves and scarf as close to the fire as possible. The landlord noted the activity and invited us to place my shoes, Chloe's boots, plus our gloves and scarves on the warm hearth. He also suggested that we arrange some chairs in such a way that we could hang jackets near the heat as well. By the time we'd finished the place looked like a hikers hostel, and I dread to think what the other patrons who steadily came into the place must have thought. Through the window we could see Daisy, poor thing, condensation gathering on tank and engine, making her take on that steamed-up-mirror look. But it was very cosy in there and with an excellent menu on offer we were anticipating a good feed and a good drying out before venturing out once more.

It's almost indescribable what a good pub lunch and a drop of local Ale can do for the inner spirit. By the time we had eaten an excellent meal, most of our stuff had managed to dry by the roaring log fire, with the notable exception of my gloves and shoes. As we got ready to head off once again, I mentally shrivelled at the thought of those moist articles that would feel warm at first, then inevitably turn cool and clammy within minutes. I chided myself for not having acquired any boots yet, but there was nothing to be done about it that the moment, so on the shoes went and out to Daisy we wandered. As she fired up and I settled into that big sprung seat, I remarked to Chloe that at least it was only misty now, not raining and we were both warm after the better part of an hour and a half in the pub. That lasted about 15 minutes as we picked our way carefully Westwards. The grey stuff descended to the point where visibility was almost zero, and as if to mock my comment that it was not so wet it made its point depressingly, clingingly, and definitely wet after all. It was also getting noticeably colder again to boot. Feeling the bonhomie evaporate we pressed on, round endless twisty bendy roads and soon I was on autopilot, huddled in that pose familiar to all open-faced helmet-no-fairing-and-it's-winter riders, until suddenly I was jolted back to reality, in the worst possible way. Round a blind bend the road simply stopped at a river!

This was another ferry crossing, the same little open air, roll-on, get wet whilst crossing, roll-off type we had come across earlier at Dartmouth. This one was even smaller and was, as I said, hidden round a downhill blind bend. It turned out that there were signs and stuff warning the unwary, but in the mist and drizzle I hadn't seen 'em. What the little chap selling the tickets must have thought I just can't imagine, as Daisy plus two screaming riders catapulted from the mist and then kangaroo'd, wobbled and finally slid to a halt about six inches from the edge. I managed to get my heart going again, eventually, by which time Chloe had climbed off the now stalled Daisy, removed her helmet and sat down by the river, flushed with the moment of excitement. The ticket seller was asking if she was allright, whilst throwing me the odd disgusted look. Clearly in his view, I was a speed-mad yobbo who should be banned from the roads without delay. There was no point trying to explain, so I stay put. After an uncomfortable wait, during which I studiously ignored the disapproving looks from the ticket man, the ferry finally edged up to the bank and I duly pushed Daisy on. Over we went, after parting with a whole £1.00, and pressed on ever West, past Plymouth and then North towards Bodmin moor, wherein nestle the Hurlers, an ancient stone circle. Again the map exceled in its utter uselessness and we almost immediately got lost.

This was a truly desolate experience. The mist on the rising moorlands made me feel very, very, insignificant and lonely although Chloe seemed unaffected by such thoughts due to the fact that we had crossed a cattle grid and were now trundling around on unfenced roads, where the sheep were free to wander as they see fit. She tapped on my shoulder before long and said that we should stop – she wanted to feed grass to them. Whilst trying to work out roughly where we were I watched her wandering up the road trying to attract a belligerent looking ewe. I could see nothing on any horizon, other than the grey veil, but I was fairly sure that we had been heading steadily northwest and as such roughly in the right direction. All we needed was to find a signpost to the single village that showed on our map, and we'd at least know that salvation was close.

Eventually, after persuading Chloe that the ewe was not going to play ball, we got going again and by sheer fluke stumbled across the village itself, St Cleer. This was a major plus, and I was suddenly confident that it couldn't be too hard to find our spot, as it was only a short distance due northeast according to the map. Would that it were that simple! We followed a likely looking road, only to find ourselves in a farmyard after half a mile. Back we went, and selected the next route out but this turned in a big arc and deposited us back in the village. Third time lucky then, and it was with no small measure of relief that after a short distance, there were the elusive stones, on a particularly desolate stretch of high moorland. We stopped, got the photo and with no hesitation headed straight back towards civilization. At Liskeard, we took a break and assessed our situation: we were way behind schedule by then, with the time approaching five o'clock and I was more convinced than ever that we'd not get all our landmarks on this foray if I was to get Chloe back to school on time. But there was nothing for it at that moment but to press on.

We found our way onto the A390 heading West again towards St Austell. We needed to get past that town without any further delays, and things really started to look up when magically the mists began to lighten, and there was even a hint that sunshine was trying to break through. Our spirits were very much buoyed, to the point, in fact, that I began to feel confident that we would at least be able to camp within striking distance of the planned place and therefore get back on schedule. The road was such a joy to ride that we opened Daisy up once more allowing her to stretch her legs after all the little twisty roads of the past two hours. The weather continued to lift and brighten, the moist air at last becoming dry breeze and as the sun finally broke through we pulled into a little petrol station with a nice café out back, filled Daisy up, then had cream tea and crumpets to celebrate this most satisfactory turn of events.

While Chloe finished off, I wandered outside to check on Daisy and make sure that everything was as it should be, using my little adjustable spanner to check on the main mounts and the obvious nuts, bolts and fastenings that I could reach. Everything was shipshape except her large ornamental horn, situated just below and behind the big sprung seat. This was flapping about on it's mounting, and was quite fiddly to tighten, but a few minutes saw it done. Daisy had fared well it would appear, and as I checked her oil level I was very pleased that she was showing no signs of any oil-leaks other than one spot underneath where the engine breather is situated. I enthusiastically pointed out these things as Chloe emerged, but the look she gave me suggested that she thinks I'm gibbering. She did however give Daisy's pillion pad a pat, and agreed that she's a 'good girl'.

Once underway again, we skirted through St Austell and headed straight on towards Truro. The traffic seemed to be inordinately heavy, so we filtered through as best we could, negotiating the half a dozen gridlocked roundabouts around the south side after which we met the longest traffic jam I have ever seen in my entire life. Oh, the bliss of being on two wheels! We could thread our way steadily past, but I was appalled at the utter congestion and assumed, quite wrongly as it turned out, that there had been an accident further out. But the real reason for the jam became apparent as we left the town behind – an endless line of caravans, stretching as far as the eye could see, was strung out along the not-that-wide road. We bowled along past these, for what seemed to be miles, expecting at each bend to find the front marker and a clear road ahead, but alas it was not to be. It took us nearly an hour, dodging in and out of the oncoming lane, to cover the 15 or so miles to Truro. I was raging inside.Bloody caravans! Turning this whole area into a choked up misery and it wasn't even summer yet!

Finally we were through it, past Truro and riding into a glorious sunset on the last stretch down to the Lizard towards the last landmark of the day, Goonhilly Earth Station, and hopefully an easy to find campsite. We were however riding much later than I'd planned, and as darkness began to close in I started to fret about the campsite, remembering the dismal failure to find one on the foray into Suffolk. I had utterly failed, of course, to research any of that in advance. But this is the West Country and we were therefore delighted to find numerous campsite signs close by. The Earth Station, a great cluster of huge satellite dishes and domes, looked for all the world like a field of fantastic giant mushrooms, and was, as a result, dead easy to find. We could see the things for miles, and on arriving there we just sat for a while and soaked up the peaceful surroundings, letting the day's weariness ebb away before I got out the cameras for the all-important photo. I congratulated Chloe on a fine day's achievements – we were back on schedule, had survived some pretty awful conditions, picked off four valuable landmarks and now could relax for the evening at the nearest campsite we could find. As the sun sank lower on the horizon and the insects began to emerge, whining, buzzing and whirring all around, we turned and threaded our way back along the tiny roads towards one of the numerous camping signs we had seen just a short while ago. Finding a camp site really was easy but I had to pause just inside the gates, in order to remove about a million bugs, moths and six legged beasties from my helmet, beard, neck and jacket before we got booked in and trundled off to find a flat spot and get set up for the night.

For Chloe this was the first real camping she'd ever done and as such it was a big occasion. The modern tent was nothing like the wood and canvas contraptions that I remember from my youth.They were, if nothing else, simple devices but despite two outings, I still struggled to make sense of the new fangled thing. In the meantime Chloe set about doing the honours with the brand new cooking equipment that she'd been carrying in the back-pack. My inexperience in preparation became blatantly obvious once again at that point, as Chloe emptied the contents out on to the grass. The bag of coffee powder had split open, and was now just a loose mess in the bottom of the pack: Worse, the sugar had joined the party in exactly the same way, and the two had mixed up with the equally mangled bag of rice. Chloe managed to salvage at least enough for a cup each, and enough uncontaminated rice for dinner, which she set about preparing. She did a grand job too, and an hour later, stuffed with improvised chili (sweet, and with a hint of coffee) we headed for the facilities block to get cleaned up.

Freshly showered, we went exploring to find the on-site bar, which was a delightful little affair, decked out like a hunting lodge but with open views to the West where the sun was making up for it's absence most of the day by putting on a spectacularly fiery sunset. Excellent beer was on offer, which I made a point of sampling several times whilst Chloe matched me with fruit juice, and we spent a happy evening poring over the map, with her doing the route finding with her finger again. I worried about the seemingly enormous distance to cover next day, heading first up to the north coast of Cornwall, then further up and across into Somerset and eventually a real distance ride home. So it was off to bed early, ready for a long, long day on the morrow. We were only mildly hampered by my failure to bring along a light of any description.

Dawn. And glory be, it was a bright dawn. The sun was just poking above the low horizon, casting the eastern sky with a fiery glow, giving the fields and distant trees, in their early misty shroud, a surreal feel. There was not a single cloud in sight, and the first birds were just trying out a few halting notes. The sight made me pause and time stood still for a magical few moments - the relief was enormous after yesterday's endurance test. We broke camp at a quarter to six after failing to have breakfast or tea due to a non-functioning stove. This was stupidity on my own part; I had neglected to turn the thing off properly the previous evening and it had leaked the vital gas away during the night. The lack of sustenance was almost the end of the world to Chloe who does love her breakfast, and for me, because I need a caffeine fix to get the old heart started of a morning! I had to promise us both a stop at a Little Chef or some-such place once we were under way. We pushed Daisy up the driveway, to avoid waking the entire campsite, but once in the lane she fired first kick and we hit the road with spirits high.

We only had two Landmarks to get on this final day of the foray, but we'd have to cover over 400 miles as well if we wanted to see our own beds that night. As we threaded our way North towards Truro I began to fret again at the seemingly impossible task. The distance itself, barring misfortune, wasn't really an issue, but of course it wasn't that simple at all. We'd get lost hunting for the landmarks, that was almost certain, we would have to detour from the main routes to find the them, which would invariably take a lot more time than one imagined and to cap it all, we couldn't forget Daisy, who was doing fine certainly, but was not sensibly rideable all day long without plenty of rests, both for her to cool down and for us to relieve our cramps! And what about all those caravans? If the previous day was any measure of what we could look forward to, then we were in trouble before we started. I chideed myself for such negative thinking and focused instead on the plus points that were surely in our favour - the weather for one thing, had changed dramatically, and as such the miles would trundle past infinitely faster than yesterday. Then, there were only two landmarks to find with long riding sections in between, again unlike yesterday, so it should be possible to avoid things like the ferries that ate up the time. No, things were definitely going to be easier.

I was so intensely wrapped up in these thoughts that we were upon Truro and heading out the other side before we knew it, looking for the left turn that would take us North again to join the A30. We were relieved to find that there were no caravans, or indeed any other traffic, which meant that we could give Daisy her head once more through the gently sweeping curves that snaked off to the horizon. The early sun was burning off the wispy mist from the fields, and a glorious panorama of undisturbed countryside surrounded us.On occasion it was so eyecatching that we simply had to stop, if only briefly, to savour the peacefulness of the scene. On one such occassion we watched a kestrel hovering, with deadly silence, almost within touching distance, until it dropped like a stone on to some unwary, and I suspect suddenly late rodent. Chloe took to 'mooo-ing' or 'baaa-ing' at the animals as we passed, causing me a few chuckles, and thus did we progress steadily through the morning.

The miles fell away as we continued North. Camelford came and went, opening up a long stretch of winding, uncluttered road where Daisy could once again stretch her legs. In due course Stratton and Kilkhampton fell behind us as we headed on towards the coast at Clovelly, on the border between Cornwall and North Devon. There we turned East once more, skirting Bideford, on to Barnstable and a planned stop for an early lunch. What a surprise that town was to both of us. For some reason, the name had conjured up in my mind's eye visions of some grey industrial town, disinteresting to visit and probably depressing, but nothing could have been further from the truth. In fact we were enchanted as we slowly trundled around the picture postcard town centre, before stopping to indulge in Cornish Pasties (even though this was Devon) followed by a big home made ice-cream each, made with real Devon cream. Wonderful, but time was trickling past and I needed to check Daisy over before heading off again, just to make sure nothing was coming adrift.

That horn was loose again, she had developed a slight oil leak around the dynamo, where it interfaces with the timing chest, but it wasn't too bad and I didn't have the right spanner or hexagon key to do anything about it anyway. A quick clean with some Kleenex would have to do, but I told myself to keep an eye on that in case it was an early sign of worse to come. Chloe was studying the map again as I did my rounds of nuts and bolts, because from here we needed to head towards the coast where our first landmark of the day should be found in the little town of Lynton. We had not been able to decipher the clue to this one in advance, and therefore had no idea what awaited us. I discussed the possible meaning of the cryptic clue that had been provided ('Raising the profile of copper and zinc') with Chloe as we prepared for the off once more, but neither of us had any inspirational ideas. We'd just have to see what could be found once we got there.

It was just after twelve o'clock when we left Barnstable, taking the A39 and continuing to enjoy the almost perfect conditions. The early promise of that fantastic sunrise had not been an empty one, and it was a glorious summer day, with the temperature rising for the occasion to give us a thoroughly pleasant experience on a thoroughly pleasant road. The hilly landscape that we were traversing could have been made especially for classic motorcycling, with that meandering roller coaster road winding its way between the profusion of greens and colours that one only sees in the English countryside. And a surprise awaited us as we approached Lynton, where the road snaked over the last hill and began a descent which took our breath away with it's sheer, raw beauty. To one side of us was a rock escarpment rising steeply from the very road and on the other is thick, wild, river bank woodland, following the course of the West Lyn River. Our road swept steeply downwards, twisting and turning as it followed the contours. Daisy's deep burbling exhaust note reverberated amidst the rocks and the trees as she loped on the over-run in third gear, and In the end I simply had to pull over, stop, and just soak up the magical surroundings.

I started to wonder how the people that live in such an area perceive their own surroundings. Does it simply become the norm, no more than just the everyday background to their lives? Do they travel to places like Kent and find themselves moved by its beauty, on the grounds that it is so different to this, their own environment? It's an interesting point, and one that I mentally filed away for a time when I'd have the chance to discuss it with a local from some equally breathtaking region, hopefully on one of the many camping occasions that were planned. Just gazing around, astounded by the peacefulness of the place those thoughts kept me distracted for a full ten minutes, before my mind once again focused on the need to get underway again. I called to Chloe, who had wandered across the road and was prodding around in the woods and we reluctantly got mounted up for the last halfmile down to Lynton.

The town was a perfect compliment to that approach road, with its 'Olde Worlde' collection of stone-built buildings nestling between stark coastal headlands either side. We trundled through the centre, but could see nothing that matched our clue, so we turned round and headed back, this time taking a different route around. Several such circuits failed to present us with anything obvious, but the surroundings were so pretty that neither of us was moved to care too much. Eventually though, after possibly the fourth circuit of the place, we stopped outside the splendid Town Hall, where a tourist information point was advertised. Perhaps, I explained to Chloe, we could get some inspiration as to the elusive clue there. Before we got inside however, we were accosted by a rotund gentleman who had scurried busily from the building, urgently addressing us as he approached. He seemed to be asking what we were doing and I suddenly realized I had parked Daisy in a spot 'reserved for the Mayor'. The gentleman accosting us turned out to be that very honorary himself, judging by the gold chain, and I braced myself for the inevitable dressing down.

Just how wrong that impression turned out to be became clear as he reached us, puffing slightly from his exertions. He was indeed the Mayor, introduced himself as such, but far from being upset that a pair of motorcycle ruffians had nicked his parking space with their nasty noisy machine, he was actually enthusing about Daisy! He congratulated us on the choice transport, was delighted to see such a machine in his town, and, pointing to the camping gear, wanted to know how far we'd come, how far we were going, professed astonishment and admiration for Chloe when he heard the answers, before asking what had brought us to Lynton. Explanations followed, and in fact we found ourselves explaining the whole story of the landmark challenge in detail. On discovering that we were also raising charitable funds, he forbade me to move whilst he hustled back into his town hall again to reappear five minutes later, waving a fiver – from the town funds – for 'your cause'! He then turned his attention to Chloe, and I watched her almost visibly swelling with pride as he announced that she was an example to all doing such a thing requiring, he was sure, tremendous strength and effort at such an age. The man's sheer enthusiasm was infectious to say the least and I found myself brimming with pride for Chloe as well. We eventually managed to get the subject onto our immediate problem, that of the elusive clue. It took him but a few seconds to answer it, with a hearty "Of course! It's the Brass Rubbing Centre! Oh, I say how clever!"

Is it? Ah… yes that fitted. Copper and Zinc makes brass, rubbing the stuff would indeed 'raise the profile' so to speak. But we hadn't seen any such place, so could he give us directions to it then? He could, did and in short order we were saying our goodbyes to this wonderful character and were under way again, full of fresh enthusiasm for the task. We found what we were looking for, noted that we had in fact ridden all round it several times earlier, got the all-important photograph and finally, reluctantly, left Lynton and it's colourful Mayor behind, riding once again up that wonderful approach road before turning east for the next leg. Exmoor awaited us. We were both looking forward to that because it's National Park land, and that meant unfenced roads and undisturbed wild countryside again.In fact, as we crossed the cattle grid that marked the boundary, it was almost like turning a page onto a different scene as the lush green moor land came right down to the road, trailing along in a wonderfully unkempt manner that would never see a curb-stone or be forced to follow a straight edge. We noticed as we proceeded along the higgledy piggledy road that signposts had given way to white stones, two feet tall, which had directions and miles engraved upon them. So we were not disappointed and it was truly a marvellous ride in the continuing ideal weather.

We eventually stopped on a high crest, took Daisy two or three feet off the road onto the springy green carpet that stretched in a bumpy panorama as far as the eye could see, took off helmets, gloves, jackets and simply sat there a while. Sheep interrupted their industrious cropping of the lush grass to stare quizzically at us. A hawk stopped it's flight and hovered nearby, giving us an unrivalled view of it's precision use of the wind currents, it's wing-tip feathers stroking the breeze as it fixed the ground beneath with powerful optics in search of lunch. I mentioned to Chloe that this was what we should have enjoyed previous day when searching for the Hurlers down on Bodmin moor, and that our current surroundings would be equally bleak should the mist and cloud descend once more. But we agreed that there was no room for regret that we hadn't got to sample it there – we've got it here now.

I layed back on the grass and thought about the day so far, and was simply gratified that it had not only started out well, but had just got better and better as the miles fell behind us. But inevitably it was time to get underway once again and it seemed only too soon that the unfenced roads gave way to the hall-marks of civilization once more, as we crossed the little cattle grid at the far side of the moor. A quick map and time check revealed that we had some 50 miles to our next, final landmark and it was already pushing towards two o'clock. I began to mentally calculate the total distance still to cover to get home trying to plot that against various average speeds in my head. I didn't like the answers and suggested to Chloe reluctantly that once we had picked off the last photograph, we would have to leave the lanes, settle for the main routes home and ride as long as possible between rests. As usual, she was far more optimistic about things, confident that Dad was merely worrying unnecessarily. After I showed her the distance to home and invited her to do some maths involving dividing the 250 or so miles by, say, an average speed of even 40mph (which caused further debate, until Chloe understood that each stop, junction, traffic light etc would reduce the average), she realised that we really were up against it somewhat. I was more concerned about riding after dark I explained, since, as she'd demonstrated in Norfolk, Daisy's electrical abilities were definitely far from ideal and highly questionable in the reliability stakes.

It was with a sense of urgency then that we set off once more, determined to push harder than we had all weekend. I fretted about Daisy's ability to take the punishment, but there was nothing else for it really and the throttle hand wound on the juice accordingly. We were heading for a hunting lodge, owned and used by King John in the 1200's, apparently. If our prior research was correct, the would be found nestling somewhere close to Cheddar, and that hop alone was going to take a good forty five minutes if we were lucky. But Daisy eased up to 75 on the straights, of which there weren't too many, and the miles steadily rolled away beneath her wheels. We arrived at Cheddar at around ten to three, having somehow missed the hunting lodge. It was however necessary to stop for a while to ease the bones, and it seemed appropriate to enjoy a pint of cider (Coke for Chloe) before doubling back to find the thing and get our picture. As usual the pathetic map we were relying on made it hard to pinpoint exactly where the lodge was, and with a myriad of little roads in this area I began to think we'd never find it. Round and round we went, to no avail, and the precious minutes ticked relentlessly past in the afternoon sun. To add to my worries, Daisy began to overheat as a result of our stop-start-stop search and in the end I was forced to a halt by a little farm shop in order to let her cool down. That at least gave me a chance to ask inside about the lodge. It's easy, I was told, as it's actually in the middle of the little town of Axbridge, which was not two miles up the road. Can't miss it – it's right in the town square, I was assured.

The information, against all previous experience of 'local' knowledge, turned out to be absolutely right, as we pulled up ten minutes later in front of the very large and ancient lodge smack in the middle of the very small town. Whilst doing my research back at home, this little snippet had failed to register, and I had wasted a lot of time looking for my own idea of a hunting lodge, which in the proper order of things should surely be in the woods? I had therefore dismissed any route that led into a town or village! I made a mental note to check such details for the next lot of landmarks, and certainly wouldn't get caught out again. That was that then, and as I took the vital photograph I enthusiastically congratulated Chloe and Daisy. The last landmark of this foray was safely in the can, (or cans to be more accurate, because in a very uncharacteristic fit of logical thinking back in the period of minimal planning, it had occurred to me that having a set of backup photographs in case of disaster would be an incredibly sensible precaution. I therefore had two disposable cameras in the tank bag). We checked the time again and I wished we hadn't - all that mucking about in the lanes had really cost us, it was now nearly five o'clock. With just over two hundred miles still to do this was no joke. We did the maths again, considered our options and came to the conclusion that if we really pushed things and took minimal stops, we could maintain an average speed of 50 mph, probably. It was not likely however, as we were both feeling the miles by then, and we were certainly not going by the motorways, so we'd have towns to slow us up, not to mention the twisty roads, punctuated with regular roundabouts or junctions themselves. Call it six hours then, which would get us home at eleven if we could keep up the pace. Of course, all this assumed that Daisy's lights would keep going!

Despite the pressure to crunch miles, it was not possible to be in the area and not ride the Cheddar Gorge. Chloe was dead keen to see it, having listened to my inadequate descriptions, and I had promised that we'd head back through Cheddar and up through the Gorge itself. This was actually an experience I had never before sampled on a motorcycle and therefore I too was dead keen. We took our time threading our way up through that spectacular monument to violent geography, revelling in the surroundings and gratified by the deep burble from Daisy's exhausts, bouncing from the rock towering above us. I still find it hard to describe the gorge, with it's sheer rock faces bordering a road that snakes through numerous 'S' bends as it climbs steeply up to the top and into the Mendip Hills. Breathtaking – and we both agreed it was a fantastic thing to do with an old classic motorcycle!

And so, inevitably, we left the gorge behind us, turned towards Bath and set about the long haul home. Picking up the A4 heading east, a harsh pace was set for Daisy and pretty soon, with Chippenham and Marlborough behind us we took a ten-minute stop at Hungerford. I tried to explain to Chloe the terrible events that took place there on that fateful day in 1987, just before she was born, when a certain Michael Ryan and his gun collection took the lives of some seventeen people before he took his own. Chloe asked the million dollar question "Why?" and I found myself unable to answer that. He took that secret with him. We moved on, continuing on the A4 past Newbury and finally we joined the M4 at Reading where we took a well deserved rest at the services. We had pushed Daisy hard and covered some 85 miles in one and half hours, including the stop at Hungerford. The horn had come loose yet again, and that oil leak round the dynamo was noticeably worse, but nothing else was amiss. I began to feel immensely proud of the old bike but considered that she was in for a real test from there, as we'd be completing our weekend with an anticlimactic and uninspiring 120 miles of motorway.

It was exactly a quarter to seven as we joined the M4, and exactly a quarter past nine when we pulled up at home that evening. That, I felt, was pretty good going for a fifty year old machine carrying two people and gear. Chloe wasted no time in claiming the bathroom, once she'd managed to fight off Sheba, our dog, for whom the disappearance of two of the family again had obviously been traumatic and confusing. Chris explained that she had been pining the whole weekend, lying in the garage for long periods with her nose carefully positioned at the crack in the doors. She had resisted any attempts to distract or cheer her up. I took my time unpacking, only mildly hampered by Sheba's demands for attention and answering a barrage of questions from Chris. Later on, as the family sat down to a very late meal, the talk was of high adventure and Chloe gave a fairly good rendition of events as they had unfolded. The Mayor of Lynton was the high point undoubtedly, and I smiled as I watched her try to explain that encounter, but it was also nice to hear her describing some of the sights and scenes that had captivated us so thoroughly up on the moors.

Chris was clearly very taken with the idea of National Park land, and insisted on a detailed account from Chloe before turning to me and asking whether he would get to see similar on his next outing. I assured him that this would indeed be the case, since one of the landmarks was buried in the hills of Cumbria. There was anticipation in his manner that made me feel enormously satisfied. My plan to broaden the kids' horizons was definitely showing signs of paying dividends already, and I was delighted at the prospect of continuing to do so. By the time the plates were cleared that evening, I was under pressure from both children to confirm the rest of the landmark campaign, and I promised that we would look at the maps the next evening – right then it was very late, and a school day next day to boot – so off to bed with them both, I insisted. Diane was clearly pleased to see the kids so keen to be involved, and as they reluctantly headed off to their rooms, I promised everyone that we would plan the rest of the challenge in the coming week, but I also had to remind all them that before continuing, we would have to check that Daisy had handled this last test without any problems!

Photographs.

Daisy ...

Chris ...

Chloe ...

The infamous Sprung Hub ...

Daisy at Le Mans

Grandad and Chloe at the Rabbit Rally

Will it fit back on ...?

Chris takes a break ...

At the dam in central Wales ....

The Angel of the North ...

At the campsite in Coldstream ...

Dawn mist in deepest Wales ...

Visiting castles ...

Chloe at the silver mine ...

What it was all about - Daisy in the Lake District

7. Fire in the Shires!

The following morning, with everyone off to school and Diane at her morning job, I wheeled Daisy out into a glorious sunny day and settled down in the drive to check her over. A brief visual inspection was encouraging, with nothing obvious to fret about, so I opened up the socket set, got my box of spanners, and set about the task of checking all the fastenings and mountings. Rocker box and cylinder head bolts had all loosened off slightly, with the beginnings of an oil-leak showing around the rear pushrod tube. This was fixed easily with but a few moments of tightening whilst carefully observing the torque settings of 18ft/lb. The horn had come loose again, so it was time to take it off and find a proper solution. After checking the threads on both nut and bolt, I decided to simply re-mount the thing, but using some thread-lock on the nut to prevent it undoing again. The dynamo had continued leaking but it was a minute's work to slacken off the clamp, then tighten the nut to pull it harder against the timing chest, and do up the clamp once again. The engine mountings and those of the gearbox took but a slight turn on the sockets to nip them all up, but the fuel tank was a different matter.

Daisy's tank is secured with four bolts to the underside, one of which was now conspicuous by its absence. They're special bolts on these older models, with a shoulder that ensures that you can't tighten them too far and thus pierce the tank itself, with the inevitable results. I had no spares and decided that Daisy could live with it until later in the year, when doubtless other such items would be joining this one on the list of things to be replaced!. Next up, I checked the chain tensions of both primary and secondary drives, needing to give each a small amount of adjustment, before turning my attention to oil. This needed changing I decided, as she'd just completed the best part of a thousand miles on her fairly new engine. Once that was done I spent the rest of that relaxed morning with a bucket and soapy water, before finishing off before lunch by giving her a well deserved wax and polish. She looked fantastic by the time I had finished.

All told, she had done rather well I considered, as I tidied away the tools and cleaning gubbins. If this was what could be expected from the old girl, then the long haul North should hold no worries for Chris and myself at all. In fact Chris was still very wary of Daisy's manners after the troublesome Norfolk experience, despite no sign of any such problems on our unplanned detour to Le Mans. It seemed she would have to deliver more than one trouble free journey to convince him that she had been properly fixed! Putting the tools away then, my thoughts turned to what else needed doing before we took to the high roads of Scotland. The tent had proved adequate, albeit a bit small, but I had suffered mightily from sleeping on the hard ground with just the thickness of the sleeping bag for padding. I had also discovered just how cold mother earth can get in the wee, small hours, as the chill from the ground had sometimes left me quivering.So cold did I get on one of the nights, that by five in the morning I had, in desperation, attempted to light the stove inside the tent, in order to heat the place a bit. That had led to the discovery that we had no gas and at that point I had given up, got dressed and gone off to stamp around the place in an effort to get warm again. Chloe had suffered no such ill effects, and I guessed this was simply age creeping up on me in yet another small way.

So, a bed roll of some sort was definitely required and I needed to consider other small items whilst at the camping store, such as a gas cylinder for the stove, an additional one as a spare, and some proper storage containers for the likes of milk, sugar and tea bags. Maps had also proved to be a problem thus far, and I began to wonder where to get larger scale versions of the areas we had yet to visit. We had managed with the 1:250,000 scale that I was carrying for both forays to date, but it had proved useless once off the beaten track and it was clear that life would be much easier with more detailed items, especially when considering the wilds of Wales, Scotland and Cumbria. Later that evening, I sat down to make a list of all these necessities, and then began looking at the choices for the next attack. It occurred to me that the school holidays were a good few weeks away yet but with Scotland and Wales both requiring more than a normal weekend to complete, and both kids determined to share the experience, I had to concede that these epics would have to wait. I had to look closer to home for the moment, and having already dealt with the southeast and East Anglia there weren't actually that many 'odd ones' left. My eyes turned to the little marks on the map in Surrey, Middlesex, Berkshire and Gloucestershire, wherein nestled a landmark apiece.Those would make for an interesting weekend's worth of adventure, I reckoned, as they lie in a logical progression, heading northwest from our little corner of the land. We could call in to see my other brother, Howard, and his family on the way through Wiltshire too. I decided to make that one a surprise visit for him and also for Chris, and therefore left it unmentioned for the moment.

As it turned out, Diane was going off to a music convention in London that next weekend, taking Chloe with her. This was something I had utterly failed to remember until the Friday morning, when I was reminded not to be late picking her up from work, Chloe up from school and delivering both of them promptly to the station. I duly did all that, and on his arrival home from school Chris was quick to accept my suggestion that we may as well take the opportunity to go camping again. Of course I hadn't had time yet to go and purchase the items on my list, but I certainly couldn't face another night without some padded insulation, so with some urgency we jumped on Daisy there and then, Chris with the back-pack on, and rode the seven miles to the camping shop, arriving just in time to stop the old boy there turning the sign on his door to 'closed'. After begging to be allowed in, he told us we must be quick, and we hurried round the place grabbing all the things that I could remember on my list, which I had of course forgotten to bring!

On the counter at the end our little stash grew. We had half a dozen plastic pots with screw on lids, a bedroll, some extra bungees and some gas cylinders. I racked my brains but couldn't think of anything else. Chris declined the offer of a bedroll, taking the opportunity to dea me another mental shock when, like Chloe before, he suggested that only 'old farts' needed such things. But the shopkeeper was pointedly looking at his watch by then, so I let the latest insult go as we shoved all the purchases in the back-pack, paid the man, and climbed back on to Daisy. Just as we were about to pull away, I remembered the thing that I had been racking my brains over, the camping light! I jumped back off and just caught the 'closed' sign going up for the second time. Under the disapproving stare that was now being aimed at me I babbled something about the need for the light, apologised for my idiocy and the inconvenience it was causing, took the first one tersely offered, waved some more money at the by now thoroughly bemused shopkeeper and finally left, slightly embarrassed, to return back home and get Daisy ready for an early start the next morning.

An hour later we were still trying to work out the best way of fitting everything into Daisy's limited storage, and getting nowhere fast. We hadn't had the bedroll last time, the spare gas or the alarmingly large gas light. There seemed to be no space for any of them no matter how many ways we tried, and we were both getting frustrated with it and each other whilst achieving nothing. Salvation came in the shape of Bill, our neighbour. He had been observing our various comical attempts to manage what he clearly saw as a simple task, and finally decided to intervene with a polite clearing of his throat to attract our attention. Bill is everything in life that I am not. He *knows stuff*. Specifically, at that moment in time, he knew all the stuff that mere mortals such as I could not hope to grasp, and made impossible and complicated things seem very, very simple. This was probably because most things are in fact very simple, but that I am even simpler than they are. Whatever the case, Bill was happy to demonstrate his clear superiority and abilities over those of his rather useless neighbour, and proceeded to make suggestions that as usual left me tingling with shame at their breathtaking simplicity, but more to the point, my own inability to see them without help.

The neatness of Bill's solution could'nt be argued with. "Lay out the bedroll" he suggested, "and place the light cross-ways in the middle".I did what I was told. "Now", he continued patiently, "place the gas cylinders, bottoms facing outwards, one at each end of the light. These will make a natural pair of end stops", he observed, "around which you can now roll the bed up, enclosing the light within". It was all true, and very, very obvious. But bill was on a roll now, and wanted to be sure I couldn't mess it up. "Secure with bungees, and you have a neat roll, containing that bulky stuff, which you can just put across the back of Daisy with the tent". I did. It did and they did, and I felt deeply stupid to have not been able to see this myself during the twenty minutes of buggering around. Bill had worked it out in seconds the smug git. I tried deflecting the shame away from myself, by telling Chris how stupid *he* was not to have thought of the obvious answe. I was rewarded with derision, and so grudgingly raided the fridge and produced some beer, handing one over to Bill as a thank you. As we drank in the evening sun, I explained to him what we were in the process of doing. It was clear that Bill was thinking I had lost some, if not most of my marbles, confirming this with a simple statement – "You're bloody mad" he said. I tried to explain the joy of the open road, the thrill of the challenge, the recaptured fun of youthful pursuits, like camping. Not to mention the camaraderie that was developing with the kids, I added. None of this seemed to convince him, as he eyed me with what looked like a concerned smile: eventually I gave up, bade him good night, making excuses about the need for an early night, long day tomorrow, up early and all that. But as I put Daisy away that evening I found myself wondering whether Bill had a point. Are we mad? No, I decided, I don't think so.

It was a bit of a novelty this, I thought, as we set out the following morning under a vast blue sky, bright with its promise of a warm and sunny day to come. Daisy had started first kick and here we were heading West on near empty roads. Early mist was hanging in the trees and clinging to hedgerows across the fields, glowing mystically as the sun slowly but surely caught up and burned off the moisture. There was a slight chill in the air, but with warmth at our back promising to grow stronger by the minute, that was sure to be a temporary inconvenience, nothing more. We were planning to cut across country all day long, following a route that would take us first to the ancient city of Canterbury, through the North Downs to Ashford, then we would thread our way Westwards through the Weald of Kent, to Guildford, before turning north to keep our first appointment at Windsor. Specifically we would be looking for Runnymede, the site at which King John put his seal to the Magna Carta, the great charter of English liberties,in the year 1215. Being so close to Windsor, I had also promised Chris that we'd go on to see the castle. I was amazed to discover that he had never even seen a photograph of the place! Well, there's no substitute for the real thing I declared, so visit it we would. From there, we'd turn West once more and pick our way across to the A4 at Reading and on into Wiltshire for that surprise rendezvous with Howard.

Daisy had other ideas. We were in the middle of the Weald, deep in rural Kent, stopped for a rest next to a charmingly rustic little bridge that spanned some ancient stream that had been gurgling along next to the winding road for the last few miles. Chris was leaning on the bridge gazing down at the clear water as it made its leisurely way along beneath him. He'd done the thing with sticks, dropping them into the current and then waiting for them to emerge the other side, and now he was looking for fish. I was sitting on a little style by the road, having a crafty cigarette whilst dreamily gazing at the countryside around me, thinking that life doesn't get much better than that. I was also thinking that my cigarette was giving off rather more smoke than was normal, which was annoying as it was interfering with my lazy inspection of Daisy against that idyllic backdrop. Holding the thing up to inspect it I was suddenly, and harshly, jolted back to reality. It was not the cigarette giving off the excessive smoke but *Daisy*! It was coming from beneath the panel on her petrol tank, curling up around the tank-bag and before my very eyes it was getting thicker! I let out a yelp as I scrambled from my perch, and Chris, yanked from his daydreams yelled a harsh query at me along the lines of "What the hell…?"

"Daisy's on fire!" I yelled back.

What followed was classic circus stuff. As I ran full tilt towards the bike, I cannoned into Chris, who was running from the bridge. I yanked the tank-bag off and flung it to the floor, but then all we could do was dance around Daisy utterly helpless. Smoke was boiling from under the panel, but I had no way of getting the thing off! Chris, by now in a blind panic, yelled at me to "do something", I yelled back that I couldn't – I had no tools and no time. The panic deepened, the smoke got even thicker, the air was thick with an acrid, burning smell and in desperation I tried to grab the edge of the panel and rip the thing off without undoing it's retaining bolt. Better that, i thought, than the unthinkable consequences of doing nothing. As I grappled desperately with the thing, it occurred to me suddenly that a fire inside a recess within a half full petrol tank was about as dodgy as it is possible to get and I bellowed at Chris to get away. He must have arrived at the same thought already, as he didnn't need telling twice!

My fingers failed to grip the edge of the panel as I heaved, but as they slipped off they caught the lead light, standing proud from the panel, ripping it from it's housing. Smoke boiled angrily up through the hole, and self preservation finally cut in – I abandoned the hopeless struggle and took flight, taking large, urgent steps in the opposite direction to join Chris down the road. We stood and watched helplessly as time seemed to be suspended. Miraculously though, as we continued to watch, Daisy's tank failed to erupt into a fireball and slowly, agonisingly slowly, the smoke began to clear. I stood trembling as the adrenalin drained away, but after some ten minutes I cautiously approached once more, ready to flee at so much as 'tic' from Daisy. No smoke. No 'tic'. I edged closer, peering gimlet-like at that hole, and suddenly noticed that the wires coming from the now dangling lead light were a melted mess, but a mess that at least was no longer burning. I continued staring at the panel, still trembling from the adrenalin rush, desperately daring to hope that the danger was over. It was, I decided, but I still wasn't going to approach the thing until it had properly cooled down. "It's OK," I yelled as I turned to Chris "It's stopped!" I nearly burst out laughing though, as I took in a scene so familiar to our last journey together – that of Chris standing forty feet away, fingers firmly in ears, a look of abject fear and deep unhappiness on his face. I walked over to him, and slid down the stone wall by the road, to sit and calm down. "Well bugger that," I offered.

After another five minutes or so, we headed back over to Daisy, and set about inspecting the damage. I gingerly tried the light switch, which was also mounted in the panel, and we were rewarded with lights without any smoke or flames. That was good. Feeling much happier, I fished around in the lead-light mounting hole, pulling the eight feet of coiled wire that allows the thing to wander, out into the sunshine. It was a sorry state indeed, with a substantial length of it melted, but it was impossible to identify what started things off. It seemed that I'd had a lucky break when I'd slipped and knocked the actual light out of its housing. That had clearly stopped whatever it was that was burning from continuing to do so! I explained to Chris that we have had a short circuit, probably due to a section of this lead rubbing against a sharp edge or something, and that to be safe we'd need to disconnect the lead, cut it back and tape the ends up.

I got on with that, but as I did the necessary, I got to thinking that I had not reacted particularly logically to this incident. Daisy has a good old fashioned battery mounting, with the power source housed in its authentic Exide box, mounted on the left hand side and actually within easy reach. In hindsight it was plainly obvious that the thing to have done would have been to simply to grab the leads and yank them off, disconnecting the battery, rather than attacking the panel in the tank as I had. As I thought about it, I also cursed myself for not equipping Daisy with a fuse, which would have prevented the problem outright. I made a mental note to do just that when we got home at the end of the weekend. On the plus side, the crisis was over with no real harm done and we could continue with our journey as planned after all, if I can persuade Chris to get back on! He did so, warily, but was quite insistent that I gave all manner of assurances that there was no possibility of a repeat performance. I showed him what had gone wrong, explained why it could not happen again (whilst mentally thinking 'at least not in the same place'!), but had to smile as he inspected things minutely with a look of doubt on his face.

We'd lost nearly an hour, I reckoned, as we got going once more. But I was so relieved to still be in possession of a functioning motorcycle that this was a small worry indeed. In fact I felt insanely happy now that the drama was over – it must have been a side effect of all that adrenalin. As we pulled away up the lane, I reminded Chris that we had plenty of time today, and that I reckoned we'd earned ourselves a slap up lunch at some country pub. He agreed with that suggestion readily and as we were somewhere in the Weald of Kent still, approaching the Sussex border, finding such an establishment wouldn't be hard. Twenty minutes later, we were seated outside a handsomely Olde Worlde Inn. It was a quarter to twelve on the clock, we'd ordered, and were both looking forward to tucking into, a good old traditional ploughman's whilst laughing together as we re-lived the horrible few minutes of panic earlier. I ribbed Chris about the finger-in-ears approach he seems to adopt whenever anything happens to Daisy, but he got awfully serious as he breathlessly told me that he really did think she was going to explode. I had to agree that I had also expected the worse in the end, which was why I too had run away! The jolly Landlord interrupted our musings at this point, as he brought out the lunchtime fare and, noticing Daisy, he spontaneously exclaimed his delight to see 'such a beauty' on his forecourt. All thought of the challenges from earlier were well and truly banished as he turned to us and said, with certainty in his voice "And I bet she doesn't give you *any* problems!" We looked at each other, Chris and I, and both of us burst out laughing. We were then duty bound to recount the story for the poor man while we ate, lest he thought we were being rude. Five minutes later, as we finish the food the stout chap reappeared with a pint of Sussex Ale and a coke, "On the house" he insisted!

It wasn't long before we regretfully left the hilly green panorama of the Weald behind us and picked our way through the urban sprawls of East Grinstead and Crawley. We could probably have cut across country on some smaller minor roads, but the last minute decision to do this foray meant that I had not got round to looking for sensible navigation aids. We were still armed only with that large scale map, which would almost certainly get us hopelessly lost on anything other than at least rural A roads. The inevitable stop-start filtering through traffic didn't take long to upset Daisy on that rather warm day, relying as she does on the fairly primitive pre-monobloc carburettor with it's quaint remote float and recalcitrant mixing chamber. I found myself having to constantly blip her throttle at each bottleneck, lest she sputtered into silence and made us play the waiting game while she cooled off. We were trapped for nearly forty minutes in the choked up towns but eventually we broke through into open countryside, still heading West, and at last I was able to let Daisy stretch her legs and breath once again as we swept past Horsham on the A264.

That was much more like it. The route we had selected between Crawley and Guildford was breathtaking, deliberately taking a detour further West than necessary, if direct transit were the aim, in order to approach Guildford from the southwest. The reason was simple, this route, cresting the Devil's Punch Bowl and the Hog's Back, was an absolute pleasure to ride. The sheer variety of landscape kept one constantly refreshed as it alternated between dense broad-leafed woodland, common ground and heathland. There was the odd lake in there as well, but more to the point we were able to pick up the beginning of the North Downs ridge, blessed with it's ancient routes which have maintained their rustic winding charms to this day in spite of now being 'A' roads. The early summer sunshine had brought forth an explosion of life all around; birds, bugs and a profusion of colourful plants made for a very soul boosting meander.

Moving north eventually, we crossed the M3 motorway and it wasn't long before we saw the little circling dots of airliners that mark the stacking airspace around Heathrow. As we got closer, I started to count the things, which were circling over a wide area before reaching the bottom of the stack and taking their slot to land, joining the long line from the West. It was amazing to think that all day long, every day, literally one aircraft every 30 seconds or so would join the final approach and head in to burn rubber on that busy tarmac. That's a lot of planes, travellers, cargo and commerce. Eventually we passed directly under the flight path and stopped to watch, mesmerised, as a seemingly impossibly large 'plane, which seemed to just hang in the air against all logic, passed over us. Amazing, if a tad bloody noisy! It was half-past two when we pull into Runnymede.

I didn't really know what to expect from a landmark so steeped in historical importance, but at first it was a bit of a disappointment. Basically the place is a park now, on the bank of the river Thames, populated with a number of memorials, including the Magna Carta site memorial itself. As we took a rest, and just wandered around, I explained to Chris how the Magna Carta had played such a vital role in shaping the social history of Britain. We read the plaque on the memorial and it was a strange feeling to be standing on the same spot some 800 years after the events described took place. Daisy, not to be outdone, had attracted the attentions of an entire coach-load of ex-forces OAP's, obviously out for a regimental reunion or some such event. They'd crowded all round her, posing with her as their colleagues took photographs or just discussed what must be their own memories of owning or riding such machines in the past. It was clear that if we approached at that point, we'll never get away, and so we stayed hidden in the trees until they eventually returned to their coach and headed off. Daisy was proudly displaying several spots of oil underneath her, and with a frown I bent down to investigate the source. It was the dynamo again and I found myself irritated by that having suffered with it in the West Country, and thinking that I'd fixed it good and proper during the week. Obviously not, as it was now taunting me once again, to which I added my own frustration that yet again I had come with insufficient tools to do anything about it. Would I never learn, I asked myself?

There was nothing to be done for the dynamo, other than to mop up the dribbles with Kleenex, so we got underway again and as promised, I pointed Daisy along the very busy road into Windsor. It really was the grandest of places, especially the entrance to the castle estate, known as the 'Long Walk'. A vast treelined avenue, along which the general public are not allowed, led up to the Castle proper, raised high at the end in all it's regal splendour. The scale of the thing was truly remarkable and it must have seemed an insurmountable challenge to any would-be attacker back when it was first constructed by William the Conqueror to guard the Western approaches to the capital, some 900 years ago. Of course, it's been extended and strengthened over the many years since, but all the same one can't help but be caught up with sheer ancient mystery of the place. We trundled around the town, which is impressively in keeping with the castle, before eventually threading our way out towards the M4, on which we had agreed to travel as far as Reading and the A4 junction.

Progressing through the afternoon, Chris recognised Hungerford as the town that we had discussed over dinner last weekend, questioning me over my shoulder to confirm that this was the place. We stopped for a couple of minutes and I wondered what he was thinking as he stood with a vacant look and just gazed around him, but I didn't want to get back into a maudlin mood though, and so we were back on the road in pretty short order. The architecture as we moved West from London changed steadily, becoming predominantly that of Cotswold stone. It was a charming effect, to see entire villages formed from the stuff and somehow the look was both traditional and highly characteristic. Alderton is such a place, nestling on the very Southern edge of the Cotswolds and as we pulled up outside the residence of the Wiltshire branch of the Ham family, I was struck by how wonderfully peaceful it was. Indeed, I was a little worried that Daisy's arrival may have disturbed the peace somewhat and could imagine the stares of disapproval, unseen, boring into us from behind various net curtains. On the other hand, brother Howard runs a Harley, so they must be used to it. Without further ado, we knocked on the door, eager to see the surprise from a part of our family that we only ever see once or twice a year.

There was no answer. That of course is the problem with surprise visits. Chris was disappointed as he had been eagerly looking forward to seeing his two cousins again, but I suggested to him that all may not be lost as I had Howard's mobile number and they may just be out shopping or some such. The village was blessed with a charming little pond at one end, and we wandered down to there to sit and rest while I made the call. Chris was dangling his feet at the edge, and this attracted the attention of the local pond bully – a very large, very stroppy, black swan. It was not about to put up with any nonsense from us humans either, and I couldn't help but laugh as Chris emitted a "Whoooa" and rapidly scrambled backwards under a swift and violent attack on his boots. The swan was there for the duration it seemed, and glaring at us with little piggy red eyes it started an aggressive backwards and forwards patrol, radiating attitude all the while and seemed to be daring us to try it on again. We decided to keep our distance.

I made the call, found out that Howard and family were at a village community event a few miles away, and after explaining that Chris and I had dropped in whilst on the way past, so to speak, he was delighted and suggested that we should head straight over to join in the fun. Well, why not? Directions were duly handed out, we left the swan to rule his kingdom and headed back to Daisy. The directions proved to be accurate, and we easily found the little village of Sherston, where we had agreed to meet. What we found there was a delightful scene. The entire village was closed to traffic and a full-on street party was under way! Chris and I parked Daisy at the edge of the cordoned-off main street and began to wander amongst all the fun, I was overwhelmed with a feeling of irrational nostalgia for the old country way of life. Nothing like this ever happens in urban areas such as Ramsgate, where we live. Even if it did, it wouldn't be the same, because the setting of a rural village in the heart of the English countryside takes some beating.

The street was full with noisy, happy people, milling about in the sun and there was plenty going on. There were traditional craft stalls, toffee apples could be bought for 50p, the products of home made baking were displayed on several stands, with all the traditional fare on offer and a colouful iced cream stall promised the buyer a proper home-made treat. There were two pubs in the street, and both had joined in with long trestle tables outside boasting a line of barrels on each, offering draft beer of various sorts straight from the tap. The garden fete atmosphere was finished off with a number of country games under way. Horse shoe throwing, guess the weight of the pig, open the box and shove ha'penny were all popular attractions. Wonderful stuff. I called Howard once again, to find out where in that heaving throng he and his brood were hiding, and followed his directions round to the back of one of the pubs. There we found a boules tournament under way, apparently an inter-village competition just for kids. Howard's two were competing and the proud parents were seated alongside one of the 'pistes' to watch. We exchanged hearty greetings but got a traditional welcome from Trish, Howard's French wife, by way of the cheek-to-cheek kiss that is the norm for that nation. Chris visibly shriveled as the same treatment was aimed his way, and we all laughed at the horror on his face. Clearly this was not a cool thing for teenage boys to be seen doing! Howard was quick to go for beer, returning to offer me a frothing jug of some local real-ale, and I settled down with them to catch up and just enjoy the experience while Chris wandered off to look around. The remainder of the warm, sunny afternoon lazily passed by, but relaxing though the whole experience was, we inevitably came to the point where we had to part company once again.

Howard and his family were due at an evening barbecue, whilst Chris and I needed to continue our quest, so we all wandered up through the street to where Daisy patiently waited, cooling from her earlier exertions. She had also decorated the road with more oil-spots, larger than the last collection and extremely irritating to my eye. Howard took the opportunity to rib me over my choice of steed, commenting that no such problems would bother him with the Harley. Why didn't I see sense and get one? He asked, smirking, and he added that it would also get me around much faster. I pointed out that I prefer to travel in style, adding that the rural surroundings he had chosen to live in must be the real reason he chose an agricultural machine to ride. I was forced to concede however, that I was getting a little perturbed about the dynamo and that in fact I was pretty certain that would get progressively worse. With a good few hundred miles still to do that weekend I considered that something needed to be done. Howard suggested that we should perhaps retire to his house once more, where I could make use of his tools to effect a running repair. It was but a ten-minute ride, and after opening up the garage they left Chris and I to it and went inside to get ready for their evening.

I found the necessary spanner and Allen key, loosened off the mounts and pulled the dynamo out from it's housing to inspect the cork gasket that served (or not, in Daisy's case) to keep the black stuff on the inside. It was a mess, and where the dynamo had obviously been allowed to vibrate, it had been somewhat chewed up. I held it up for Chris to see, and it was obvious that the sorry thing was not going to seal anything again. I couldn't just bolt the dynamo back in place without a seal – the things acts as a spacer, and even if it didn't it would spout oil by the bucket-load. The problem was that I didn't have anything that would remotely do the job. Chris surprised me then, by suggesting firmly that we couldn't even consider giving up. We'd come too far, he still hadn't camped yet since starting this campaign (the Rabbit and Le Mans being too organised to count in his opinion), and anyway, there must be a way to fix it? This was a very different attitude to that which he had displayed in Norfolk!

Howard reappeared just as we were having that discussion, peered at the mangled gasket and suggested that we could attempt to seal things with Hermatite liquid gasket, a tube of which he happened to have in the shed. This wasn't as obvious as it may sound now. The cork dynamo seal is very thick and I'm not sure whether a thinner seal would prevent the drive pinion of the dynamo from rubbing on the inside of the casing. I tried the dynamo in place without any seal, and gently turned the engine over. I was rewarded with a graunching noise that confirmed my fears. We scratched our heads, and considered what might be done, but the only thing I could think to try was a very thick layer of the liquid stuff, let it go off, and try not to do up the mounting too tight. Of course, whilst doing all that I'd have to pray that it would then make a good seal. It would be pressure that could confound such a bodge, I told Howard. Ask any old Triumph owner about crankcase pressure and bad push rod tube seals. A bloody nightmare on a good day, and could easily cause this attempt to fail dismally. but it was the best plan available however, and so we carefully squeezed a fat donut of the sticky red goo all around the mounting boss and left it to go off in the sun. I was only marginally dismayed that the tube in question looked as though it had actually been used to seal Noah's Ark!

Chris had wandered off by this time, to catch a few extra minutes with his cousins, Sammy and Alex. Howard and I had a cup of tea, while he returned to ribbing me over Daisy. After a while we returned to the task in hand, refitting the dynamo in its proper place. But as I gently did up the nut, and watched the red gunge squeeze out all round the join, I was utterly convinced that this would not work. I wiped all round the joint with Kleenex, removing the unsightly excess, and the end result did at least look like a solid seal. I then primed Daisy, started her up and we both peered critically at the engine. At least there were no horrible noises emanating from the timing chest and after running for a few minutes at revs, there was no sign of any problem with the seal. We decided to declare it a good bodge and without further ado, Chris and I said our goodbyes, mounted up, and headed off into the Wiltshire countryside. At Howard's insistence, I had taken the remaining gasket goo, the old cork seal, the spanner and Allen key, just in case we needed to bodge things again and they now resided in the tank bag. After a few miles, I stopped to inspect the dynamo, still paranoid that our field repair simply would not hold, but all seemed to be in order and I began to relax a bit.

The shadows were growing longer, as we set off once more, and Chris reminded me that it was nearly half past six, and wasn't it time to make some decisions about camping? He'd not forgotten the experience in Suffolk, where we had run out of light and had been very lucky to find that pub. He wanted to be sure of his long awaited chance to do the tent thing this time. I couldn't argue with his logic, and after looking at where we needed to get to the next day, we decided to press on as far as Cirencester and find a campsite there. I assured Chris that this was a very popular tourist area, and as such there should be a plethora of campsites around every other bend. I hoped to hell this was indeed the case, and his look of cynicism wasn't encouraging. To put him at ease, I calculated the distance to the rough area, on the map, and he was somewhat reassured once he realised that it was only fifteen miles or so away. We would cruise at 50mph easily on these not too twisty and apparently empty roads and so we'd be there by seven for certain, I thought, as we set off once more into the early evening sunshine.

We made good time indeed, stopping once more, very briefly, to check on the dynamo which seemed to have capitulated and was no longer displaying incontinent tendencies. We trundled into Cirencester at ten to seven, and it didn't take long at all to get through the place and out of the other side, heading towards Gloucester and hopefully a handy campsite. Against all the odds, we stumbled across the much wanted camping sign almost immediately and turned into the place without a second thought. Chris perked up considerably as we signed in at the little hut by the entrance, handing over six pounds for the privilege and receiving strict instructions regarding where in the field we could camp. This seemed a bit unnecessary, as it was in fact a large field with, as far as we could see, no other campers at all. There was plenty of space all round, but the attendant was quite assertive in his instruction that we must camp *there*, as he pointed rigidly to a spot by the hedge that marked the boundary. He also instructed us, gravely, that we must be particularly vigilant when setting up, making sure that we stayed within the pegs that marked our slot, and do not stray beyond them into the empty hundred yards or so of space either side.

Clearly, here was a chap who takes his responsibilities very seriously indeed, and having no wish to detract from his moment of authority, we readily agreed that we would indeed be careful. Once outside, Chris was agog at what he'd just witnessed. "What's wrong with *him*?" he asked, glancing back at the hut. I answered with a shrug and a grin because I found myself recounting an old Billy Connolly sketch, in which he ranted about car-park attendants who's sole purpose in life was to be irritating. The description fits our campsite attendant perfectly and we have a quiet chuckle at the thought that, as Mr Connolly suggested, he probably has a limp! No matter, we were there and in plenty of time to enjoy the evening sun whilst sorting ourselves out for the evening. But a timely growl from my stomach reminded me that I hadn't eaten since that early lunch and it was high time I did something about that. "Come on" I enthused, "let's get set up and then we'll go and find dinner!"

Twenty minutes later I was cursing. Why did we only have one sleeping bag? It was almost unbelievable, but it turned out that we had managed to leave one behind. It was more than unbelievable, especially after all the efforts we'd gone to in our attempts to fit everything on after buying the extra gear. I was at a loss to understand and spent five minutes stomping around checking and double checking. Chris, in typical teenage fashion, dismissed the discovery as unimportant. He didn't need one, he assured me, and this statement just served to irritate me further because I know it's nonsense. We spent a while bickering about it uselessly. He was adamant that I was just making a fuss over nothing and I was equally adamant that he knew not of what he spoke, and told him so. I realised that the debate was pointless, I was still hungry, time was ticking past and I therefore I abruptly terminated the argument in favour of sorting out dinner. The problem of freezing to death in the small hours could wait. We had two choices; we could go and find a supermarket, and buy the ingredients to cook ourselves a meal, or we could search out a pub and buy a meal there. I left the choice to Chris and he quickly elected to find a pub. He went back up in my estimation, marginally, as a result.

We secured the tent, shoved everything except valuables inside, and mounted up on the now unburdened Daisy. Before I could start her however, our friend the car-park attendant came urgently out of his hut and headed our way, with one arm in the air bearing an accusing finger. We were promptly admonished that it was not acceptable to start 'that noisy thing' inside the confines of the campsite and must push it outside first. I looked around the empty field and with my temper already frayed from the missing sleeping bag , not to mention the subsequent argument with Chris, I was in no mood for this pillock. I pointed out that there was nobody here to be disturbed, and that in the unlikely event that there were any later on, or when we left in the morning, we would certainly observe the request. Right now however, I was hungry, and tired, and had no intention of pushing anything anywhere! With that I glared at him, gave Daisy a hefty kick, and she answered immediately with her throaty bark. I nearly fell off laughing as Mr. Jobsworth, possibly realising that he was on very thin ice, turned abruptly and stumped away and I noticed that he did indeed have a pronounced limp! That simple observation completely restored my good humour. The world was working properly after all.

Rural Wiltshire in the early summer is a wondrous place, and that is especially true of an evening. We headed out looking for a place to eat, and as luck would have it, happened upon a long straight road running between dry stone walls that simply begged me to wind Daisy's throttle on. We relished the echo of her deep exhaust note bouncing back from the stones on either side. The evening air was warm and fragrant, the surroundings idyllic and it was not long before we found a perfect compliment to the experience in the shape of a very large country Inn, seemingly in the middle of nowhere, as is so often the case. Round the back there was a large beer garden with plenty of tables, and we were able to park next to this area, choose a table, then get to the serious business of studying the menu and sampling the ale. Chris went for a chilli, and I couldn't resist the steak in Stilton sauce. Daisy was attracting a fair gathering of admirers too and Chris sidled over to the small group to bask in the glory of being the pillion on the appreciated machine. He was soon enthusiastically discussing the Landmark with several of the crowd and I happily left him to it. It appeared, from the gestures during the conversation that much admiration was being offered for the lad that had clearly travelled so far on that little pad – quite the celebrity so it seemed. The drinks and meal arrived in short order so, after finally attracting his attention with a series of arm-waving and pointing gestures, Chris reluctantly left his fan club to go their own merry way and joined me to eat, flushed with satisfaction and somewhat puffed up with pride. He enthused to me that he had been asked many questions about Daisy, and had been able to answer them all, including showing off the ingenuity of her sprung hub suspension, which, he continued, had flummoxed a couple of the younger enquirers. "Why" he asked, round a mouthful of Chilli, "does she attract so much attention? It's just like that guy at the other pub who gave us those drinks!" he added. He seemed to like the idea of fame, however small the dose, and I let him ramble on while we finished our meal and drinks.

After a while, my attention was focused on the rapidly dying sunlight, which was busily fading into a glorious misty sunset. I reminded Chris that we couldn't trust Daisy's lights and as it was beginning to get a bit murky, with our route back consisting of the little back roads with no street lighting, we'd better get a wiggle-on. I went inside to settle our tab, and managed to buy a couple of bottles of ale for the tent. Chris would be allowed to try his first taste of parentally approved English Ale this very evening, but I would save that for a surprise later. We had enjoyed the evening thus far, but the return ride to the campsite was an experience beyond all expectations. We rode directly West, heading into a deep red sunset glowing above and within a hazy horizon that merged land into sky in a misty, shimmering blur. This was fantastic enough, but we were utterly captivated when a large shape emerged from the mirage. For a fleeting moment, on that eerie, silent road, the thought of UFO's flitted through my mind, but slowly the shape took on familiar form and became recognizable as a giant hot-air balloon emerging lazily from the distance. We stopped to watch it approach, but we were in for a treat as another, then another emerged from the already surreal surroundings. Pretty soon, it became clear that there was a whole bunch of the things, and the Western sky seemed to be full of them, drifting along no more than a hundred and fifty feet or so up. It was the most amazing sight set, as it was, against that glorious hazy backdrop and made all the more surreal by the complete lack of any noise either from them, us or our surroundings. I found myself wondering what it must be like from their perspective and realised that I was envious of them.

We sat there for a full fifteen minutes watching the spectacle, until I noticed with a jolt that I was now having to strain my eyes into the dusk to see anything at all. I reluctantly told Chris that it was high time for us get a move on again and I was forced to turn on Daisy's lights, for all the illumination they offered, as we set off once again down that long straight road. The line of balloons stretched from horizon to horizon off to our right and that was the perfect ending to the day. Even the jobsworth site attendant had shut up shop and gone by the time we pulled into the campsite – which now had two more tents cluttering up its acres of space. We sat outside our own tent and broke out the beer, Chris taking his with a surprised "Thanks Dad!",proceeding to affect a false bravado as he tried his first sip. "S'allright" he assured me, but his face was a mask of uncertainty. As the last light faded, we could still see the occasional flare from the balloons, as their occupants adjusted the fill but I thought they'd have to land before long, or they would be brave fellows indeed to risk it in the dark!

Chris dismissed any attempts to give him the single sleeping bag when we turned in later, and buried himself beneath our spare clothes, jeans and jackets instead. There was no point arguing with him further and so I left him to it, and retired to doze off in relative comfort. I woke at around midnight to find a shivering Chris fidgeting, grumbling and vainly trying to cover himself more effectively. He was bravely trying to survive the unpleasant cold without making a fuss by the sound of things, but after waking up a bit I realised that I couldn't just leave him to suffer. I turned to face him in the dark. "I expect you're freezing then?" I said, with perhaps a hint of smugness. The pitiful moan that came in response was enough to confirm this, but there was no mileage in saying 'I told you so'. I needed instead to work out what to do, but first off I gave him the sleeping bag, which, on *that* occasion, met with no argument. He wasted no time getting into it while I attempted to find, then ignite, our newly acquired gas lamp. I was mightily put out on getting the thing lit, to discover that Chris was already sound asleep. "Bloody charming, thanks dad and good night" I muttered to myself as the night chill I began to make itself felt.

I sat there and wondered what to do next. I needed layers, so put on my jeans, three pairs of socks and all three shirts, before curling up under the rest of our clothes and the riding jackets. It wasn't enough. In fact, It became apparent pretty quickly that I was going to get extremely cold, and no amount of fidgeting and arranging was going to make things any better. After half an hour of that nonsense, I sat up shivering, hugged myself, and desperately tried to think what else I could do. Chris was snoring deeply by then, just to add to my misery. I re-ignited the gas light and then found the little stove and lit that too, hoping that these two would at least heat up the inside of the tent sufficiently to stave off hypothermia. They did in fact achieve this with startling speed, rather too efficiently in fact, and within ten minutes I was sweating profusely in my three shirts. That was fine, I was no longer on the endangered list. What to do next though? I couldn't go to sleep with those two things burning and if I turned them off it would be no time at all before the cold came back. I cursed my stupidity for leaving one of the bags at home, for the fiftieth time, before settling on the best of several bad options – I'd let the heat build up for another ten minutes, and then take my chances once more under the pile. I soon dozed off in the muggy atmosphere but woke with a jolt within an hour, freezing once more. No trace of the heat remained and so once again the entire exercise with lamp and stove had to be repeated. The night dragged past slowly. I was forced to carry out the tedious ritual every hour or so, until eventually the deep dark outside began to give way to the first hints of daylight, almost imperceptibly at first. I could also hear the first stirrings of the great outdoors as a blackbird tried out a few halting notes and something snuffled around in the hedge behind our tent.

Chris snored on, oblivious to all. I decided to make one more attempt at sleep, but the next awakening would be it. That would be the time for a cup of tea and an early start to the day's adventure. I poked my head from the tent at six o'clock, tired, desperately cold and very miserable. I found it hard to take in how such a warm sunny day had given way to such a dismally cold damp night. I had been starkly reminded just how cold it can actually get at night, even in late July! Looking out at the early morning, my spirits were lifted on two counts, and they needed to be after the endurance of the night. Firstly, Daisy hadn't spontaneously combusted during the night, and secondly, it was clear that the Eastern sky held the nothing but the promise of another fine sunny day. A swollen, blazing sun was edging up over the horizon, with not a single cloud in view. Despite the nightmare of the last eight hours, I found myself thoroughly heartened by the spectacle of the mist-shrouded fields and woods, bathed in the golden glow of dawn. A heavy dew had fallen in the night, but that simply gave the whole scene a magical sparkle.

I woke Chris, who's never been good at mornings, and tried in vain to get him up so that he could witness the scene oustide our tent. I abandoned the attempt as a waste of time, and decided to leave him be for another thirty minutes. Instead I settled for getting a mug of tea on the go and breakfast things sorted out, congratulating myself that this time I had remembered to bring everything required for a good breakfast. By the time Chris surfaced through the opening, I had scrambled eggs, bacon and beans well underway. We sat together as we ate, watching the day grow brighter and after a second mug of tea it was time to clear up, pack away the tent and load Daisy up for the day.

I thought that before doing any of that, we should just fire the old girl up to make sure all was well. She answered my first kick with her customary deep bark, and as she sat warming up, the heavy dew on her engine, exhaust pipes and silencers turned to steam, which drifted off into the crisp air. Chris appeared to be in suspended animation. He was dawdling around as we packed up, listlessly 'helping' in slow motion. I ended up doing the lion's share of everything and my attempts to chivvy him along were met with a bad tempered, tetchy response, which of course made me equally tetchy. We bickered and grumbled at each other until Daisy was ready to go, and I reflected that it was an ironically fitting end to what had, after all, been a truly crappy night. But the open road awaited us, and in an effort to lighten our mood I spread the novelty map out whilst enthusing about the weather. We looked at the thing and discussed suitable routes. Or rather, I suggested suitable routes while Chris grunted in monosyllables by way of response, each of which could be taken as a 'yes' or a 'no'. I suspected they actually meant 'don't care' but I was not going to get wound up, I decided. Instead, I made a show of putting on an air of jollity. We were, I declared, ready to roll!

Chris completed the morning's performance by getting his helmet strap tangled, then stuck, which culminated in a bad tempered display of exaggerated gestures and general weight throwing as he stomped around trying to free it. I sat on Daisy, watching, feeling increasingly exasperated at the sudden teenage strop, but eventually he managed straighten things out and came across to take up his seat, pausing only to flick me a belligerent stare as he did so. The look seemed to challenge me with an unsaid "Yeah what?" Finally we were away. At this time of the morning there was little by way of traffic to worry about and we put Cirencester behind us in no time at all before turning NorthWest towards Gloucester. We were looking for a stately home, known simply as 'Helen's' near the village of Much Marcle (which I considered to be a wonderful name). The good thing about that day's riding was that it was almost all going to be in an area that I have never previously visited, therefore the joy of discovery would be certain.

Looking at the map, it also appeared that we would spend most of the morning in good open countryside, and as we put Gloucester behind, heading west to Ross-on-Wye, that promise was delivered in spades. The 'A' roads that we found ourselves on were not the big dual-carriageway types that bore the pants off me. No, these were wonderful twisting, turning, sweeping roads alternately bordered by open pasture punctuated with banked and wooded cuttings as they followed a roller-coaster geology. That lot made for an exhilarating and enjoyable ride, and even the sun delivered on it's early promise, bathing us in a glorious warmth that chased away the chills of the night in no time at all. Motorcycling just doesn't get any better than that, I considered, but that train of thought was prematurely derailed because right then the noise started.

Strange noises are nothing new to anyone that regularly rides an old machine like Daisy, and as is often the case this one started quite suddenly. That particular noise was not of a type, or indeed volume, that immediately concerned me, but the sudden appearance of *any* noise on an aged motorcycle could be the harbinger of doom. The experienced rider knows this, and never simply ignores such a thing.So, I found myself slowing down and cocking my head from side to side, in an effort to pinpoint the source. Of course, as soon as I did this it stopped and as soon as I shrugged away my concerns and wound Daisy's throttle on again, there it would be again, just on the periphery of hearing, almost inaudible, but definitely there. I continued along at a slower pace than the 60mph we had been cruising at and began analysing the sudden irritation. It wasn't really a mechanical or metallic noise, more like a sort of rumble or rub that comes and goes, always just evasive enough to leave me frustrated as I tried to identify it. No amount of hard listening and head-tilting helped, and so we carried on, me fighting the beginnings of a slight paranoia. In fact, we carried on as far as Ross, but there I took the chance to pull up by a little shop where we could take a breather and, more importantly, I could look Daisy over for anything obvious.

At least Chris seemed to have brightened up, and was quite perky as he conned money out of me for 'something small' from the shop. I took the chance, as I rummaged around in my pockets, to ask him about that noise. "What noise?" he responded. Ah. I explained further "There's a strange noise, sort of rubbing or something, can't you hear it when we're riding?" He gave me a look that suggested I'm going senile, took the proffered coins and turned away. Over his shoulder he said "There's no noise dad. You're imagining things!"

I had to admit as we got ready to set off again, that I had been unable to find anything amiss. I spent about ten minutes trying to find something loose, checked that nothing could be rubbing against a tyre. Even checked the chain tensions. Nothing suggested itself as the source. I started the engine and listened hard from all angles for any hint of the noise – nothing. I span the back wheel and critically examined it. No noise. 'Fine', I thought, but as we pulled away, I couldn't quite shake the niggling feeling that there was trouble ahead. The roads continued to offer a thoroughly good ride as we swept northeast, and it was not long before we found our Landmark, Helen's stately home. It was closed, and a sign at the entrance invited all would be visitors to not enter, thank you very much. That was OK by me as I couldn't see Chris being particularly enthusiastic about such a place and I'd rather be riding on a day like that anyway. We took our photographs of Daisy in front of the friendly sign, which at least had 'Helen's' at the top, and then sat with the map and started to talk about the rest of the day. I explained to Chris that we only have one other landmark to visit, and it was, rather handily, on the way home, so with most of the day still awaiting us we could take our time. Taking our time, I suggested, meant riding South through the forest of Dean, because it was there, and we could.

We were soon glad that we did, as that was a very special experience indeed. On a bike, it was almost indescribably good, so I won't try to describe the mixed foliage, broad leaf woodland that we picked our way through. Suffice to say it was deeply satisfying and, I was sure, good for the soul. But the real pleasure came after the forest, in the shape of the A466 from Monmouth, which is where we had ended up, following the meandering river Wye along Offa's Dyke Path. The scenery and geography that we encounterd on this road was simply fantastic, in a closed-in sort of way. The road was hemmed in by the river, with wooded banks on one side, and rock escarpment or further woods on the other. There were no sweeping views or open plains, but it was breathtakingly beautiful to ride, for all that. Go there, do it for yourself - you can thank me later. Half way down, we found a large pub, right on the Welsh border, proudly proclaiming it's Welsh-ness with flags and banners, but more importantly right then was the fact that it served food and beer. We stopped to sample both, sitting outside admiring the view across the river, whilst Daisy 'tinc – tinc'd' as she cooled off. Marvellous.

We followed the Wye all the way down to where it connects into the wide estuary of the river Severn, close to Chepstow. From there, heading east, we crossed the river via the famous old bridge (not the new thing which carries the M4) which was pretty spectacular in itself, spanning as it does the great flat estuary shallows, but all the more so when undertaken on a classic motorcycle. The feeling of open exposure to the elements on the central section, even in that ideal weather, was quite pronounced. But I got distracted from that. As we climbed the Welsh side to the apex of the bridge, my nerves were jangled once again by the return of the irritating noise that had so plagued me earlier. It was a jarring note which upset my otherwise euphoric state of mind and I cursed out loud. But not for long – as we coasted down the English side of the bridge, I leaned over to shout at Chris that he must, surely, be able to hear it this time, only to discover that it was HIM making what I have thought of as the 'rubbing' sound. He was humming some sort of tune in a funny sort of way, and it was arriving in my ears, distorted by wind, as that elusive noise! "Bloody hell – you Sod!" I yell into the wind. He stopped his humming to lean over my shoulder to shout "What?" but I was laughing now, partially through relief that Daisy wasn't in the early stages of disintegration, but mainly because of the absurdity of what had begun to be a real worry. I decided that it would keep and yelled "Nothing!" as I turned my attention back to the road.

We continued on our way in peace, blissfully lacking that noise! Onto the M4 then, for a short distance because that was no place for a fifty something year old motorcycle. Past Bristol, we turned off towards Bath, where we picked up the A4 heading east once more. I was getting to know this road rather well by that time. Entering the fascinating City full of rich Georgian splendour, I marveled, as I always do, at the grandeur from another age. Compare this to any 21st Century architecture and there is just no contest – the modern stuff loses hands down. Where did we go wrong, and why? I stopped to show Chris Royal Crescent, which, let's face it, is bloody impressive. Isn't it? He actually agreed and wants to know why it's only old buildings that are built, and look that way. Good question, which caused me to lament the loss of magnificence in our apparently advanced society. Progress, I told Chris, has its price – that price is the sacrifice of grandness on the altar of profit. Shame.

It's was after two o'clock I noted, as we left Bath behind, heading for Chippenham then Marlborough. Somewhere around there we'd be turning South into the Berkshire countryside to begin hunting down, if our clue solving of earlier was correct, a steam museum near the town of Grafton. The last time I had traversed this route Eastwards, Chloe and I were against the clock, but this time we were in no rush and I let Daisy lope along at a leisurely 55mph. Chris must have been happy on the back there, because the 'noise' was back! I tilted my head surreptitiously and sure enough he was away with the fairies humming some racy tune that I couldn't pinpoint. "Having fun?" a yelled over my shoulder, yanking him out of whatever inner universe he had been inhabiting "Yep!" came the enthusiastic reply. Well, so was I, great stuff. At Marlborough we found the A346 heading towards Burbage but I pulled over at the first available point in order to study the map.

This, I told Chris, could be a bit tricky. The red circle that marked the spot we needed was in a blank bit of map with no apparent roads shown. That was not a total surprise, and I was starting to get the hang of winging it with compass now, so I discussed tactics with him that went along the lines of "If we can get to Grafton, *here*, and take any left turn heading north, the Steam thingy is only about two miles" Chris looked distinctly dubious. He was, after all, a veteran of the same sort of vague navigational notions from the earlier Suffolk adventure, and had swapped intelligence with his sister, after her West Country foray, regarding Dad's apparent lack of directional abilities.

"Why don't you get a better map?" was his considered response. "Well, it's a bit late for that" I pointed out, although I secretly had to admit that it really would have been a sensible move, *before* we had set out. We managed not to bicker too much about the lack of a good one, and got underway again with my compass plan being the only one available. Finding Burbage only five miles on, we turned left and began looking for signs to Grafton. When it appeared, I was somewhat dismayed to discover that it was pointing the wrong way, assuming I had read the compass properly and we were in fact on the road I thought we were. We stopped, and I got the map out again, for all the use it would be. Chris was looking at me with *that* look again. Clearly he thought his father was a dolt of the first order. I was beginning to agree with his unspoken sentiment as I stared at the useless thing. I didn't understand how Grafton could be *that* way. Time ticked past, as it tends to do, rather aggresively, when you can't afford it to.

So, the map clearly showed the place, but not where the sign in front of us said it was. Bugger. I realised that if this sign was correct, then we had already gone two miles or so north of the place anyway, so where was the bloody Steam museum? There had been none of those little brown signs that one expects, directing the would-be visitor to such places. Neither had we passed any crossroads or turnings, along which the thing may have been hiding. I turned to Chris and explained my thoughts "What do you reckon?" said I. "Get a proper map" came the sullen reply. That was unhelpful "Bloody smart-arse - come on, get involved, tell me what you reckon we should do!" I replied with barely concealed exasperation. He shrugged. I looked hard at him, and he decided to stroll over and take a cursory look at the map. Incomprehension showed on his face, so I tapped my finger on the map and explained the quandary again. "It's obvious, it must be down that road," he announced after a minutes contemplation, pointing to the road which the sign suggests goes to Grafton.

I hadn't thought of that, because it still seemed wrong. I wasn't convinced, but we gave it a try and just one minute later we did indeed come across one of the much sought after little brown signs. I decided that my first comment only minutes earlier was in fact right after all – Chris was a smart-arse! I told him so in good humour, and he mumbled something about me being a bit of an old duffer. He'd definitely been talking to his sister! We followed a tiny road for about half a mile, over a stunning little picture-postcard bridge and there at the end was not only our landmark, but another Triumph rider as well. A fellow landmarker, I enthused to Chris, we must introduce ourselves as we get our photographs. We rode over to him and parked Daisy up next to his much more modern machine. In fact, his was one of the new Hinckley Triumphs, from the current Lincolnshire factory that was going from strength to strength in a slow but steady climb back to prominence, and it makes for an interesting contrast seeing the two side by side. Obviously the owner was thinking along the same lines as he introduced himself as Simon, and quipped "You've brought granny out to see her granddaughter then?" There was actually some truth to that, we both agreed, because it was the Speed Twin, unveiled in 1938 that was largely reckoned to be the model that set Triumph on the course to greatness and along the way changed the face of motorcycle design for several decades thereafter.

It transpires that Simon is not a landmark hunter after all, but is just out for a ride. He was a member of the Owner's Club however, had heard of the landmark challenge but didn't really know much about it. Chris, seeing another chance to display his knowledge and indeed bask in the glory of participation, was eager to explain the details and recount the story so far. I realised as I listened that he truly was proud of his involvement in the challenge, and also that of his sister as he explained her own adventures thus far to the now amused Simon. We spent a good twenty minutes there, lapping up the afternoon sun in the wonderfully peaceful surroundings, but it was time to get going again on the final leg home. I looked at the map again, but Simon produced a much better one and offered to share his local knowledge regarding the best route towards home. He was amazed when I told him where home is and looked pointedly at Daisy, then at his watch, then at us. The look said a lot, but what it said loudest was that Simon thought we were mad.

His instructions were very clear, at least. We'd need to go back to Burbage, then take the main road South from there, joining the A342 to Andover after about six miles. From there it was simply straight on to Basingstoke where we'd pick up the A30, which was the Daisy-friendly alternative to the M3. We discovered that the museum was closing, and couldn't go in, so I told Chris that we may as well get going and at that, Simon offered to take us as far as the junction with the A342, where he would be head in the opposite direction. Rather than getting lost in all these little roads, we readily agreed. He asked what speed should he keep down to, but I assured him not to worry - Daisy would cruise happily at 60 mph or even above. He didn't look convinced! He mounted up and pressed his finger on the little button that whirred his engine into life, then sat with a big grin as he watched my own starting routine with Daisy. Petrol on, choke lever (under seat) a quarter turn, ignition advance/retard lever on the handlebars to half retarded, lean under tank and press the tickler button on top of the ancient carb float, ease over compression and give the kick-start a mighty heave. Daisy responded immediately and then I had to knock the choke back to full off, push the advance/retard lever to three quarters advance, before I grinned back at Simon and gave the thumbs up as he shook his head in amused disbelief.

Fifteen minutes later, as agreed, we waved goodbye to our guide and continued at a steady pace into the glorious early evening sunshine. I estimated that we'd get home at around eight o'clock if we took the twisties rather than the motorway, and that is what we did, eventually picking up the same route through Guildford and the Weald of Kent that we had used on the way out the previous day. We stopped at the same pub that we had lunched at, but this time the landlady of the establishment was in charge, so there was no free beer. We stopped again at the little bridge, so recently the scene of near disaster, and Chris recounted the story with me, asking, "what would really have happened if Daisy had stayed on fire?" What indeed, I wondered, but in answering I suggested that it never pays in life to wonder or worry about what might have been, just accept and be very grateful for what *is*.

8. Northern Landmarks and Punctured in Durham

You can't take a fifty-something year old motorcycle, ride it two up, loaded to the gunnels, all round the place with no maintenance and absolutely no preparation. It's obvious to anyone that this is asking for trouble, and if you actually manage to make it without problems, you will almost certainly find a host of them on checking over the machine back at home. Things will have come loose, fallen off, started leaking or simply broken. I had been assured by many that this was the case, almost written in the scriptures, so it was. These thoughts haunted me as I opened up the garage on the Monday, to give Daisy a full check-over. I was feeling mildly guilty at my lack of proper attention to Daisy's mechanical wellbeing in the last few weeks, having hardly looked at a nut, other than the necessary dynamo fix in Wiltshire, since putting in the new engine. But Daisy was clearly made of stern stuff I discovered, as with mounting respect for her I found nothing amiss.

There is a school of thought that says any regularly used machine will 'settle down' during it's first few thousand miles from a rebuild, at which point nothing comes loose any more and only things like the chains and tyres need any real attention. It would appear that Daisy had attained this much sought after state of being – there really was nothing to do to her except a slight adjustment to primary and final drive chains. Even that troublesome dynamo was still on as firmly as it could be, and the really impressive bit was that she didn't seem to have leaked any oil, anywhere. I was absolutely delighted with that, and my determination that the landmark trophy would be ours was now underpinned by a growing confidence that Daisy really could simply breeze through it all.

That evening, brimming with enthusiasm once again, I started to think about the next adventure, to find, record and cross off the numerous landmarks in Scotland, Cumbria and the North of England. There were a lot of pushpins in the map up yonder, and they were well and truly scattered, but after a while we had the beginnings of a plan. We had to have a plan this time, or chaos would result, so an evening of umming and aahhing saw one thrashed out, at least in theory. If all went well our plan would see us complete a large anticlockwise sweep, starting from our jump off point in Cambridge. The problem was one of logistics, and although we could in theory work our way up-country from South to North, this would involve a huge amount of to-ing and fro-ing from East to West and back again, and would actually require a large number of additional miles for each decisive move North. No, far better, we decided, to find a steady route North, from which we would only divert for landmarks to the East, leaving any to the West for our return leg Southwards, unless they were very close.

Of course, now that we had the long Southwest, Wiltshire and French trips under our belt, we could use that experience to sensibly predict how far each day would take us. I explained to Chris the effect of having to leave a given route to divert in search of landmarks, but he tersely reminded me that he was on the back in Suffolk, and could well remember that particular fun. We had also learned that regular breaks made the whole experience far more enjoyable. Where Chloe and I had stopped regularly to absorb the delights of Cornwall and Devon, and the same with Chris in Wiltshire, we had remained comfortable throughout the day, but on the last days, pushing for longer in order to get home, Daisy's antiquated seating and rider positioning had made themselves felt in spades. I talked this through with the kids, and we settled on a limit of three hundred miles a day for all future adventures and having decided that, we were able to put some timings on a rough schedule, starting at seven o'clock each day (as in wheels turning on the tarmac – preferably with Daisy packed with all of the various items that we were meant to have with us) and ending no later than seven in the evening, by which time we should be choosing a spot for our tent.

It all seemed dead easy when approached like that and, with increasing enthusiasm we settled down to drawing up a plan for each day, starting with Day One, a nominal Saturday morning, and plotting the whole thing from there. We were aided immeasurably in that exercise by the use of some computerised route planning software on the family PC, another trick that I had failed to utilise up till now. That approach, for the first time, would give us the luxury of having some idea of just how well/badly we were progressing once out there on the road - a comfort I had not had with Chloe in the Southwest, and the lack of which had led me to fretting far more than perhaps I should have done!

Planning for the great Scottish leg got underway then and, after a couple of evenings involving much map scrutiny, head scratching, debate and argument we had agreed that the start point should still be the lay-by in Cambridge that we had used earlier, and the route from there would be the A14 initially. With no intention of suffering a long and boring motorway stint on the M1, we would instead be sticking to the A1 for the main trek north. The plan was to pick off four landmarks on the way up to Newcastle, where our first overnight stop would be made. From there, we would pick up the A697, make for the Scottish border at Coldstream, onwards to Edinburgh, Perth and then a long haul through the Grampian mountains to our second overnight stop at Elgin. By that time, if all had gone well, we'd have a further three landmarks in the bag. Day three would take us round past Inverness, across the Moray Firth and up into the Highlands for roughly forty miles, before turning back on ourselves and heading South again, along Loch Ness, Loch Oich, through Fort

William and finally on to Stirling where we'd stop. Two more landmarks will have been visited along the way, in theory. On day four, we would continue Southwest, back into England, through Northumberland and into Cumbria before jinking Southeast once again, then down through the industrial Northern sprawl that is Preston, Bolton and Manchester. In theory, we will have knocked off another five landmarks by the time we camp, somewhere in the region of Runcorn or Chester. Finally, we will meander through the Midlands heading for home, picking off a further four landmarks on the way, making a grand total of nineteen in the week which, when added to the twenty already in the bag takes us a quantum leap towards completing the entire challenge! Simple, we rashly agreed.

Having constructed the grand plan, I was able to print off strip-maps and route directions from the computer and was astounded that it ran to thirty-six pages. This seemed ridiculous to me, but once I started to read the things it became apparent that the actual directions are very detailed and I realised that I won't really need any of those. The strip maps that accompanied each page of drivel would, by contrast, be extremely useful. They contained far more detail than our by then dog-eared map of Britain and it was certain that the two used together would offer a far better navigation aid than we had been used to so far. During the whole planning process, Chris had remembered National Parks, and wanted to look at the big map with me again insisting that I pointed out the areas that would be unfenced roads and cattle grids. He seemed to be fascinated by the thought of such an arrangement and as we looked he began to grill his sister once again about her own experiences on Bodmin and Exmoor. I smiled to myself as I listened and reflected on the fact that to Chris and Chloe open National Park land was indeed a novelty. They had only ever seen the countryside 'at arm's length' really, what with fences and 'Private, Keep Out' signs everywhere you go.

I remembered an episode when they were both much younger, when we had taken a picnic and wandered off into the wilds of Kent to find some real countryside. We had found an idyllic little copse, surrounded by green fields and woodland so had stopped the car on the verge for our picnic. We could see nothing that even hinted at civilisation and all was peaceful as we happily sat watching the kids exploring the hedgerows and woodland. Suddenly, seemingly from nowhere, a well-to-do Lady of the green-welly set appeared and in short order proceeded to lay into us verbally. Her language was shocking, as she lambasted Diane and Myself for daring to stop and enjoy ourselves in 'her' countryside. She accused us of 'being out of our element' and scolded us for bringing our 'shitty suburban brats' (they were the actual words she used) to a place where they were neither 'suited nor welcome'. Our tormentor was clearly going to make a point of seeing us 'orf', and harsh words followed as I invited the inbred throwback to do something interesting, and possibly amusing with her head. But our relaxed afternoon had been utterly spoiled and we never took the kids to the countryside again in the same carefree way. To this day, I have no idea what sparked such an aggressive and unnecessary tirade, especially as we had been very careful to make no mess, and had seen no signs or anything else to suggest we shouldn't be there. We were doing nobody any harm, as far as I could see. I recounted the story to Chris and Chloe as they sat there poring over the map and Chris admitted to a vague recollection of the dreadful harridan before exclaiming suddenly in an alarmed voice "There won't be people like that in the National Park will there?" I could only hope not.

Finally, the big day arrived. School was out for the summer and we had six weeks in which to do the remainder of the challenge. There was nothing left to plan, buy or fix and I declared us ready for the big trek north. Chris was almost bursting with anticipation and with no reason for delay we set off very early on the first weekend of the holidays. We wanted to get to our base camp and be ready to hit the road by seven o'clock, which meant a five am start from home, but at least the traffic was very light as a result. We made good time and after arriving at the lay-by, getting changed into riding gear, extracting Daisy from the interior of the long suffering Espace, we soon found ourselves exiting Cambridge on schedule. It was one of those days for which motorcycles were invented, warm even at this early hour, with the promise of a long balmy day reflected in the golden shimmer dancing in the misty fields. Daisy was positively purring along beneath us as we settled down to a steady fifty-five mph heading towards Peterborough and the A1.

Our first landmark was not much of a detour from our main route, and waited for us some seventy miles North. I congratulated myself for making the effort to actually do some planning that time round, happy in the knowledge that we could take a leisurely ride in order to stay on schedule and get there by nine am. That's what my computer directions told me, I recalled, and it seemed like child's play to me as the sun strengthened, burnt off the early mist. Leaving the A14, we turned North onto the A1 and began the long haul. After putting the initial motorway section behind us, we were soon passing Peterborough but before long we pulled into a rest area, where we got ourselves a mug of tea and I could slope off for a quiet ciggie. I told Chris that I had travelled this road many, many times in the course of my working life, and it was blessed with more little tea stalls than any other road in Britain, I reckoned. They seemed to be in every other lay-by, sometimes a caravan, sometimes a shack, the occasional porta-cabin and a few proper cafes, but all offering a good cup of tea and trucker-sized bacon rolls. This one was a caravan, with an awning, and we presented ourselves at the chin-high counter in order to acquire some traditional traveller's fare. As we waited, the smell of sizzling bacon drifted over to mingle with the earthy smell of early morning mist, and we sat quite happily just enjoying the experience. It wasn't long before a pair of king sized baps, stuffed with bacon, and two Styrofoam cups of tea were exchanged for five quid – which I thought was extremely reasonable.

As we ate, I showed Chris the map and remarked on the fact that we were going to spend nearly the whole day on that one road, give or take the odd diversion for the landmarks. Not quite route 66, but an impressively long road by Britain's standards, stretching as it does from London all the way up into Scotland. He wanted to know if there were any National Parks on the way. The idea really had caught his imagination, and he looked disappointed when I told him that it would be a good few days before we saw any of that. Our immediate focus returned to that day's plan and in particular, our big map showing the landmarks. We calculated that we had covered some thirty-five miles already that morning, and had approximately the same distance again to the first official stop of the day. It was just after eight, which meant that we'd easily stay within our planned schedule, and with that, we get togged up and were back on the road again in short order.

Daisy really was running faultlessly, shrugging off her heavy load with no fuss at all, settled at a relaxed fifty-five once again. It seemed like no time at all until we left the A1, just before Grantham, and headed East into the lush green lanes of the Lincolnshire/Leicestershire borderlands. Proper English countryside was that, a gentle rolling landscape, criss-crossed by ever smaller roads with their high grassy banks. The springtime explosion of growth had given way to the wild colours of summer flowers, butterflies and numerous buzzing things proliferated all around us. I slowed Daisy to a sedate meander, which allowed us to take our time in savouring that veritable Garden of Eden and I also realised that for once, even out there in the small lanes, we were not lost. In fact, our target was extremely well signposted. We had no trouble following the little brown heritage signs as we threaded along numerous little lanes to arrive at the landmark, Belvoir Castle, almost bang on time and very relaxed. As Daisy was parked up in a suitable place for photographs I reckoned that this place was not so much a castle but rather more like a stately home. Certainly it had turrets and crenellations, but it was lacking that essential raw brute feel of your proper castle. What it wasn't lacking though, was a place in history.

After taking our photographs, we wandered around outside and found several information plaques that informed us that the original structure was believed to have been built in the eleventh century by one Robert de Todeni, who's main claim to fame was that he had served as William the Conqueror's Standard Bearer during the Battle of Hastings. The story board took us through a potted history of the place since those early origins, telling a tale of medieval upheaval, treachery, treason and war. I found it fascinating stuff indeed and enthused to Chris that this was just one local story plucked from centuries of upheaval that is English history. He gave me the 'old fart' look, but then got interested himself as I read out the bit about one particular family who lost their ownership of the place when, in 1464, Lord Thomas Ros, the then Lord of the Manor was executed for his support of the Lancastrians during the Wars of the Roses. I found that I was experiencing the same eerie feeling that I had felt at Runnymede and wondered aloud if, with all turbulent events it had seen, the place was haunted.

That captured Chris's full and undivided attention and, as we wandered back down to Daisy I found myself deeply debating the existence, or not, of ghosts, ghoulies and things that go bump in the night. He was particularly taken with my line of reasoning that suggests that ghosts are quite possibly restless spirits, yanked from life before they were good and ready, or with unfinished business that must be cleared up before eternal peace could be achieved. I explained, by way of example, that having your head lopped off for liking the wrong colour rose could, by some, be construed as a good enough reason to stick around and scare the pants off of the living. What I could promise, I assured Chris, was that we would be visiting a number of places that have equally deep and tumultuous history attached, thereby making them equally good candidates for a good haunting. I smiled inwardly because I couldn't help noticing that as we walked, he kept flicking a worried look back up towards the castle and in a moment of wickedness I suggested to him that if he really wanted to investigate the possible existence of ghosts, then I was sure we'd be able to camp at one of them and keep a vigil. His interest, it seemed, did not extend to actually staking out a dodgy old ruin, and he dismissed the suggestion rather quickly with one of those looks and a firm "er…*no* Dad!"

Back at Daisy, who was gleaming in the early sun, we had attracted the attention of another set of admirers. An old boy and his equally ancient wife were remembering their own younger days, which apparently featured a Triumph 'just like this one'. It's amazing how many folk had one, or at least think they had one, and we spent a little time chatting to the current veteran, with Chris taking the lead with his by now familiar and enthusiastic diatribe into the merits of all things Daisy. While they were twittering away I pulled the wad of strip maps from the tank bag, shuffled the used ones to the bottom, and studied our next leg which would take us back to the A1. From there, we'd go North again for about eighty five miles before taking another detour to pick off landmark number two of the four we were hoping to get in the bag that day. With Daisy able to cruise happily at sixty to seventy mph I reckoned this would take a couple of hours, including the detour, if the old backside holds out and we don't have to stop for a stretch too often.

The old boy was showing no signs of leaving however, lost as he was in a dreamy haze of nostalgia that was being fuelled by Chris's enthusiasm. I started to make obvious getting ready to go motions coupled with an exaggerated inspection of the watch, and eventually Chris got the message and began to prepare himself. The old boy stayed until Daisy was prepped and kicked into life, and as she firesd up he turned to his wife and exclaimed "Cor, 'ark at that! If only we could turn back the clock, eh Lil?" I was amazed to see what looked like a tear in her eye, as she put her arm through his and squeezed, so I felt it was time to go before they both started. With a wave to the old couple then, and a big smile, off went again. We couldn't follow the brown signs this time, and I couldn't remember the twisty route we had taken to get there, but the A1 was due East and we were once again thankful for the little novelty compass as we picked our way across a myriad of little crossroads and meandered amongst the fabulous greenery once again. It was not too long before we found it, and turning North I wound on the throttle once more, listening to the exhaust note deepen as we climbed through the gears until Daisy was thrumming along happily at a steady sixty-five.

Now that we had put the far Southern section of this road behind us, it began to dawn on me that the A1 is actually quite a pleasant road to ride. Our schedule, which was oh so important on setting out, seemed to become less so with each mile, as we simply settled down to enjoying what, after all, we had set out to do - ride. The café's, tea huts and caravans continued to populate the numerous lay-by's, which gave us plenty of opportunity to take a rest and be tempted again by bacon sarnies and large mugs of tea. The miles fell away steadily, ever Northwards until suddenly, and without warning the (M) part of the route imposed itself on us as the road turned into three lane motorway once again. We stuck to the near lane, as all the traffic sped up around us but after a while, with everything going so well, I decided to get the ordeal over with and get us back onto the smaller sections as quickly as possible by letting Daisy stretch her legs a bit. Seventy five, eighty and eighty five duly ticked up on her ancient speedometer, at which point the thing decided that that was quite enough of that thank you and the needled starts to bounce wildly between twenty and ninety, not to mention all over the place in between. It became impossible to read, but I was revelling in the sheer joy of the first real test of the rebuilt engine, which was making no fuss at the demands suddenly placed upon it.

Now, it must be stated that the speeds that are indicated on a speedometer as old as Daisy's should be taken with a large pinch of salt. If the thing is telling you that you are travelling at eighty miles to an hour, it is more likely that you are progressing at more like seventy. However, on that road, on that day, during a particularly brave five minutes we actually overtooke number of slower cars. Daisy was making a most satisfactory howl, but I had to be honest and admit that the vibration was awesome and it seemed appropriate, after a while, to ease back somewhat and give the old girl a breather, not least because my fingers and feet were tingling with the first signs of the dread numbness that one can expect from such frivolous abandon on an old machine like that. The speedometer agreed, evidently, it's needle settling down to a gentle wavering once I got back down to an indicated seventy. The vibration was much less harsh at this more sedate speed, and I fought off a slight pang of guilt for treating the old girl so harshly, silently promising that we'd sit at that speed and no more from then on. It seemed to be Daisy's 'smooth spot' - she felt totally at ease, unstressed and had a wonderful exhaust burble that could not fail to please. I realised that I was grinning like an idiot, a situation I suspect was well known to many owners of classic machinery.

After a while, the motorway did the decent thing, and duly gave way to dual carriageway with lay-bys once again and we settled down once more to an enjoyable ride. Everything was right in the world, life was marvellous, there was not a hint of anything other than sheer enjoyment stretching ahead. Even the traffic, what there was of it, seemed to be behaving in a fairly sedate and non-threatening manner. I couldn't help but grin even more as a familiar noise intruded on these thoughts, but it no longer caused me to worry because it merely meant that the young man on the back was happy and away with the fairies again. I was yanked from this reverie by a sudden cessation of the noise and an urgent tapping on my shoulder. Chris was attempting to yell something, which I couldn't hear in the wind-rush but he was agitated enough to suggest that all may not be well at the back there. As I dropped off the throttle and looked round I couldn't ascertain what was wrong immediately. Judging by the gestures though, i thought I'd better pull over onto the shoulder.

All became clear as we coasted to a halt. Chris had noticed that we were about to lose our tent and baggage, which was hanging off the side of the bike at a wild angle. I had considered getting a proper rack and panniers for Daisy, before setting out on these adventures, but somehow I had not got round to it. The panniers we had with us were soft throw over types which, whilst eminently suitable for use on a broad dual seat of the type fitted to the vast majority of motorcycles, were faring rather less well on the rigid mudguard of our mount. The whole lot had slipped to one side and was barely hanging on at all. We had to take it all off, reposition the panniers and tighten up all the straps before putting back the tent, bedroll and bits, with bungee straps re-applied as best we could manage. It all looked pretty solid again and declaring it sound, we took the opportunity to check the route sheets. We'd made excellent progress, and I enthused to Chris that we should arrive at our next jumping off point soon, to look for what I believed to be an air museum of some sort. By my calculations we had put over a hundred and forty miles behind us since starting out, and it was not much past eleven o'clock, which meant we were easily on schedule for our day one target of being in Newcastle by evening, even with the detour we were about to take. What we didn't know, *couldn't* know, was that there was trouble ahead. I should have realised that it was all going too well.

Leaving the A1 and heading East for fifteen miles or so, the expected air museum was uncovered with consummate ease and we got the all-important photos without any drama so decided to take a rest before setting off again. Relieved at the rapidity with which this particular landmark had surrendered its location, we broke out some crisps and a Mars bar each whilst contemplating our next leg, which would circumnavigate the historic town of York to the North before heading East yet again almost as far as the coast. I had not identified the next site from the clue, which refered to Adam and Eve putting up a tent in the garden or somesuch nonsense. None of us could think of anything remotely useful or likely, whilst carrying out the research back home, and it had been agreed that we'd just have to wing it on the day, hoping that something obvious would shows up once we got there. It really didn't seem to matter. We'd made such good progress that morning, the sun was shining and no problems seemed imminent. Twenty minutes later we discovered Eden Camp, and obviously that was where 'Adam and Eve set up their tent'. A large sign assured me that this was, in fact, the country's most popular theme attraction and I found it strange that I'd never heard of it. Chris was all for exploring the place, as he would be I suppose, but our schedule didn't allow for that and anyway, I had by now discovered somewhere infinitely more worthy of a visit, only some fifteen miles to the Northwest if my map is to be believed, and therefore worth a little detour,. 'Scagglethorpe' it said, and I could only marvel at such a splendid name for a village. We simply had to go there, I enthused, just because it was there and we could. The withering glare of incomprehension somewhat doused my spirits. Clearly the old man was having one of his moments, the look said, and was not to be encouraged.

I looked again at the map, and had to admit that it was quite a detour really, and I was slightly saddened that I was alone in my delight at the quirky place-name. Oh well, back to York then, or at least round it once more on our double-back trek West to rejoin the A1 yet again. The weather was playing ball, getting warmer as we progressed through the day and Daisy was still behaving remarkably well, so all was well with the world. But the going started to get tougher then, as we began a series of long climbs ever Northwards, leaving the Yorkshire moors behind us and enjoying the sheer freedom of a relaxed ride in increasingly interesting country. I marveled at the enormous power stations looming on the horizon, built to feed the ferocious appetite of an industrial explosion in years past, and I wondered what it was that they now feed, given that the huge manufacturing and steel industries had largely given way to a lesser breed of lighter activities. These thoughts were interrupted however, when I noticed, seemingly for the first time, that a tingling vibration had crept up on me and the beginnings of a pins-and-needles sensation was setting in. I lifted my hand and the sensation was markedly increased and I took the first opportunity to pull in to yet another lay-by. Happily, the duty tea hut was in residence, and Chris was happy to trundle off to do the honours after I explained that we'd got some loose nuts and bolts somewhere that needed some attention.

That was easier said than done. The spanners, woefully inadequate collection though they may have been, were buried in one of the panniers, which in turn were supporting the camping gear. It all had to come off, and the contents removed to get to the bottom where the sad little bag of rusty implements had been hidden. There was one mighty adjustable spanner as well. I spread the motley collection on the ground and started the process of checking the forward engine mounts. They seemed good, so I moved onto the underside and rear mountings, but they too were solid. That was curious, I told Chris, who had returned with some steaming cups. I fully expected to find some loose nuts, to explain away the vibration, and the absence of anything even hinting at slackness was worrying, for if that's not the cause then what is? Will it prove to become a drama later? I moved onto the gearbox mountings hoping that the culprits would show themselves there, but they were also solid. Stranger still. I sat back on my haunches with the tea whilst my paranoia took over, populating my mind with disintegrating clutches or crumbling bearings.

Chris had a more relaxed approach; "You imagined it," he suggested. Resisting the impulse to bounce my half full coffee cup off his head, I explained about the definite vibration through the handlebars and the tingling fingers, but he remained sceptical. I explained why such things should never be ignored but he was unmoved. I gave up, and got on with being paranoid. After checking for any obvious signs of any other traumas, and only discovering that Daisy's big ornate horn was about to fall off again, I reluctantly had to accept that there was nothing useful I could do and so we packed everything back up again, reinstated the camping gear on top, and headed once more out to the open road. As we accelerated up the slip road, taking her up through the gears, my attention was immediately focused on that vibration. It was still there, and I knew that it would fester in my mind like a cancer until I could find an explanation for it.

Back on the main carriageway, my mind churned and it came to me that over the past few months I had come to know Daisy intimately. I knew all her little foibles and characteristics, every little noise and rattle (of which there are always a few on any old Triumph) was known to me, and I realised that the current object of my attention was actually not that bad – just not usual. But if I had learned one thing in my many earlier years of riding a variety of old bikes, it was that the appearance of a hitherto unknown rattle or vibration was almost always followed by a drama of some sort. There was nothing I could do right then though, so we continued on our way, but I began to mentally chew my blanket (an old family saying – I had a granny, bless her, who when worried about something, which was nearly always, would sit in the corner with a blanket on her lap, and busily chew the corner, even though she had no teeth!) deciding that I would have to investigate a little more once we had managed to make camp later on. By mid afternoon we were approaching the general area that marked our first overnight stop and the road had once again become motorway. We pulled up in the services at the Bishop Auckland junction to get our bearings, study the map and generally decide what we should do next.

We only had one landmark left to get that day, and according to the map the thing couldn't be more than twenty miles away from our current position. It was another cryptic and crafty one, but we had been able to solve it in advance with the help of the online ordnance survey website. We'd had no trouble with the others, in fact the day had gone exceptionally well thus far and as it was only half-past three we decided to press on, get the thing discovered and photographed, and then take the first chance to camp that presented itself. I told Chris that we should camp as early as possible so that we could investigate the source of that vibration. His response, "I still think you're imagining it Dad - I can't feel it" didn't really help. But, buoyed by the progress of the day my confidence was high and I wasn't really too worried about much at all. I'd find the source that evening and fix whatever was causing it, and we'd go on tomorrow to another highly successful day's adventure. I was about to discover that I was entirely wrong in this belief – and about a great many other things!

It started there, the general downturn in our fortunes, because that next landmark was conspicuous by it's absence. We simply couldn't find the thing. It was ten past five, and we had been riding round in circles for an hour utterly failing to find anything remotely matching the clue 'Sounds like a pigeon loft of warm metal' it said, and right on the map reference, or at least very close, we'd found a place on the Ordnance Survey called 'High Forge' - a heritage site by all accounts. It was a very well hidden heritage site, we both agreed, as we pulled up for what seemed like the fifth time at a road junction which we had already traversed from every conceivable direction. I was pretty sure that we had now tried every single road within a three-mile radius, and there were only two notable things to see, other than endless cornfields. One was a particularly uninspiring industrial estate, seemingly completely out of place in the otherwise pleasant countryside and the other was a famous landmark indeed, but not what we wanted – the Angel of the North stood impressively, albeit a tad rustily, on the horizon. We are both getting fractious by then and it seemed pointless trundling around any more lanes, so we decided that the best bet was to enlist some local knowledge and accordingly set off to the nearest place to us, the village of Stanley, a few miles to our West. We found a large pub just on the outskirts and suddenly a pint of cellar temerature real-ale seemed like an incredibly good idea, whilst hopefully picking the brains of the locals.

"No, can't help you, sorry" This was the third local we had talked to, after extracting a blank from the barman and his assistant. I stared into my beer and began to wonder what to do next as nobody, it seemed, had ever heard of High Forge, or a local heritage site of any description. As I studied the faces, It occurred to me that in the present cloth-capped company, we must look a proper pair of Charlies. A couple of soft Southerners, who had appeared from nowhere on that old wheezing motorcycle, with a tent and not a lot else, asking obscure questions about non-existent forges. In an effort to demonstrate that we were not in fact barking mad, and therefore salvage at least some self esteem, I explained about the landmark challenge to our by now small audience and in desperation we showed them the clue seeking any ideas as to what it could possibly be. "No, sorry …" was the collective response. This was almost beyond belief and I turned to Chris, "Right, let's 'phone Ken Talbot!" I declared, which was met with the predictable response from Chris, "Who?" But I was striding outside by then, heading for the mobile 'phone and only slightly perturbed by the several locals who, not wanting to miss some good free street entertainment, were following gleefully.

Ken Talbot, assisted by a number of his stout fellow members of the Birmingham and Wolves branch of the Triumph Owner's Motorcycle Club, was the creator of our current problem. He was the organiser and official contact for those of us stupid enough to actually take up the challenge. I had his number along with all the clues stashed in Daisy's tank bag, right there with the 'phone, which was an unusually sensible precaution that I had taken in an unprecedented fit of clear thinking and good planning whilst packing for the trip. I certainly couldn't face another hour of hopeless meandering around the hills with only a rusty angel and some cows, not to mention a decidedly irritable Chris, for company. A call to Ken was clearly the thing to do so I found the number, and dialed the digits, giving the now gathered audience a raised eyebrow and an expression that I hoped would suggest that the person on the other end of this call had got some explaining to do. I connect to whatever cleverly hidden mast serviced the area, and in short order I heard the brusque tones of the man himself.

"Ken... Is that Ken Talbot?" I enquired, beaming at the now rapt audience. "Aye, who's this then?"

Explanations followed , and I ended by telling him "We've been all over the bloody place now, and we've stopped at a local pub right here, and there's no sign of this forge and nobody's ever heard of it! I know it's on the maps, but has any of you actually ever seen the bloody place?" I realised I was sounding tetchy, and there was a moment of silence, then Ken offered some help "Forge? What forge?" another pause "It's not a forge you want young man, no, it's a bit bigger than that, it's a steelworks, the Dovecote Steelworks, see?" I let that information sink in. "What! There isn't a steelworks anywhere near here either!" I exclaimed, "Just fields – are you sure this map reference is correct Ken?" If nothing else, our Ken was a patient man and wasn't at all ruffled by the gibbering madman raving down the telephone at him. "It certainly is, and it's definitely there!" he assured me in a steady confident drawl. "You can't miss it, bloody great place is a steelworks," he added. "

All I could think to say was "Well it's bloody well camouflaged then!" and I couldn't help noticing that our audience was looking particularly happy with the exchange, as several of the cloth caps nodded with barely concealed mirth. I asked another important question. "Has anyone else doing the challenge had a problem here?" Apparently not, as Ken confirmed no other callers have asked about this one. Great. Just marvellous, I thought, but our Ken turned out to be charitable soul and offered me a lifeline. "Listen, if you can't find it, that's OK. Get a photo of something recognisable from the immediate area and we'll accept that. It's about participating, and getting folk out on their bikes lad, so we'll not punish you for summat silly like this!" Well, that was something at least. I thanked him, promised we'd have one more try at finding the thing, and if not we'd get a photograph of something else recognisable. "How about the Angel of the North from across these fields?" I suggested. "Aye, whatever, but just enjoy yourself!"

The call ended there, to the evident disappointment of my new fan club, and I beckoned Chris over to explain the plan. We checked the time and was irritated to discover that we had lost nearly another hour, hadn't found our last photo of the day, hadn't found a campsite yet and still had that vibration to track down before I could truly relax that night. But on the plus side, it was a glorious summer evening and we at least had a solution that was definitive, so I teold myself to take Ken's advice, stop fretting and just enjoy myself. We got our gear together, bade the still present audience a hearty farewell, and headed back out for one more look around. It occurred to me that the industrial estate we had seen earlier, looking so out of place, may well be hiding the steelworks within it's boundaries and with no better plan I suggested to Chris that we try to find it again.

That was not quite as easy as it sounded,winding our way through themyriad of little country roads, but before long the rusty angel appeared once again on our horizon and we knew we were close. Riding up through a little copse and round a bend at the top that I recognised from our earlier criss-crossings of this area, we swept down the other side to break into a wonderful sun-soaked little valley, bordered by meadow each side. I realised in that instant that nothing else in the world actually mattered right then. The vibration, our schedule, the elusive landmark – all of that faded into insignificance as we simply enjoyed the experience of being lost in picture postcard surroundings, just us and our old motorbike. We swept on, through the valley bottom, took a long right hander up out of the other side, broached the top of a another wooded hill, down into a sweeping bend the other side ... and suddenly all hell broke loose.

The normally sure-footed Daisy just lost it completely, without any warning. Her rear end jerked violently, then jinked sideways, yanked Chris, with a yelled "Woooah!" out of whatever reverie he was enjoying and caused him to grab hold of me violently. Shocked out of my own daydreams, I found myself suddenly fighting the handlebars, which had taken on a life of their own, and we careered towards the verge, narrowly missing the trees to our left. Then we were plummeting down the hill, completely out of control, with Daisy bucking and sliding beneath us. She went into an almighty and violent tankslapper, the handlebars whipping from side to side and in that moment I was certain we were going to come off. There was no time to think, react or do anything remotely sensible and all I could do was hang on as the frightening toboggan ride unfolded. And then it was over, as fast as it had started, with us careering to a sliding halt at the bottom, skewed diagonally across the road, hearts pounding and knees trembling like crazy. I think Chris had actually nearly swallowed his tongue, judging by the gurgling noises coming from the back but I was in shock and just sat, motionless, for about twenty seconds. Neither of us moved or spoke but eventually we came round.

"What the hell…?" I began, but Chris lets loose his tension straight over mewith a violent exclamation. "Bloody hellfire! ….!" and with that he catapulted from the pillion and stumbled off to the verge, discarded his gloves on the road and pulled violently at his helmet before thumping down on his backside to glare at Daisy. I dismounted in a less theatrical manner, pushed her over to the verge, and the squashy, wobbly drag drew my attention to the fact that her rear tyre had blown, which explained the sudden descent into chaos. I dropped her on the side-stand and followed Chris's example, divesting myself of gloves and helmet. I reached with a trembling hand for the tobacco tin but found that I couldn't actually control my fingers to roll one due to the shakes. I looked across at Chris, and without knowing why I said "looks like I picked the wrong day to give up smoking!" It wasn't likely to break the ice right at that moment, and indeed it didn't.

Chris looked pretty shaken up.

"Are you OK?" I ask.

"No I'm fucking not!" was his the terse response. That brought me up short. Strong language indeed from a fourteen year old in front of his father, but I let it go under the circumstances. Finally, once the shakes had subsided, we got round to inspecting Daisy. A puncture it was all right and in the sprung-hub rear tyre at that. That was absolutely the last thing we needed and was as depressing as it could get with a rigid framed motorcycle of this age. The process of getting the rear wheel off is a protracted, torturous and dirty affair at best, requiring at least two pairs of hands and ideally a decent tool-kit and workshop. There was no way I was going to attempt a repair out here in the boonies, with night drawing in, so I decided to waste no time at all and make use of my recovery insurance, get them out to pick us up and take us to the nearest campsite. I made the call, but immediately ran into problems as the controller attempted to establish our whereabouts.

"Where exactly are you?" he asked the question which, I had to admit was a remarkably good one.

"We're in the middle of the countryside" I replied "er… about five miles South and a bit sort West of Newcastle" I added. Obviously, that wasn't particularly helpful, but those people must get a lot of idiots like me 'phoning them, because he sounded awfully patient as, without a pause he smoothly went into his routine.

"That's OK sir, but we'll need to give the driver a bit more, so, do you know what the last town or village was that you went through?" I explained about Stanley, and the pub.

"Great, so you're definitely between Stanley and Newcastle. OK, can you see any features or landmarks near you?" I nearly laughed at his use of 'landmark' but suppressed it and explained that on the horizon to the East of us was the Angel of the North.

"Right, OK sir, I think I know roughly where you are, so this is what I'll do – I will give your details to a local recovery company, with as much information as I can about your location. I am going to suggest that they telephone you directly and hopefully you won't be too hard to find" He went on to tell me not to leave the vehicle (as if we would – where would we go?) and that we could expect the call within thirty minutes. I thanked the guy, who had impressed me with his handling of our situation, and with nothing else to do I explained to Chris what the score was. We settled down to wait.

I sat and thought about the task ahead of us - getting that back wheel off. I knew it was a painful job at the best of times, and with the paltry tool-kit we had with us it was not a comforting thought at all. Then there was the tyre, which is a struggle to get off and on again, and likely to be quite a challenge out here in the wilds with only Chris to help. I sank into a depressed state of mind but was brought round by a deep rumbling sound approaching from the direction we had just come. As I stood up, a guy on a Harley came over the hill and slowed to a stop. Explanations followed, and it's clear from the look he gave us that our new friend thought we were quite mad. We obviously didn't look too well equipped, because having explained that we intended to fix the thing that evening and then carry on Northwards, he began questioning me about my readiness for such a problem.

"You've got a spare tube or heavy duty repair kit with you?" Good grief, what does he think we are amateurs? I had a superb repair kit, there in the panniers, and I scrabbled about inside looking for it to show off our preparedness for such things. It wasn't there. Strange, I could have sworn it was in the left pannier, with some big tyre levers. I switched to the other side and scrabbled about in that one but it was not there either.

"Must be in the tank bag." I said, beginning to wonder. It wasn't. I began to feel pretty stupid and I could feel my face redden as I was forced to admit that, in fact, we don't after all have a repair kit of any sort.

"But you've got a spare inner-tube, surely?" No we didn't and I mumbled this dreadful admission as I realised how foolish I must look to have come on this trip with no way to deal with a puncture. I looked at the incredulous rider, expecting derision of the highest order, but without further ado that knight of the road declared that it was not a problem – he'd go and get an inner tube from his garage which, he assured me would fit. With that, he promptly about faced and headed back off leaving me with a mixture of feelings. I was utterly embarrassed at our ridiculous plight, but that was tempered by a feeling of pride to be a motorcyclist, as I pondered that his actions were entirely typical of the breed. It's built into us, I reckoned, no matter what we ride or where we're from – or indeed how stupid the object of our assistance appears to be!

These thoughts were abruptly interrupted by my mobile, and it was the recovery company. The guy was in Stanley already, which was impressively fast, and wanted to know more about our location. I explained about the pub we had been at, and he knew where that was, so I described as best I could the route we had taken from there. No problem apparently, he knew exactly where to find us, and ten minutes later we heard the truck approaching. He took one look at Daisy and exclaimed "Well, I'll not be fixing *that*! Where are you from and where do you need to get back to?" We explained the plan, we just needed to be taken to the nearest decent campsite, and with that he proceeded to load her onto his truck. Fortunately, minutes later, our other Harley-mounted saviour returned and I was left speechless as he proceeded to hand over not just the promised inner tube, which was indeed exactly right for Daisy, but tyre levers and a foot pump as well! He explained that he lives not far away and has had the tube hanging in his garage for ages. We watched as the recovery driver makes things secure, and settled down to chatting. Chris came to life again and explained where we've been with Daisy on the other forays so far; I reflected that it does actually all make for a good yarn, to which this episode will only add flavour.

The recovery man finally declared us ready, and as I enquired as to how I could return the pump and levers, Harley guy insisted that we keep them, and would accept no payment for them or the inner tube. As he straddled his ride once again and fired the engine, he pushed up his visor and offered a piece of good advice. "You really ought to get a repair kit and fix that other tube for a spare!" I nodded and grinned enthusiastically and we waved him off. Hurrah for Harley-riding Mark from Gateshead – you know who you are, and you are a credit to your peers. The recovery guy had insisted that we unload all the gear, so now we had to shove it all into the back of his cab, before we could settle onto the big bench seat up front. We confirmed once again that the nearest campsite is where we wanted to go and without further discussion he made his way back onto the A1, turned South and delivered us, after a while, to a campsite right on the Durham junction 10 miles or so South of Newcastle. He wished us luck as he headed off, leaving us to check in, and all I wanted to do was get the tent up and find some food. It was a quarter to nine by the time we'd unpacked and got ourselves sorted, and dinner was the next priority. As we knocked up spaghetti, with some mince and a tin of sauce that we had bought at the site shop, it was obvious that I'd not get anything much done to Daisy that night. I was suddenly exhausted anyway, and Chris looked pretty tired, and so by mutual agreement we decided to leave everything until morning and accept that the day's schedule would have to go to hell in a handcart.

As the sun finally disappeared over the western horizon, I stared at Daisy with her flat tyre, and tried to think the job through. She was made in an era when solidity, strength and of course cost were the main design criteria for a working motorcycle. Quick access to such things as the rear wheel were not high on the agenda: the thing was surrounded by solid bits of metal fixed firmly in place with a plethora of stout bolts. I wondered if there was a trick that would allow me to get that wheel out more easily, but I couldn't see it. I got up and went over to her, crouching down in the last of the light for a quick inspection, but it was depressingly obvious that there would be no shortcuts. It was then that I notice a little sign stuck in the grass nearby, next to the little looping road that ran round the site. It said 'No way out' and I reflected that nothing could be closer to the truth!

An early start was essential so we were up at seven. A mug of tea was a prerequisite to any serious activity and that was sorted out before I got round to dealing with Daisy. It was a warm morning with a bit of light cloud, but there was enough sun coming through to glint off the heavy dew that had fallen in the night, making the first ten minutes of contemplative mental preparation rather pleasant. But I couldn't put it off any longer and, pausing only to focus Chris on the task ahead, I strode purposefully over to make a start. Daisy's rear stand, which resides right at the back and serves to elevate the rear wheel from the ground, had sunk into the earth overnight. I needed that to be firm and so we pushed her over to the road, where things were more solid. I explained to Chris what was to be done, and which bits were going to be painful; then we got on with it. The process went like this; Disconnect chain, remove brake arm securing bolt, remove the mudguard stay retaining nuts, loosen the flange nuts that join the two mudguard halves which will allow the rear section to be lifted clear of the wheel, loosen the main wheel nuts. When all that was done, placing any removed parts safely out of harm's way, we could lift the mudguard clear and pull out the wheel.

Easy to do, allbeit time consuming, but I know from previous bitter experience that the real challenge would be getting it all back together again. That very heavy back wheel, with it's rotating central spring-box, has a little locater bar which has to fit 'just so' into a little slot in the frame, which of course is hidden and inaccessible. That would have to be done whilst keeping the mudguard clear, pulling the two rear frame lugs apart to accept the hub width, holding the brake arm in the right place, lifting the extremely heavy wheel and pushing the whole lot into position. Difficult enough in a good workshop with stout able bodied assistance, but quite a challenge on the edge of a field in the middle of North Yorkshire, with a very slim toolkit and an inexperienced fourteen year old apprentice. Fifteen minutes later, phase one was successfully accomplished. The wheel was out ready for inspection. Unfortunately, the removal of chain and brake arm had left my hands and lower arms smothered heavily with thick greasy oil. I despatched Chris off to find anything that he could by way of rags or paper towels, whilst I began to survey the next, almost certainly challenging, task – that of removing the punctured inner-tube.

By the time Chris returned I was surveying with a degree of dismay the remains of Mark's tyre levers, whilst cursing the fact that the tyre itself was still firmly in place. The levers were simply too small, had quickly given up the unequal struggle and had bent. I only possessed some smallish screwdrivers, one of which, having been brought to bear on the recalcitrant tyre bead was now also bent. I cursed again. Clearly I needed bigger, stronger weaponry if we were going to make any progress. It was seven thirty on a Sunday morning and we were in a field just off the A1. The nearest town, Durham was five miles away and the on-site shop at our camp ground wouldn't open for another hour. Chris was moping around getting bored, I had no obvious way of getting the tyre off and our schedule was looking to be in tatters. Bloody marvellous, I should have known that it had all been going too well yesterday.

I suddenly remembered that we hadn't had breakfast yet, and there were bacon, eggs, beans and bread in the tent, bought the previous evening at the shop. With nothing else to do until that shop opened again, so I could find out where the nearest Halfords was, it seemed the sensible thing to do and my stomach growled in agreement. I call over to Chris to get the stoves fired up and tried to put on an enthusiastic face as I wandered over. Yes, a good breakfast would make all the difference I enthused. We cooked up a handsome feast and a fresh brew to wash it down, but as we sat down to eat Chris was getting morose about our current predicament. He was convinced we'd be stuck here all day, and with nothing to do or see, that was a boring prospect indeed and he made his thoughts well known. "Rubbish" said I, with a bravado that I didn't really believe myself, "We're close to Durham, which is a city. There's bound to be somewhere we can get big tyre levers and then we're sorted!" He fiddled with his breakfast and grunted, before an inner thought occurred to him. "How do we get there then?" he asked, but I was already ahead of him there. "We're going to call a taxi from that shop, and the driver will know where to go!" I declared triumphantly. Another grunt, and I had to admit that it was not the very best plan in the world, whilst cursing myself again for forgetting to pack the puncture kit and stout levers that I had prepared at home.

We finished off our breakfast in silence, then cleared up the rubbish before collecting the dirty stuff and heading for the wash-block where the fairy liquid dealt with it, as well as the grease on my hands and arms. We needed to take a shower before hitting the road, but I pointed out to Chris that there was no point doing that before we'd fixed Daisy – we'd get handsomely dirty again trying to put her back together! Once the shop opened, we discussed our predicament with the proprietor, who quite rightly pointed out that although there most certainly was a trading estate not that far away where we'd get what we needed, nothing would be open until ten o'clock, what with it being a Sunday. More time wasted then, and I began to think that fate was conspiring to spoil our day in no uncertain terms, but there was nothing to be done about it except call the local Durham taxi firm and book a cab for nine forty-five. It was, of course, late. In fact it was nearly a quarter to eleven when we arrived back, thankfully with a set of three stout car-type levers and a heavy duty repair kit, and after handing over the best part of fifteen quid to the cab driver, including waiting time, both of us were keen to get straight at the job.

Getting the tyre off now we had proper tools for the job was easy, but getting the thing back on again was less so, especially as I was acutely aware that pinching the inner tube would be extremely bad, given our circumstances. But eventually it was done and the donated pump was brought into service without delay. I explained to Chris that we needed to leave the thing for a while, just to be sure that it was going to stay up, and in the mean time we applied a patch to the punctured one that we'd just removed. Both stayed up, which was at least a minor victory, but we approached Daisy again with a degree of trepidation for what was to come next would not be fun at all. Chris held the rear mudguard out of the way, while with his other hand I had him holding one of the levers, to insert 'twixt frame and wheel in order to pry the frame lug out past the spindle bush. This was incredibly hard to do, especially as I had to have the other one ready to do the same on the opposite side, whilst at the same time trying to marry up the extraordinarily heavy wheel to it's lugs, all whilst keeping the little locating arm straight and stopping the brake arm going out of position and getting tangled with chain guards and frame. The first two attempts were nothing short of comical and ended, in each case, with the wheel jammed at some obscure angle and a goodly number of my fingers jammed with it. On the third attempt, the wheel slotted into place, only for me to discover that the brake arm had become jammed in the wrong position. It all had to come out again. It was something like the fifth attempt and some twenty minutes later that the nightmare thing finally slotted into place, and we sat back on the grass, tempers frayed, glaring at the thing with malevolence. But it was in and the relief was palpable - the rest would be plain sailing.

I rolled a cigarette, studied my oily black arms and the lacerations to my fingers whilst rattling off a silent mantra of things I'd like to do to the bloke that designed this particular wheel arrangement. My watch told me that lunch time had been and gone, so we'd lost half a day so far, but I consoled myself that the rest was just so much meccano, and we should be on the road within the hour. Little did I know that what we'd just suffered was only Daisy's opening salvo in what was to become a battle of wills – man against machine and may the most belligerent win!

9. Mountains, Rain and Perilous Descents!

Finally we finished the job, packed up the tent and after a miserable attempt to get clean in a cold shower-block with lukewarm water, we finally got under way once more, making our way out of the campsite and turning North once more. It was a quarter to two, and we still had get the landmark photograph that we had been forced to abort the previous evening. I'd agreed with Chris that we were not about to go hunting for the cursed steelworks again but would instead find anything that was recognisable nearby. The Beamish steam museum was close enough, we agreed, being on the outskirts of Stanley, and then without further ado it was Scotland here we come! I confessed to Chris that I had never been there before, so it was to be a first for both of us and I was looking forward to it more than ever having overcome the trials of the morning.

We were soon past Newcastle and, anxious to make up for lost time, I opened Daisy up as we pushed onward into Northumberland. The weather was holding up well with a light but warm breeze caressing us as we finally peeled off the A1 onto the A697, and struck out for Coldstream and the Scottish border. I reckoned it to be about seventy miles and if all went well I saw no reason why we couldn't ride later into the evening in order to make up for lost time. After all, we had not been riding this morning and as such were still pretty fresh. Chris was happy with the plan and we made good steady headway for a while, but our luck was obviously on the turn downwards because Daisy started to miss-fire. That was all we needed, and I tried the usual tricks to clear the problem like dropping a gear and winding open the throttle to clear the carburettor, but to no avail. With only a paltry thirty odd miles behind us we were forced to stop once again.

We found ourselves in a truly nasty lay-by full of rubbish, which made a sharp contrast to the picturesque Northumberland landscape of gently undulating greenery. I explained to Chris that we'd be here for a bit whilst I investigated the cause of the misfire, and he agreed to get the camping stove out for a brew. I began to tinker with Daisy, but after prodding various bits I couldn't find anything obviously wrong. We seemed to have a good spark, and with Daisy's antique ignition system there was only the magneto to worry about, and that appeared to be fine. All I could think to do was change the plugs and generally clean the points and all the HT connections. By the time I'd done that Chris had the tea made and as I let mine cool a bit, I start the engine. It seemed to be better, with a couple of experimental revs showing no signs of the dread miss-fire, so we finished the tea, packed up the stove once more and set off again, hoping to hell that the problem was cured. Fat chance, was the answer that hope. Daisy was not happy at all and I began to fret about what else I could do. We proceeded slowly, inside the hard shoulder of the road, trying to pinpoint something, anything, that would give me inspiration. I discovered that as long as I build up the revs slowly, the misfire doesn't seem to occur, whereas any attempt to accelerate normally produced an immediate faltering sputter. I was loath to stop yet again, opting instead to build up speed until we were cruising along at around sixty-five or so. That was fine as long as we hit no junctions or roundabouts that forced the whole frustrating charade to be replayed over again. Chris was leaning over my shoulder enquiring, "what exactly is the problem?" and I could tell he was getting despondent again, as well he might.

We still had a long way to go, or, if we were forced to turn round we were a long way from home! But progress was being made and so we just pushed on until eventually, as we pulled into Coldstream, Daisy forced me to deal with the problem by stopping dead and refusing to start again. There was a sign just in front of us that said 'Welcome to Scotland' and we had stopped ten feet short of it. An omen, or just a quirk of fate? We took stock of our situation, and agreed that it was not looking good. I had to confess to Chris that short of some obvious fiddling, I was at a loss what to do next but at least we could see what appeared to be a pleasant little campsite not far away, right on the far bank of the river Tweed. That was the obvious first move, I suggested. We'd push Daisy down to it, set up camp early and once that was done we could consider our options. What looked like a short distance turned out to be nearly a mile's walk as the road looped first into the town, round through the main street and down to the river via a back lane. I was exhausted by the time we got there and my spirits droop even further when I realized that our luck had completely gone as a dark threatening sky began to creep over, bringing with it a steady drizzle.

By the time we got our camp set up, the light had faded to nothing, the drizzle had intensified into light rain and there was no option but to leave Daisy until morning. Chris was holding his spirits up remarkably well, bustling around helping me with the tent and then asking if we could get to the supermarket and buy 'something special' as he put it, to cook for dinner. I agreed that this was a damned fine idea, after all there was nothing else we could usefully do right then and I reckoned we'd certainly earned the most slap-up feed that could be concocted on a camp stove. Even though it was still fairly early, darkness was crowding in remarkably fast as we walked up the little lane towards the town, to stock up with the makings of yet another Spaghetti Bolognaise, Chris's favourite food, some chocolate goodies for afters and a fourpack of Newcastle brown ale to finish off. We sat under the little porch section of our tent, listening to the steady patter of rain, but buoyed all the same by the feast that we had just consumed. After dinner, with the time still only seven o'clock, I suggested a walk round the ancient town, with it's historic attachment to the Coldstream Guards, and we set off along the river bank path up towards the town.

Out of the blue, Chris piped up that if nothing else, at least we were in Scotland and the talk turned to Scottish people. Chris wanted to know if their accent was 'worse' than that of Newcastle, the people of which, to our southern upbringing, spoke an almost foreign language. I decided to lead him on a bit, and described not only a very different accent to our own, but also a slightly fairy-tale picture of the violent history between England and Scotland garnished with a depiction of your average Scotsman, who, I said earnestly, tended to be towering ginger-haired brutes of men that, to this day, harboured a deep grudge against Englishmen with a particular distaste for soft southern Englishmen. This was received in contemplative silence, as we trudged up the hill, but any questioning of my tale would have to wait, for there, beckoning warmly in the dark, was a very pleasant looking little pub. "Let's go in there and have a drink" I declared, and moved purposefully across the road. Chris however stayed put. "Come on" I enthused, but he was definitely looking uncomfortable and I suddenly realised that I must have overdone things on the raving Scotsman front.

I crossed back over to reassure the poor lad that I had been pulling his leg, mentioned that I could see a pool table through the window, something I knew he enjoyed, and with that he follows me in, albeit somewhat warily. The first thing I saw as I entered was a huge Scotsman leaning on the bar, with a shock of ginger hair, a brutal looking face and an array of aggressive looking tatoos. Even I was taken aback slightly by the sight of that mountain of a man, but for Chris it was simply too much. Before I could even turn to say anything, he'd gone, straight back out of the door like a human Exocet, leaving me standing in the doorway feeling rather self conscious. The huge man turned and studied me, as I stood there in indecision by the door and, straightening up, he let loose a loud belch before turning his back on me. It was enough, and I quietly exited in pursuit of Chris. I had to walk fast to catch him up as he retreated rapidly back down the path and no amount of persuasion would get him to go back up to the town, so we spent the evening in the tent with a slightly strained atmosphere and me feeling rather guilty to have overstepped the mark and genuinely worried the lad.

We were up at seven, and it was raining. A steady, unrelenting downpour, but there was nothing for it, so I struggled into all my clothes, jacket and waterproof trousers and out I went to look for the trouble that had caused us to stop the previous night. As I'd already done HT leads and plugs, I reasoned that the problem must be with the magneto itself, and wasted no time before pulling off the cap. It was immediately apparent what the problem was, because the points assembly, which had evidently fallen apart, dropped out and disappeared into the long grass. I scrabbled about trying to find the bits, then discovered that the little rivet that held the contact itself onto the points arm had come off, causing the little round contact itself to rattle around in the cap. It was also apparent that the remaining assembly was loose and flapping about. I gathered up all the bits and retreated back into the tent where Chris was just beginning to come round, and after lighting our little gaslight I set about reviewing the situation. After numerous attempts I eventually managed to affect a repair on the contact by poking the bent rivet top back through it's proper hole in the points arm and peening the edges back over. The result wasn't at all convincing, but the thing was back where it should be and I hastened back outside to replace the assembly in its rightful position, reset the points gap and tighten everything back up.

So, petrol on, flood the carburettor, and with one hefty kick I was delighted to hear the engine roar into life. I grabbed my helmet, told Chris that I'd be two minutes, and set off for a test ride around the town. There was no sign of the misfire and I returned back to camp with an absurd feeling of triumph and achievement. But reality soon asserted itself as I began to prepare breakfast. The repair was, at best, a bit of a desperate bodge and realistically I had to wonder how long it was going to last. If it gave out again, which could be just a few miles into the day, would I be able to fix it again, or would it be broken irretrievably? Did I even fancy being in that position, out in the sticks in what looks to be increasingly appalling weather? As the bacon and eggs sizzled away and I turned my attention to the kettle, Chris finally crawled out from his cocoon, and immediately grilled me for details. I answered his questions regarding the cause of Daisy's woes and the fix I had applied, as well as voicing my concerns, then we discussed what to do. Our schedule, which took a big hit yesterday, is now even more over-optimistic than before, and I explained to Chris again that there was no guarantee how long the fix would last. Should we carry on or do we strike for home? "Well", I say, "isn't that why God gave us recovery services?" Chris agreed, having lost none of the enthusiasm he had displayed when setting up camp the previous evening, so onwards and upwards we'd go, we declared. Bulldog spirit and all that.

We broke camp and with the time just nudging nine-thirty set off towards Edinburgh. Out on the road, I was relieved that the miss-fire had definitely gone, at least for the moment, and the journey looked like it would be uneventful, if a trifle miserable in the constant drizzle. Our next landmark was due South of Edinburgh and from there we had to continue on into the city itself for another one before we could cross the Firth of Forth and venture further into Scotland. Chris remarked, as we stopped for a breather, that he thought there were supposed to be a lot of mountains in Scotland, but now we were there he was very disappointed. I had to explain to him that we were only in the relatively low Southern region, and that we wouldn't see much in the way of mountains for a while yet. But see them we would, I promised, telling him that he should keep an eye to the North as we approach Edinburgh and cross the Firth. "How long will that be?" he wanted to know, a suppressed excitement about the lad. I was seriously looking forward to my first experience of the Highlands too, and there was no denying that I shared Chris' eagerness to get there, but before that we had two Landmarks to knock off.

We arrived at the rough spot on my strip-maps, but we had no idea once again what we were looking for. 'Where little Bob set the press rolling' the clue had suggested, but as we scanned the area we could see nothing that suggested itself. Up and down we went, finding nothing. We had passed some small side roads however, and it seemed hopeful that one of them would yield up what we needed, so we systematically began to quarter the area in what was becoming a familiar routine. Half an hour later we were still none the wiser, but I'm determined that this time we're not going to lose too much time and decided, once again, to place the call to Ken for some inspiration. Ken was at work apparently, but his charming wife was obviously well used to landmark calls and very quickly identified the clue, telling us what it was we needed to look for. "It's the Robert Small print works," she informed us. This didn't help much, as we'd seen nothing of the sort as we did the circuits, but at least we now knew and could seek some of that 'local' knowledge. We thanked our informant, and headed to the nearest petrol station to seek enlightenment. "Never heard of it" was the rather disappointing answer we got, and several other locals professed to the same complete ignorance of any such place.

Eventually, having lost nearly an hour buggering around yet again, I decided to get a photograph of the village sign just up the road, as proof of us being there, and moved on. At least the next one should be fairly easy, I told Chris, for it's the Royal Yacht Britannia, and that can't be hard to find surely? It wasn't, although the process of weaving Daisy through the nightmare traffic of the City left me feeling pretty fraught and strained, and we have to get out of the place again yet. Finally, by mid afternoon, we were through Edinburgh, and striking out towards Perth on the M90. As we approached the place, the dark shape of the looming Grampian mountains filled the horizon to the North and West, the higher ridges and peaks shrouded in grey foreboding cloud and Chris, his excitement growing, was constantly tapping me on the shoulder to point out particular peaks or features. Perth passed behind us, we branched at last onto the A9 and headed straight into the mountain range proper. The long climb began; noticeable particularly as Daisy's exhaust note deepened with the uphill work and it seemed that with every metre we rose the weather was getting correspondingly worse. I began to regret, yet again, my failure to purchase proper heavy-duty bad weather clothing. Both our jackets, being straight forward leather, were soaked through and seemed to now weigh several tons apiece. Our gloves and bootshad capitulated completely, and the flimsy waterproof trousers we each had were simply not up to the unequal battle with the Highland weather. Every seam and join was, by then, liberally funnelling water to the most inconvenient of places.

We struggled ever higher, the sky darkened further, until eventually I was forced to turn on Daisy's paltry lights and just when I thought things could get no worse, the heavens opened, Scottish Highlands style.We were battered by some of the heaviest rain I had ever seen to the accompaniment of violent blustery gusts from every direction. There had been a marked drop in temperature too, and we were soon desperate for a campsite. It seemed an eternity before we found the blessed sign that promised respite and followed it. Sure enough, a camp ground appeared out of the maelstrom and pulling up at the entrance lodge, we all but fell from Daisy as she came to a sodden halt. I turned to look at Chris, who I was sure must have absolutely had enough of this adventure. Our eyes locked, and I was truly amazed when an ironic half smile broke out on his face, as he made a theatrically exacerbated gesture, flung his arms wide, surveyed his own disastrous appearance then uttered a sharp exclamation; "Bloody hell!" he opined.

Having booked in, leaving something akin to lake Wichita spreading around us in the little reception, we were directed along the path down to a river bank, to what in better weather would have been an ideal site. The rushing river Tay tumbled and roared along not ten feet from the spot we were given and we set about unloading the sodden mass that was supposed to be our tent and belongings. There is nothing more miserable than trying to put up a wet tent in torrential rain and this particular occasion was, without doubt, the most depressing experience of the whole challenge so far, with not just all our gear soaked through, but all our spare clothes too. We huddled in the badly erected tent and took stock of our situation; the clothes were are in were sodden, all our spare clothes were sodden and our bedding was equally unusable. What we need right then, was a mug of tea, but that just led to another depressing discovery – "Where's the bed roll?" I asked Chris. "What? – I dunno!" came the answer. I looked around, and then crawled outside into the downpour to look for it, but the roll, which had contained our gas cylinders, was nowhere to be found. It became obvious that the thing had fallen off, somewhere back on the road! "Just bloody marvellous" was all I can think to say.

So, with no tea or food that could be cooked (the little shop on site had closed just as we had arrived) we decided to venture out to the local town in search of a warm dry place to eat. The local pub was three miles away but provided us with a steaming hot steak & kidney pud which restored us somewhat, and whilst we ate we hatched a plan to get a lot of change and spend the rest of the evening in the launderette trying to get warm and dry whilst in theory we watched our clothes and bedding spin round and round in the big dryers. At least that idea worked out exactly as planned, and we hogged all three dryers feeding bedding into one, all our clothes into another and jackets and boots into the third. We then changed out of our damp set and shoved them in for a session. Sitting there feeding coins into the machines, I reflected that I had never felt lower in my life. Not very much was said for a while, but we shared the opinion that neither of us wanted another day like today. We both agreed on one thing, which was that if the weather hadn't improved by the morning, we would stay put and stay dry, schedule or not.

I woke at six thirty, to find that the river had swollen overnight and was nowgenerating a quite unbelievable roar as it tumbled and crashed over the rocks close by. But it was immediately apparent that the weather was much improved and I poked my head out to see broken cloud scudding across the sky in the fresh cool breeze. The site shop wouldn't open for another hour and a half, so I decided to forego breakfast, opting to get an early start in an effort to make up for lost time. After several attempts I managed to rouse Chris only to be rewarded with a very grumpy teenager as a result, but the mention of a day's riding in the mountains soon had him up and about. We broke camp amidst the glorious panorama of dark mountains shrouded with raggedy clouds, and in short order we had packed up and were off towards the peaks for what we both hoped would be a fantastic day's riding, up to Elgin on the Moray Firth to the East of Inverness. As we resumed the long climb, Daisy toiling beneath us, it was not long before an urgent tapping from Chris drew my attention to our first sighting of a snowcap in the distance. "That is what we're here for" I shouted, and suddenly I was absolutely delighted that we had pressed on after all, as the stunning landscape spread out around and below us.

We simply had to stop, numerous times, in order to marvel at the stark, dark beauty, which to us soft Southerners is a completely new and wonderful experience. On one occasion, parked at the top of yet another steep rise, we were utterly captivated by the sight of a large cotton wool cloud scudding along below us, eventually breaking across the road we had just ridden, spreading it's way upwards towards us like a special effect in a Hammer Horror film. I moved next to Chris as he watched this display in awe "You wanted wild National Park Chris? – Well you've got it mate!"

Daisy took the morning's hard work in her stride, although at numerous times I had to drop down a gear and settle for a slow, laboured ascent up yet another long, long incline. At the top of those, I invariably stopped to allow the old girl to cool down, but with so much to take in this seemed to be a bonus rather than a chore. By mid morning, we had left the Grampian range behind us and found ourselves picking our way down, between the Cairngorms on our right and the Monadhliath range to our left, so that no matter what direction we looked there were distant peaks shrouded in cloud, set in a glorious panorama of raw heath. Bright yellow gorse bushes competed with the purple heathers to make for a colourful vista all around, and the air had a crisp clear quality that is never to be found in our normal daily lives. I suddenly realised that Chris, who had been asthmatic since he was two, had not produced his inhaler at all in the last two days. That was a situation I hadn't seen for many, many months.

Eventually, Daisy could take things easier, as we finally broached the highest point of the snaking road and begin the long descent towards Inverness. The landscape became less stark as the white peaks were left behind us, but I wondered whether Chris would have a permanently cricked neck as he kept a constant awestruck gaze over his shoulder. The morning's ride had made everything suddenly worthwhile, but we were about to enjoy an even better highlight of the day. Leaving the A9 at the point at which it turns northwest towards Inverness, we joined the A95 Northeast towards Elgin and our next landmark. We found ourselves in a much gentler environment of pleasant rolling green hills and one of those lazy twisty roads that we all dream about. What happened next would make for a memory that I will never forget.

Coming over the crest of a hill, down into a sweeping bend the other side we could see a railway line coming across from the East which turned to run parallel alongside our road about a mile away. There was an old steam train chuffing across the low valley and as we got closer to the point that road and rail met, heading the same way, we ended up side by side with the engine thundering along at a good lick, not fifty feet away. I was almost immediately overwhelmed by the sheer sense of nostalgia and let out a childish whoop as we hurtled side by side up the straight. I was not alone in my delight either, as the old buffer driving the thing (a strange profusion of whiskers, overalls and oily rags) started hanging off his foot plate and waving at us madly in between various gestures of appreciation for the old motor bicycle that had, from nowhere, suddenly joined him and his equally old contraption. We grinned and nodded back and suddenly he was giving me the 'throttle' signal. He wanted a burn up! Unfortunately before we could establish the winner of such an unlikely race, the railway line peeled off to the East once more and the train with its eccentric occupant were gone, as quickly as they had appeared. It had been a strangely exhilarating few moments though, and made for the icing on the cake of what had already been a stunningly good day.

The next landmark, bizarrely, was a petrol station. The clue had urged us to 'fill up under the sign of the Jolly Roger' or something like that, and all became clear as we came across the Buccaneer service station just outside Elgin. Taking a rest there, we shared some food and tea from the little shop, and congratulated ourselves on our progress so far that day. We have covered only seventy or so miles, but much of that had been hard terrain for Daisy and it was only lunchtime anyway we agreed. The remainder of the day looked positively easy by comparison; West towards Inverness for forty odd miles, North once more, taking us over the Moray Firth and along the raggedy coast line for another thirty or so, and finally a short detour inland a bit to where we hoped to find the Shin Falls, our final landmark of the day. From there we planned to come back down to Inverness and begin our southward leg at Loch Ness, camping at the first place we could find. Easy, we both agreed, and before long we were off once more. Over the Firth at Inverness we went, and onto a delightful coastal road. Daisy was still running fine, and I had a fleeting thought that the repair, affected so long ago at Coldstream, was obviously holding.

Those thoughts were interrupted as we were treated to yet another sight that neither of us had ever seen before. The stark, imposing silhouettes of a number of giant North Sea Oil platforms, 'parked' in an estuary. That sight captivated us because up that close the things really look pretty impressive. That surprise gave way to another delight, in the shape of a long, low, multiple arched bridge stretching across the estuary for what seemed like half a mile or so, and I began to wonder as we burbled across, just how many surprises and pleasures one can experience in a day? Eventually, as we'd planned, we cut inland once more, following the superb road that took us up to Shin Falls, where we stopped for a very late lunch. The place is apparently famous for it's spectacular salmon run, and we followed the signs to a wooden walkway that wound down to the face of the steep rapids where the fish power their way up to their spawning grounds upstream. Standing feet away from the roaring torrent, it seemed unbelievable that anything could swim against it, let alone still have the energy to do anything afterwards, but we failed to see any salmon leaping the falls.

We stayed for ten minutes or so before heading back to Daisy, but half way back up Chris had a shock when a wizened old Scottish lady, looking tougher than my leather boots, possessing a beard nearly as good as my own and wielding a sharp piercing voice, grabbed his arm in a vice like grip, fixed him with an intense stare from gimlet eyes and demanded

"Jeearseeum?"

He stuttered and tried to back away, giving me a desperate glance that beseeched me to help him out of this sudden, startling confrontation, but his captor was not to be ignored.

"Th' *fush*!" she elaborated "Jeearseeum?"

For a second, Chris looked like he may dive in blind panic over the walkway safety rail, but the tough old harridan had him in a grip of steel, and before the situation could get out of hand I stepped forward to help him out of the hilarious situation.

"Fish, Chris – the lady is asking did you see them!" Seeing a sudden way out, he finally responded to her saying "Oh! No….no, we didn't see any fish" and with that she snorted at him, mercifully released her hold, and hurried on down the path. I was, by that time, trying not to burst out laughing as Chris shook his head, tried to straighten his jacket, whilst his cheeks flush a deep red. He set off up the path at a vigorous and exaggerated gait, and I followed at a more sedate pace, chuckling. At the top, Chris was slouched by Daisy glaring intensely at his boots with a deep scowl, but on seeing my face, still barely controlling a smirk, he stomped off exclaiming "Shut up Dad! Just go away!"

I decided it was best to let him cool off, and told him I was going to find the gents. I was not prepared for the next surprise of that day full of the things, but there it was. I went into the gents in a hazy sunshine, to come out less than five minutes later to an absolute downpour. The sky had suddenly turned dark, almost from nowhere, and we were back to the awful weather of the previous day. "Bugger", was my immediate thought. I had been looking forward to the late afternoon ride back down to Inverness, and on to Loch Ness but with the weather deteriorating so suddenly, with a rapidity that was truly startling, I was deeply depressed at the thought of another miserable soaking like the previous evening. Chris was sheltering by the shop doorway, and I ran through the maelstrom to join him. "Where did this lot come from?" I asked. "It just came – and I'm not going out in it!" was the reply. I tended to agree, and so we wandered into the dining area for another pot of coffee in the hope that things would settle down. Half an hour later the rain had eased to a steady drizzle but it was clear that this was it for the day and so we reluctantly come to the decision to press on back down to Inverness and stop at the first campsite we could find. Neither of us was impressed with the idea after the experience of the previous evening but things couldn't be as bad as that could they? We set off shortly after, heading South for the first time in four days, hoping to get a reasonable distance and find a haven before getting too wet. We were about to discover Lady luck had other ideas.

Rural roadworks can be a pain, but this lot seemed to be more painful than any I had ever encountered. We were on a high, twisty road heading back to the East coast above Inverness, and had been hopping between a series of stretches that had been dug up for a hundred yards or so each. This was the third set of red lights in ten minutes, and I vaguely considered that we must have been lucky earlier, coming the other way to have hit green lights all the way. We waited, I had my chin tucked down to keep the drizzle out, and as I stared vacantly at the rear lights of the car just in front of us there was a 'thunk' noise and Daisy, without warning, lurched forward – straight into the back of the thing! Caught utterly unprepared for that, I lost balance and felt Daisy falling, made worse by Chris on the back struggling to regain his own composure. Over we went, in slow motion, to end up in a straggly heap behind the car. The owner was out in a flash, exclaiming something that I couldn't quite decipher, but rather than demand what the hell we thought we were playing at he helped me bring Daisy upright again. Chris scrambled over to help too, having been ejected sideways.

"What the hell happened" he demanded, but the cause of the mishap was obvious from the floppy lever on Daisy's left handlebar – the clutch cable had snapped! I quickly pointed this out to the car driver, in an effort to show that I was not an inconsiderate maniac, and he seemed to understand that this was an unavoidable incident. We both inspected his car, but there was no damage either to it or to Daisy, and after assuring him that there was nothing we needed by way of further help, he was on his way.Chris looked despondent, but I cheerily assured him that far from being a problem, this was in fact cause to celebrate clever forward thinking. I had anticipated the possibility of such an occurrence, based on previous experiences from my younger days, and had taken precautions before setting out on any of the landmark adventures. There was a spare clutch cable taped to the broken one. Fitting it at each end only took a few minutes, and we were soon ready to go once more, but as we pulled away Chris leaned over my shoulder and gave me a slight chill with the comment "What do we do if *this* one breaks as well?" Good question, but not one I wanted to think about!

By the time we got back to Inverness, and found the top of the long road that runs the length of Loch Ness, the rain had become persistently heavier and we were soaked through yet again. We struggled on as far as Drumnadrochit, with no sign of a campsite along the way, but in truth I had already decided that camping in torrential rain for a second night was not an option I favoured. Having said that, I was not at all clear what we would do instead but I pulled Daisy up to the curb in order to try and take stock of our situation. It was grim, that much was clear, as yet again I cursed the very inadequate provisions I had made for bad weather. We climbed off stiffly onto the front forecourt of some kind of Loch Ness Monster visitor centre, and surveyed the rain swept street looking for inspiration, but there was nothing to see in the gathering gloom other than the little pockets of light under each lamppost where a dim shiny glow highlighted the myriad of constant pock-marks created by the relentless raindrops.

My spirits drooped further, but I suddenly felt really sorry for Chris, who had sauntered off into the doorway of the building to seek shelter. This was all meant to be a great adventure, something that he'd looked forward to over the previous weeks and although we'd certainly had some fine experiences, he has had to pay a pretty steep price in terms of endurance.It had not been quite the idyllic escape that we had planned. All in all he'd handled it pretty well and I resolved to try and make the best of things, starting with the need to try and lift our spirits.I joined him in the doorway and with a confidence that I didn't really believe myself I said, "Right, bugger this. We're going to find a hotel. We'll get a room with a bathroom, and it must have a warm bar, and we'll sit in there and get a bloody great feed, and then we'll sleep in warm comfortable beds! – What do you reckon?" He looked at me, and I nearly laughed out loud as I watched a little river of water running down his nose, dripping off the end. "Where?" he answered morosely "There aren't any here." He added, and it seemed that he had a point.

We had to get lucky. We deserved it, and as it transpired we couldn't get much luckier than finding 'Fiddler's Bar'. As we'd stood in that miserable doorway, I had caught a snatch of laughter from round the corner and immediately set out to investigate. And there, like an oasis of dry warmth in a cold, wet desert, was possibly the most welcoming sight I had ever seen. It was an Irish bar. More to the point it was a warm dry Irish bar with a little sign outside it that said 'B&B', and another that said 'vacancies' underneath. I urgently called to Chris, pointing out the stunning find and suggested that without wasting any more time we push Daisy round there and book ourselves into the place pronto. They had one room left, but it was a twin with en-suite facilities the man assured us. I assured him that I didn't care if it was the proverbial stable out the back, because right then anything that wasn't a tent, wasn't wet, wasn't cold and, most important of all, possessed a bar and served food was simply bloody wonderful. It turned out to be even better than that: the place had a lock-up garage for Daisy, just across the road.

We unpacked everything and ferried it all into the little room at the back of the bar, and before long the place looked like a back street room in Chinatown with clothes draped from or over every possible surface. Chris took the first use of the shower while I went down to put Daisy to bed and then, once I'd freshened up as well we headed down to the little bar enthusiastically, with Chris burbling that I had promised him a big feed, and he intended to abuse the offer mightily. We had the full works of starter, main course, dessert, washed down with Guinness for me and bitter-shandy for Chris. Compared to the last few days and against the backdrop of rain drumming on the windows, that, we agreed, was absolute heaven. Although tired from the day's exertions, we were in no hurry to turn in, quite happy to just relax there chatting away about the day's events, the highlights, the low points and I realised that I haven't sat and just talked to Chris like this for a long time. It felt great to do so and I was happy to stay there as long as he was, or until the bar closed. Eventually it did, and we spent the last fifteen minutes before turning in just standing on the fire-escape to our room sampling the crisp clear air and chuckling over the funnier parts of the day, like the frightening woman that had captured Chris at Shin Falls. I eventually went to bed feeling strangely contented.

The view from our window was well worth waking up for. We had arrived in darkness the previous evening in a shroud of mist and rain, which had entirely concealed the dramatic skyline around Drumnadrochit. But that next morning it was there to see in all it's splendour. The rain had given way once more to broken cloud, threatening in parts but with plenty of bright, clear patches and it looked fine for the morning run down the length of Loch Ness and Loch Oich to Fort William. Breakfast was traditional Irish fare and after that we collected all our gear which, after hanging all round our room for the night had dried quite well. The jackets were still fairly damp, but hopefully the morning ride would soon see to that. I pushed Daisy from her shelter and remarked to Chris that she looked strangely clean. That Scottish rain must be better than our stuff, because after a day's wet riding she normally looks like she had come last in a ploughing competition on account of getting stuck in the mud. Chris piped up with an observation of his own – hadn't I noticed over the previous few days how *soft* the rain was in Scotland? He was right now I came to think about it. We were soon underway and heading down the long and pleasant road that runs alongside Loch Ness. We stopped briefly at the famous Urquhart Castle, with it's eerie tower that featured in so many photographs of this most mysterious of Scotland's Lochs, and it looked in the flesh exactly as I recalled – dark, lonely and foreboding. The weather was holding up for the main part with only occasional drizzle, but it was infinitely more bearable than the rubbish we'd endured the previous day.

Eventually leaving the home of Nessie behind us, we pushed on down to Loch Oich, our next landmark and another piece of gruesome history. This was the well of seven heads, and history tells us that in the proper tradition of brutal treachery and murderous intent that passed for political correctness in the 1600s, two brothers of the MacDonald clan, daring to lay claim to the Chieftainship of Keppoch, were stabbed to death by some seven of their own clansmen, whom, we must presume, had other ideas about who should be running the show. That little coup went unchallenged for a couple of years, but then for some reason it was declared to have been not quite cricket by the Privy Council in Edinburgh, who issued a 'Fire and Sword' death warrant against the perpetrators. Unfortunately for the seven they lived amongst the kind of people that weren't about to pass up the chance to exact a legally swift and brutal revenge, and they were promptly hunted down and executed using the well tested method of lopping off their heads. Of course, it was considered only right and proper to display the macabre exhibits afterwards, but being a bit messy the story goes that the heads were washed in the very well that Chris and I were now looking at, before taking up their new role as decoration in nearby Invergarry castle. Eventually they were moved to make a fine display on Gallows Hill in Edinburgh, presumably because someone thought the place needed brightening up. A Gruesome story was that, and it was amusing to see the look of horror on Chris's face as I read off the details from the little plaque by the well. For all that, it was a strangely peaceful place and we decided to knock up a quick brew before continuing our way South once more.

Our next landmark would see us back in England once more, but the afternoon's ride to get there would take in yet more famous, or at least well known places that are probably familiar to most people. Fort William, Glen Coe, Loch Lomond and Glasgow were all on route and I couldn't wait to get at it. I showed Chris the map, and decide to build up the anticipation and give him something to look forward to; "You know what's at Fort William?" I asked him. "Dunno ... a fort?" was his less than inspired answer. "More mountains" says I, "bigger than any you've seen yet" I added. That got his attention, as I knew it would, judging by his enthusiastic recounting of our elevated experiences in the Grampians and Cairngorms over dinner the previous evening. "Do you know what the highest mountain in Britain is?" I asked. He didn't, so I pointed it out on our map, or at least I point out the place it should be on our map, if the thing was any use and had any detail worth mentioning. "Ben Nevis" I declared "and not only are we going to see it today, but in fact we have to go round it". Suddenly young Chris seemed in a hurry to get back on the road heading for what surely must be the best experience we'd have on this adventure. I was to be wrong about that, it would turn out, but at that moment I was every bit as eager as Chris and so we set off with renewed vigour and a heightened sense of anticipation.

Unlike the previous day, the skies were much clearer and we were able to see the Nevis range on the horizon long before we got amongst them. It seemed as though we were riding towards them forever, making no progress at all as they grew in our vision only millimetre by tiny millimetre. But it soon became apparent that this was merely because they are impressively large (maybe not by the standards of the Alps or Himalayas, sure, but to us they were magnificent) The last five miles into Fort William had us utterly captivated by the natural beauty of the range, off to our left, and we were thankful for our luck that in the clear skies the snowy peaks made for a display of grandeur that was both awesome and breathtaking. I found that I'd slowed Daisy to an almost pedestrian speed as we picked our way past those silent giants, because that was not an experience to be rushed. Fantastic.

We stopped at Fort William for fuel and a cup of coffee, before reluctantly taking a last look back and putting it all behind us. I felt a sadness to be leaving, and sensed the same in Chris, both of us knowing that we may never be back, but as we headed South once more the feeling was soon lost in the contrasting splendour of the ride through Glen Coe and across Rannoch Moor. In a very different way, that was nothing short of breathtaking with fantastic views, wonderful roads and it was just an all round uplifting experience. In the middle of nowhere, we found a Scotsman in his traditional national finery, playing the bagpipes in a lay-by, overlooking a deep valley. It was a charming sight and although the guy was obviously a tourist attraction, paid by the tourist board to be there, we declared him a landmark anyway, got him to sit on Daisy for a photo and he seemed pleased to oblige. Then we were off again on the long run down to Loch Lomond and what an experience that was too. The loch seemed to be almost impossibly large, and the road hugged the Western shore all the way down, passing through deep wooded sections on the way. There were little lay-bys right on the waters edge every so often, and pulling into one of these I was amazed to discover that after eleven miles riding along the shoreline we were still only half way down it's length.

It was incredibly peaceful up there, and I suddenly realised that all thoughts of our original schedule had gone out of the preverbial window during the past few days. It simply didn't seem to matter any more, even though I had arrangements back at home that I should keep. With Chris on holiday from school, I found myself thinking - so what if we were two days late? I could always rearrange things rather than rush this experience, and certainly the thought of returning to any kind of routine after the freedom of the open road seemed a poor reward to be hurrying towards. I determined there and then to take things easier where the surroundings demanded it, and stuff the schedule. That decision lifted my spirits even further as we mounted up and set off once again towards Glasgow, after all, that was what it was all about, what I had set out to achieve when I had changed gear in life – freedom and spontaneity.

Approaching Glasgow, we were dealt another flash surprise that seemed to sum up the Scottish weather. From almost nowhere, a dark foreboding sky closed in with a rapidity that was startling and as we entered the city the heavens opened once more. This time, with our new relaxed approach to time, we pulled over quickly and dived for shelter in a bus stop. If I had thought the rain was heavy as we ducked into the thing, then what followed was nothing short of biblical. The noise from the rain drumming on the shelter roof was so loud that any conversation was rendered all but impossible and we simply stood watching the incredible sight of a two foot deep fog of spray created by the huge raindrops hammering into the ground. It looked surreal, an impression that was strengthened as something akin to a river rose before our very eyes and flowed past us, engulfing two thirds of the road and lapping up over the curb to submerge the pavement right in front of our feet. Traffic slowed to a virtual standstill as we watched and unbelievably the thundering on the roof increased yet again, beyond anything imaginable. By that time, the bottom four inches or so of Daisy's wheels were engulfed by the torrent of water flowing past us, and I realized that once again the tent and all our clothes would be hopelessly wet. I wondered idly whether Daisy would actually start again after such a dowsing, but there was absolutely nothing to be done right at that moment but watch, which is what we did for nearly half an hour.

Almost as suddenly as it had arrived the downpour slowed and promptly stopped as if someone had turned off a tap. I suddenly realised how dark the day had become as the sun broke through again and illuminated a spectacular rainbow that reached right across the sky. The clouds disappeared almost magically, and we watched as the torrent flowing past us slowly receded to leave a curiously fresh smell in the air and the inevitable sound of dripping water all around us. "Bloody hell that was really bad," exclaimed Chris and that just about summed it up I reckoned. "Well, it's gone" I replied, as I headed purposefully out of the shelter "and after that little lot, we'd better see if she'll start!" Old British motorcycles are not known for their waterproof electrical systems and it seemed almost impossible that the magneto on Daisy could possibly function after such a drenching.

I positioned the kick-start and took a big heave knowing with almost total certainty that nothing was going to happen as a result. In fact, so convinced was I that the deluge will have got into everything, and so certain was I about the futility of the gesture, that the deep bark that met my effort startled me and make me jump. Amazed, I gave her a couple of blips and, as she responded crisply, I grinned at Chris and made my feelings known "Wahey!" I enthused "Way to go Daisy!" I added. Chris viewed me with a fishy eye and shook his head, but I didn't care, and leaving her ticking over, steam broiling off her exhausts and cylinders, I retrieved my helmet and gloves then attempted to chivvy Chris along. "C'mon, let's make a dash before the next lot gets us!" This at least he understood, and within minutes we are off once more marvelling at the fact that other than the shiny roads, all signs of the dreadful weather had completely gone, with even the rainbow disappearing almost as quickly as it had popped into existence.

As we followed the main ring road through the City, I was taken with the feeling of space and openness of the place, which didn't fit with the mental image I had developed for some reason, and the earthy smell produced by the rain made the experience rather pleasant. As we left the more industrialised Southern limits I had to make a choice of routes into Lanarkshire, where our second landmark of the day, which I believed to be a beam engine, was waiting. The M74 is the most direct route, and would take us straight down to within a few miles, whereas the A73 meandered off to the East before turning back to cross the motorway at the same point that we would turn off to reach our next stop. Having already come to the liberating conclusion that the touring experience was more important than any schedule, we took the 'A' road and settled down to a sedate progress through the green expanse of the Southern Uplands, with not a care in the world.

Pretty soon I discovered that this wasn't quite such a good idea as we struggled with the results of the recent cloudburst. Some sections of the road, where natural dips occurred, were still underwater and even the clear sections often had a slick covering of mud that was running from the hedgerows and banks. Progress slowed to a virtual crawl in places, and I found it mentally hard work keeping Daisy's upright and her wheels firmly in line as we negotiated treacherous stretch after treacherous stretch. On more than one occasion we had a heart stopping moment as one or both of the wheels twitched away from us and it took an inordinately long time to reach the motorway junction that signified that we were only ten miles or so from our next target. To our North another dark band of weather was building, and it was hard to decide which direction it was heading so as we rode we kept a constant eye on it, having no intention of being caught out in the open in another flash flood, but it seemed to be moving East to West in a direct parallel to our own course.

A steady climb took us to the little cluster of cottages that is Wanlockhead which, at fifteen hundred odd feet above sea level has the distinction of being Scotland's highest village. In years past, this was a centre for lead and gold mining, going back as far as Roman times and continuing right up to relatively recent times. Things finally came to a stop sometime in the nineteen fifties, but the history has been preserved for posterity in the form of a delightful living museum encompassing the majority of the village, allowing visitors to walk the entire place and finish up marvelling at the well preserved beam-engine dating back to the eighteenth century. It was an enlightening experience, capped off by the wide vista of rolling hills all around and a crisp fresh quality to the air that took some beating.

The place was so peaceful that Chris and I spent over an hour wandering around, absorbing the strange contradiction thrown up by that little oasis of industrial concentration, surrounded by nothing but raw nature for miles. Eventually we made our way back to Daisy, took a look at our maps to work out what would come next, and my spirits were buoyed even further as I explained that we were now heading for Cumbria and the lake district, which was not only one of my all time favourite areas for sheer natural beauty, but also contains large areas of that National Park he had been so looking forward to. We took stock of our progress so far that day, and it was a surprise to find out that we had already covered some two hundred plus miles since leaving Fiddler's bar that morning.

Our next landmark was hidden amidst the Coniston hills, but it was one of those we'd not been able to identify in advance. Not only were we not sure what it actually was, but we would have to ride nearly a hundred miles to get there. As it was already gone five o'clock, and after agreeing that we should shun the motorway, in preference for the meandering 'A' roads, it seemed unlikely that we'd reach it that day. But, so great was the anticipation, we agreed that we'd make the effort and ride until the light went somewhere around nine. We were able to pick up a meandering road that wound its way South, all the way to Dumfries and with the late afternoon sun illuminating the patchwork of fields that stretched to the horizon either side of us it made for a wonderful ride. Daisy reveled in the relaxed canter, providing us with a most satisfactory soundtrack as her exhaust note bounced from the stone walls that enclosed the roads. And so it went. Slowly descending from the heights of Wanlockhead, across the lower lands that run to the coast of the Irish Sea and, in what seemed like no time at all Dumfries fell behind and we turned slightly East to round the inlet that dissects the land between Scotland to the North and England to the South.

Next stop Carlisle then, and a much needed petrol stop where there was also a pleasant little café. We decided to get a meal before our final leg of the day into the Lake District proper, because there would be no such places amidst the wilds of the Cumbrian hills. As Chris finished his meal, I took the chance to do some quick checking of nuts and bolts but finding nothing particularly amiss, I topped up Daisy's oil tank instead, noting that she had consumed half of what I had fed her the previous day. That was nothing particularly unusual and certainly nothing to fret over, other than the cost of the stuff, but I couldn't find the preferred 20W50 multigrade in the station's shop, and have to settle for a 15W40 instead. As I poured the fresh stuff in, I caught myself hoping that Daisy didn't take the addition of a thinner oil as an invitation to leak it out of any weak joints. Chris emerged just as I was doing up the cap, ready for the off once more, but then I thought about what was ahead and signaled to him that we should go back into the shop. "We need to get something for supper, and stuff for breakfast, so we'll get it here in case we arrive at camping too late,"

That done, it was back out on the road and underway once more, straight into the sun which was slowly sinking ahead of us. It was just past seven when I noticed the looming peaks of the Coniston hills for the first time, away to our front and left. We had studied the map back at Carlisle and decided that the best way to our target would be to take the A595 South West, skirting the northern edge of the Lake District National

Park, before turning West and then South at Cockermouth, into the park proper. From there we'd get to enjoy the marvellous unfenced roads that would lead us to our spot in the hills. Chris was ahead of me, tapping urgently on my shoulder to point ahead and shout something about mountains over my shoulder. I gave him a thumbs-up and just after that we bumped across the cattle-grid that signalled entry into the wilds. Almost immediately the banks either side of us closed in and although this served to narrow the road, the absence of any fencing gave us the opposite feeling, one of open expanse.

We slowed to a sedate crawl, threading our way into the wild beauty of the low hills and almost immediately had to stop, just to take in the surroundings. We had to wheel Daisy onto the lush springy turf in order to allow any other vehicles that should happen along to pass, and after ditching helmets, gloves and jackets we simply wandered a little way up the nearest slope to enjoy the fantastic view. It occurred to me that this was, for us, the ingredient that had been missing in Scotland. The closeness to the surroundings offered the ability to simply stop, walk twenty steps and be right in it, up close and personal. Most of our experience of Scotland had meant that whilst the raw natural landscape was grander and far more spectacular, we had mainly been on bigger roads, with very few smaller ones obviously available to ride and on the occasions we had been able to stop like this, there was inevitably a wall or fence that prevented us from truly feeling a part of it all. What the Lake District lacked in the scale of its splendour, it made up for in sheer availability. It was the difference between say *admiring* a favourite motorcycle from afar, or actually *riding* the thing for real – both may give satisfaction but they're not the same thing at all. We wasted a whole twenty minutes at this spot, sitting at the top of a rocky, turf-studded outcrop, watching a stream tumbling past just below us. Some sheep eyed us vacantly from under a nearby tree, deciding evidently that we weren't edible, and therefore not worth further attention, so they wandered off higher into the hills. I could have sat there all evening I reckoned, as the sun sank low behind us, casting long tall shadows across the area, but we needed to find a place to camp before it got too dark. And this was the reason for my earlier eager anticipation, because I had got a surprise waiting for Chris that I had kept quiet about. The fact is that we would be doing proper camping tonight, out on our own in the wild. There are no campsites in the national park area, but instead of skirting round it until we got to the south side, camping at a proper site and then in the morning cutting into the park to find our landmark, I intended to enter the area from the north and simply get lost right up in the heart of the place. We'd find a spot such as this one, preferably complete with a stream tumbling past, and just set up camp right there. It would probably be the only time we could do it like this on the whole challenge and quite possibly the only time I'd do it in my life. Having dismissed the schedule as not important any more, I did not intend to miss the chance to really do things properly. I studied the strip map, and realised that we were in trouble if we expected to be able to use it to any great effect in this area. Most of the tiny roads were simply not shown at all and in particular our landmark was shown as occupying a large white square with no roads anywhere near. But I wasn't worried about it; I had identified this one at home, I knew that it was on little more than a track known as the Hardknott Pass, and I knew that it couldn't be that hard to find surely?

I showed Chris the map, and suddenly wanted to unveil my little secret; "This is where it gets interesting" I told him, "we can carry on down using the big roads, and there will be campsites down here" I pointed at the area. "But we've done enough of all that, and as the weather's marvellous and we've got food, I thought we might head straight into the national park, where we'll almost certainly get lost and just camp in the wild when the light starts to go!". His face registered a conflict; He was clearly excited at what I'd just suggested, but his natural instincts were telling him that there's something wrong with the idea and he voiced the obvious concern, which had also been bothering me slightly.

"We can't Dad, it's not allowed and we'll get told off," he declared. I wondered if, like me, he was remembering that dreadful woman who'd raided our picnic all those years ago, but I was ready for that and I'd made up my mind.

"Well, we spend all our lives being told what we can or can't do. If it's fun, you can't do it these days, but just for once we've got the chance, and we're going to do it anyway" I surprised myself as I said these things, but it's true - just for once I really was going to do what I wanted to do, no matter what. Chris was looking far from convinced however, and I almost regretted bringing him up to be so observant of the laws of the land and society that we live in.

"Look" I said, tapping the map, "This area really is the wilds. There are loads of tiny roads criss-crossing the whole place and by the time we get down here" I showed him the area just north of our target, "There will be no-one around to bother us. And we'll make sure that we are very careful to make no mess or leave any sign that we've been there – nobody can complain about that!" I could see that he was still unsure, but his underlying eagerness to actually do what I was suggesting won the internal struggle, and with a shrug he quietly reached for helmet and gloves and looked at me with an expression that said "Come on then". I fired Daisy up, and discarding the maps I fumbled in my pocket for the little compass, which I slid into the see-through panel on the tank bag. This would be our only real means of heading in the right direction but I realised that right there, right then, it simply didn't matter. I didn't actually care where we ended up that night and with that, I selected first gear and slowly bounced off the springy grass, turned left into the National Park and set out with a feeling of complete contentment.

Progress was promptly halted round the very first bend however. We entered a stretch of tiny road with high stone walls either side of the narrow tarmac - and found a large horned obstruction standing in the middle of the road between them. We stopped, for there was no way round the thing, and I had a fleeting panic that the huge hairy behorned beast may be the male variety, which might also take exception to us disturbing whatever deep bovine contemplation it had been occupied with. Its jaws, which had been lazily working, stopped the side-to-side motion as its ears cocked forward and a keen, piercing stare was directed at us. I noted the bulging udder with relief, but although the cow decided that we were not very interesting and returned to its industrious chewing, it showed no sign of moving. We sat and stared at the beast; and it, in turn, continued to idly watch us. I waved my arms and tooted Daisy's feeble horn.This caused the chewing to stop momentarily, but my failure to follow up with something more worthy of reaction soon saw the slow grinding return and a complete lack of any other movement. We appeared to have a standoff, but the cow had the advantage in that it had nothing else to do and nowhere else it wanted to go!

"What do we do?" asked Chris after several minutes.

"Bloody good question" I replied, "and one to which I have no ready answer! I'll have to get off and try to get it moving I suppose" but as we put Daisy on the stand I was anything but confident because after all, what exactly does one need to do to get a cow to do anything at all, let alone move, if it doesn't want to?. I approached the thing cautiously, speaking as I went and hoping that it would get the hint and back away. It didn't move, but the jaws stopped again and I was subjected to the keen stare once more. "Shoo" I suggested, flapping my arms and stamping my feet from only five feet away. The cow stared but moved not one inch. "Bang!" I tried. "C'mon SHOO!" I added, jumping around like a mad thing. I was reluctant to go any closer. The cow continued to stare, whilst continuing to move not at all. I realised that I was getting nowhere and I was completely out of ideas. I returned to Daisy and Chris, shrugging my shoulders and feeling helpless, but mercifully, before either of us could speak the cow decided that it had had quite enough entertainment from this gibbering human doing the rain-dance and with a disdainful glance at us it sauntered idly past , ambling slowly round the corner, pausing to deposit a steaming pile as it went. Charming, but at least the road was clear once more and with Chris sniggering that the cow had made me look stupid, we mounted up and got underway once more. Half an hour later, I was standing at the top of a sharp rise surveying the immediate area to the side of a road that could only barely make the claim, being little more than a raggedy edged tarmac strip snaking higgledy-piggledy amidst the rolling landscape. To our left the ground rose sharply into the lower levels of much higher hills and a tumbledown array of loose boulders interspersed with spongy, springy grass that populated every flat surface. Through the middle of this, and running off down the slope to our right, was a delightful rushing stream, splashing and tumbling it's way from the higher peaks to the low valley that we had just ridden through. There were a few sheep standing higher up the hill, inspecting us intently as their jaws worked busily from side-to-side and I could see the little road stretching away below us, looking like a carelessly thrown bootlace on a manicured lawn. We were on a wide flat ledge half way up the rolling landscape, and it seemed the perfect spot to make our camp because we were able to get round to the other side of the jutting promontory formed by a large boulder, and effectively be out of view from the road. The view was simply stunning and I could think of no better place to spend the night. Chris had already climbed up to where the stream broke over the outcrop of rock to tumble in a little waterfall down its face, and I'd never seen him look happier. Simply put, it was an absolutely fantastic spot.

As I sat some while later, watching our little stoves hissing away in the last of what had turned into a glorious sunset, I knew that this evening would remain etched in my memory for ever. It was one of those times that you just know you will never, ever forget and I felt privileged to be there. We had no real idea where we were, and it mattered not. All thoughts of a schedule or even the next day's ride were somehow irrelevant at that moment. Supper was nearly ready, tinned Irish stew that we had grabbed at the shop, we had two cans of Newcastle Brown Ale for afterwards, and a full compliment of breakfast ingredients. We had nothing to do that evening but watch the sunset, eat, drink and then just talk and so it went. The darkness, when it came, was absolute but glancing upwards we were thrilled to see the amazing panorama of the Milky Way, clearer and crisper than we had ever seen before. The general pollution down south means that we had never seen such a sky, so we got our sleeping bags out and just laid out there in the open air, inevitably ending up telling ghost stories until, much later, a deep rhythmic breathing suggested that Chris had fallen asleep. I continued to lay there staring up at a billion pin-pricks in the sky, but as the bright point of a satellite passed across the starry vista, I was reminded that even out here in the wilds we couldn't escape modern civilisation *completely*.

The next thing I knew I was waking with a start to see the first hint of a fiery dawn to the east – the beginnings of the new day. I sat up and realised that during the night a heavy dew had permeated the sleeping bag. It was soaked through and now that I had moved and disturbed it the water collected in the creases, sending icy trickles running inside in a most uncomfortable way. I tried to ignore it and lay down again, but the damage was done and I couldn't get comfortable again. I got up, found the kettle and stumbled off in the chill air to fill it with some of the water from the stream, which I guessed and hoped should be fairly pure. I decide to make sure it was well and truly boiled, just in case, and once it was on the stove I began to sort out the stash of breakfast food we had bought at the shop in Carlisle. With that lot on the go, I woke Chris so that we could hang the sleeping bags over the rocks and hopefully get them at least partially dry in the early sun, which was just making it's first tentative appearance on the horizon.

It's hard to describe in mere words what unfolded before us as we waited to eat. The low ground falling away beneath us was shrouded in a layer of early white mist, but it was one of those surreal bands that hung about four feet above the ground and was only a few feet thick. The air was clear underneath and above and Chris pointed out a tree, a few hundred yards away, with just its trunk and its uppermost branches in clear view and its middle shrouded in white. The mystical ribbon was lit up by the low sun, which itself was set in a fluorescent pink sky. A few thin clouds moved slowly across in the distance, their edges fiercely silhouetted in fire, and all around us we became aware of the absolute calm stillness , that most magical point at the end of the dark night - the breaking of dawn. Neither of us said much, for there was nothing to say at such a moment and then it was gone, the spell was broken and the new day had arrived. The odd quiet cheep or chirp that had been discernable for the last ten minutes had, almost suddenly, become a constant and loud twitter all round us as various birds awoke once more. The sun had fully risen above the horizon, banishing the eery twighlight, chasing away the mist and we were, we realised, hungry.

Breakfast was ready, and was soon devoured hungrily followed by a mug of coffee. Soon after we broke camp and prepared for the day's ride but before setting off we scoured the area to ensure that no sign of our stay was left behind us as I explained to Chris that it simply wouldn't do to leave a wrapper or even a teabag behind to spoil the next visitor's enjoyment of the natural splendour of that little spot in the Cumbrian fells. Finding nothing, Daisy was fired up and allowed to warm and then we were off once more on that little strip of raggedy tarmac, looking for the Hardknott Pass further south and our landmark. Twenty minutes later I was thinking that this must be the challenge organisers' idea of a little joke. We had found the start of the pass without much difficulty, and we'd also found a little sign for the Roman Fort half way through the Coniston hill range,skirting the heights of Harter Fell. The road, if it could be called such a thing, was almost indescribable. It was even narrower and more raggedy than the ones we had been picking our way along since yesterday, but worse by far was its route, which followed the bumps and curves of a myriad of small hillocks, outcrops and dips as it wound it's way up into the fells.

At several points, we were faced with a sudden sharp change of direction, incorporating a steep rise or drop which, often coupled with an acute angle to the road made for some hairy riding on a 1948 machine. At one particular perpendicular hairpin we had to stop and actually unload Daisy, as I cautiously took her up what appeared to be a near vertical rise, seasoned with a right angle bend five feet up just to make things interesting. I would imagine that on a modern trail bike this road would be huge amounts of fun, but a 1948 clunker with hardly any suspension and pretty poor brakes made it a dangerous experience in places. We reached the fort, eventually, but it was hard to believe that it was only two miles along the pass to this point, because I felt completely exhausted. Worse still, we had to turn around and go back along the thing to reach what, only half an hour previously, I had thought of as tiny roads but now considered to be the heights of sophisticated civilization by comparison. The fort itself was barely more than a raised floor plan of stone foundations, but for all that it was very clear to see what it used to be like. Built in around AD130 or so, it was believed to have been a very remote outpost indeed and one had to wonder why on earth they built the thing here. Presumably it served as a staging post for patrols and traders, a haven of respite on an otherwise tough and hostile route between population centres. Who knows, but the size of the thing and the number of structures within suggests that it was a fairly imposing place in its prime.

Looking along the pass from the fort, I couldn't help but wonder whether the Challenge organizers had ever actually been to that spot themselves, or was this just a ready landmark picked from the map with no realization of just how remote and tricky it is to actually get to. If they were aware, I would have to say "nice one boys – remind me to bring you here on Daisy's pillion some day!" But like anything in life, there was a benefit to be had from the effort, and there was absolutely no denying that our current spot took some beating in terms of being a sheer uplifting experience. In most directions there was no sign whatsoever of humanity, just the rolling foothills overlapping each other as they built up to the high peaks all around us. The imposing height of Scafell Pike dominated our view, reminding me that we were actually standing on the lower slopes of some of the highest ground in England and it was quite simply fantastic, but after a while, inevitably, we had to go. I looked back along the pass with some trepidation as Chris jumped onto the back once more and we began the return to civilisation. We took it easy, but before long that horrible, almost vertical right angle bend was before us again and we had to stop to survey the task ahead. It was downhill this time, and once again I took the decision to unload all the gear and walk it down, leaving Chris at the bottom to wait for me to climb back up and retrieve Daisy. I edged towards the top of the drop, and eased onto the sharp slope but we gathered pace in seconds. Panic set in just before the cambered bend, as Daisy's brakes stopped working with a startling rapidity, failing miserably in the uneven struggle to hold our momentum. I suddenly understood the true horror and meaning of the term 'brake-fade'. We were already going too fast, and even though I had her in first gear with the clutch out, both brakes anchored on as hard as I could, we were simply gathering speed and heading straight towards a rock face where the road does it's right angle turn-and-drop. There was absolutely nothing I could do. To this day I am fuzzy about the details of what happened next other than abandoning all attempts at braking, jamming the heels of both boots into the tarmac whilst I physically attempted to heave Daisy round the bend. It wasn't enough. We hit the stone wall in a side-on slew and by rights it should have ended there, but incredibly we bounced off it and we're suddenly careering down the slope past the bend, accompanied by bits of rock and mud from the wall, and straight towards Chris, who, white faced and panicked, took flight up the grassy bank. I narrowly missed the gear that we'd stacked at the bottom and mercifully came to a halt some thirty feet further on where the road rose once more. I could smell the harsh burnt tang from the brakes and I could feel pain in both my arm and leg. The trembles set in as I heard Chris running up the slope behind me, breathless, and the most ridiculous thought popped into my mind; "He'll need his inhaler" was my rather peculiar observation.

We stood Daisy by the road and inspected the damage. Her clutch lever had been bent where it had hit the rocks and the left hand handlebar rubber had been ripped at the end and had bits of stone stuck in the tear. Similarly the footrest rubber had been torn at the end but miraculously there appeared to be no other damage at all. At least, to the bike. My jacket had a large grey/brown scrape down the entire length of the left arm, and both my jeans and left boot had suffered a similar scrape to match. Neither the jacket or jeans had actually torn, but the fiery sensation up my leg told me that the impact had been quite hard. The biggest thing for me was the adrenalin flood that made me feel almost physically sick and totally spent as I slumped into a sitting position on the road and reach for the tobacco tin. I was about to voice my feelings but Chris literally took the words from my mouth – "Bugger that!" he exclaimed, but the outburst broke the tension and suddenly I found it hard to suppress a maniacal laughter which welled up within me. Probably it was sheer relief that we were in one piece.

Eventually we got back to the relative civilization of small single track roads that at least had the benefit of following a more sedate geography, and we skirted around the northern edge of Lake Windermere before stopping for an early lunch. We'd earned one I reckoned, and we also both needed to visit the gents for a call of nature that would not have been acceptable in the hills. I took the chance to inspect my leg, which was still feeling chaffed and raw, noting that indeed it had an angry looking pattern of scrapes and the beginnings of a lovely bruise on the knee. Back outside, we found a picnic table bathed in sunshine in the beer garden, sat ourselves down, took stock of our progress so far and began to plan out the rest of the day. The next Landmark was seventy odd miles to the southwest, at Skipton, which is only twenty odd miles North of the great urbanised sprawl that stretches from Leeds, through Manchester and all the way to Liverpool. We studied the strip map and it wass good to see that a large part of the route would take in the Pennines - the 'roof of England' I explained to Chris. That was certainly something to enjoy, but we needed to decide whether to take things easy and camp to the North or press on and get past the heavily urbanised areas before making camp that evening.

We agreed that pressing on South would be harder than it might sound, because there were two more Landmarks on the Northern side of Manchester and Liverpool that would require a diversion straight across country, East to West, and only once we'd claimed those could we turn South to pick our way through the inevitably busy built up areas. After much debate, we decided to take our time, make the most of the fabulous riding roads, pick off the three targets and stay to the North. We'd be able to call it a day early for once, hopefully finding suitable camping somewhere in the green belt between Preston and Liverpool. Having made that decision, it was clear that with only a hundred and fifty miles to cover and all afternoon to do it, we could take our time over lunch, set a steady but unhurried pace through the Pennines, take time to enjoy the surroundings, before covering the last fifty miles which encompass the three landmarks and then finally find a campsite fairly. Hopefully early for once. With those happy thoughts bouncing around, I turned my attention to the menu, and enjoyed the rare feeling that the only thing I needed to worry about was whether to have the ploughman's or the steak and ale pie!

The afternoon ride was both uneventful and every bit as enjoyable as we had anticipated. As we climbed steadily into the Pennine district, it was noticeable how the landscape differed vastly to that of Scotland and Cumbria. It lacked the stark imposing peaks, offering instead wide open high spaces from which grand views could be had in just about every direction. The hedgerows and grassy verges of Cumbria had given way to endless dry stone walls enclosing a myriad of little byres and outbuildings made of the same stuff. These remote structures seemed to populate the many fields for miles, presumably serving as rudimentary food stores or shelter for the countless sheep and cows that dot the landscape all the way to the horizon. We stopped numerous times, just idling the time away and marvelling at the remoteness of these high slopes, but even when we were moving I kept the speed down to around fifty and simply drank in the freedom of so much natural splendour and space.

As we picked our way ever Southwards, however, another impression began to assert itself. I began to develop the distinct feeling that these rolling hills would be no place to roam in winter, as even on that summer's afternoon the odd cloud passing over made the shadowed areas look bleak and foreboding and there was a distinctly raw edge to the stiff wind that played across the high vista. I couldn't help but notice that the few trees up there were bent and gnarled, presumeably from an eternal struggle against the constant force that would have them over if it could. But eventually the land began to fall away and we saw the first signs of civilisation once more as we dropped into the chocolate box prettiness that is the Yorkshire Dales. James Herriot country I recalled, and I suddenly understood why he wrote so much, so passionately, about the place and his life there. I remembered devouring every one of his books back in the seventies, when I could only imagine in wonder what the places he described so vividly would actually be like in real life. Well, now I knew, and it was no kind of disappointment.

All good things come to an end though, and we eventually found ourselves at the far edge of the Dales on a featureless road that led to Skipton, a few miles from which the Embsay steam railway awaited my cameras. We found the place easily and I positioned Daisy on the road next to the little ticket office, got the vital pics, but short of taking a train ride into the Dales there was nothing else to be done there so within minutes we were off again, heading towards the Western boundary of Halifax where we'd hopefully solve another unidentified clue. We had to ride about twenty miles, through a strange mixture of heavy suburbs interspaced with startling raw countryside, often switching from one to the other and right back again in the space of a mile or so. We made a wrong turn somewhere and got sucked into a nightmare one-way system that deposited us in the middle of Halifax itself, from which a Herculean struggle was required to escape from again. We seemed to go round the place about five times, and, although I swore each time that I'd taken a different road, it was only a matter of time before we ended up back in the centre again. I cursed as we passed a familiar filling station yet again, from yet another different direction, and decided that to trundle off in some arbitrary direction yet again would be hopeless because all roads seemed to come right back here. I had given up on the compass, being unable to maintain a Westerly route from that point and as we needed petrol anyway it seemed sensible to stop, fill up and try to explain to the attendant where we wanted to get to and ask for advice.

Now, understand this. I am no kind of racist. I happily accept that we live in a multi-cultural Country, but I must confess that nothing in all my years had prepared me for what transpired next. Quite simply I discovered that it was possible to be considered foreigner in my own homeland, and an unwanted one at that. This was quite a shock, and maybe I've led a sheltered life in that respect. It happened when I tried to converse with the attendant. He didn't appear to speak English, or at least not any kind of English that I have ever heard, but worse than that I got the distinct impression that it was deliberate - I was not at all welcome here. Was I over reacting? No, I don't think so. Any doubt about that was removed when another customer pushed past me and began a heated conversation with the attendant, and both of them began making exaggerated gestures in my general direction. I was left in no doubt whatsoever that whatever else was being discussed, I was not about to be invited home for tea. As the customer, a thuggish looking young man with rather more gold jewellery and face furniture than might strictly be necessary for mere decoration, continued his amazing tirade, we made eye contact. I was doubly shocked as I recognized something that has thankfully been almost non-existent in my life - hatred.

At that point an older guy touched my arm, and in clear English he said in a matter of fact way "They want you to leave - it would be best if you did that". I couldn't believe what I was hearing and what I actually wanted to do was punch furniture-face straight in the ear hole, but with a fourteen-year-old standing outside waiting, in what must now be declared as hostile territory, that was not an option. I held my hands up in what I hoped was a placating gesture, took the map from the counter and backed away saying "Fine - don't get so excited - I'm going!". The two stopped their jabber and stared at me but with no intention of allowing the situation to develop into any more of a drama, I headed for the door with a swelling anger barely controlled within me. I strode over to Daisy, grabbed my helmet and swung my leg over her, but couldn't stop the outburst.

"Bastards!" I declared, staring at the shop. "Bloody arseholes!" I added, and Chris, who hadn't got a clue what had just occurred within, immediately wanted to know why I was cursing. I just wanted to go, and I was short with him as a result "Just get on" I told him, and he was sensible enough to just do it. With his feet barely settled on the pegs I had let out the clutch and we were mobile. A hundred yards up the road I took a left turn and then a right, left, right, left and so on until we suddenly broke out into countryside again. I stopped at the first available point, killed the engine and walked over to the fence to stare across the fields, still seething about the unbelievable and deeply disturbing events that had unfolded just a few miles back. Chris was clearly unsure what had gone on and hung back next to Daisy and I realised that I owed him an explanation, so I turned back and began to recount the story. As I told him what had happened it sounded incredible even to me and Chris added to that feeling with a string of questions that could only come from one naive to the ugly reality of modern Britain "Why do they hate us? We haven't done anything to them have we?" seemed the most poignant, and was a question to which no easy answer was available, or at least not in a lay-by on a small road in North Yorkshire. We agreed to put the whole dismal experience to one side, for later consideration.

I managed to refocus on the business of escaping Halifax, in order to re-enter the place in a more orderly fashion. From what I could work out, we had come out on the Northern side of the built up area again and, determined not to get sucked back into that nightmare one way system, I suggested to Chris that we should continue to head north for about five miles where I hoped we would hit a junction with the A6033 - the road we should have connected with earlier. This would take us to the West of Halifax before turning in towards the town. Our Landmark should be on route, right on the outskirts. The clue was ambiguous to say the least, being simply 'amiable' but as we finally rode in on the right road the answer was blatantly obvious when we were invited to 'Please drive carefully through Friendly'. I took the landmark photographs right there and as I zipped the two disposable cameras back into their pockets in the tank bag, a sudden thought occured to me that lifted my spirits no end after the unsavoury incident earlier on. I laughed out loud as I turned to Chris and told him the good news.

"Hey, you know that petrol station back there that didn't like us?" I asked, "Well, we came out getting one over 'em because I've just realised something - I didn't pay for the tank of petrol!"

Mood well and truly lifted then, we set off into the late afternoon, back out into the lush green countryside, heading for an agreeably early camp. We had accepted that we'd have to do a bit of motorway to our last landmark of the day, skirting through the southern edge of Blackburn and on towards Preston on the M65. Somewhere between the two we'd be jinking north for just a couple of miles to find Hoghton Tower, a renaissance manor house. The place was closed when we found it, but the photographs were taken at the entrance to the impressively long driveway and that was all we needed. The good news was that we now had all evening to decide where to go for the night's camp, the bad news was that we were pretty much surrounded by urban brown-belt with Preston to the west, Blackburn to the east and Manchester, Bolton or Liverpool to the south. We had no local knowledge to assist in the decision making and without that it was hard to know what to do. I lay out the large scale map in order to look at the landmarks we'd be chasing the next morning, but with both of them situated to the south of the sprawl, it would clearly make no difference where we go from here as long as it's not North. Chris did not agree.

"Why can't we go North - why can't we go here?" he said, pointing to an area higher up the map.

"Well, it's in the wrong direction see? We're heading down *here* tomorrow!" I tapped my finger on the first landmark. "So? You said we didn't have to rush at anything and that we could take our time if we wanted to, so why does it matter?" I looked again at the area he had indicated, and had to concede that it looked to be far less populated and far more inviting than any other direction and it was clear that the lad was right. I had been behaving as if we were back on that schedule again, always looking at the next target instead of the best experience and it was daft when only fifteen miles or so the 'wrong way' there was open country and what looks suspiciously like National Park again.

"OK, you win!" I confessed, "Go on then, you choose where to go, and go there we shall – within reason!" he simply continued to tap a petulant finger on the same spot he had already highlighted. The immediate problem was how to get out of that urban jungle. There were no obvious roads that would take us straight up to where we wanted to go and it seemed that we'd have to do another stint of motorway, this time on the dreaded M6. My eye caught a place name that I felt was a worthy target, and Goosnargh is on the Southern edge of the Beacon Fell National Park. Couldn't be better, so with no further ado we set forth into the late afternoon sun in search of another inspiring place to camp, this time early enough and in weather that was good enough to really enjoy it. The M6 had other ideas about enjoyment however, for we joined it at just about the worst possible time of day, slap in the middle of the evening rush hour. We didn't even manage to get off the slip road before the huge tailback began and brake lights were all that could be seen for what looked like miles ahead.

We edged out into the slow river of metal, eased into the gaps until we had worked our way over to the outside lane. A big BMW motorcycle with panniers and top box glided past us, filtering between the stationary cars, so we tucked in behind it and began to ourselves filtered through the nightmare of congestion that is the modern British motorway in rush hour. I found my mind wandering as we threaded our way through: we had just spent a night under the stars, had awoken that morning to the wilds of Cumbria where no car, house or even much tarmac could be seen, had spent the whole of the morning threading our way from there up onto the heights of the Pennines and down into the Yorkshire Dales, hardly seeing any other vehicles for much of the time. We'd revelled in the uncluttered freedom of the ride. Then came Halifax and the disturbing events there, followed by urban congestion, motorway, more stop-start frustration in the middle and now this. I knew that the 'morrow would bring a lot more of the same, because there was no avoiding that huge sprawl, but right there, right then I simply yearned to be back in the green lanes and could feel a huge almost irrational impatience building in me as we followed the BMW at something less than twenty miles per hour past endless cars, vans and trucks.

The six miles that we had to cover on that blighted road seemed like sixty, but at last the sign appeared that heralded our exit, and with a huge relief I filtered back across and finally broke free up the slip road towards the promise of freedom once more. We ambled into the smaller lanes and got happily lost, until we stumbled upon a camp-site which looked absolutely ideal, nestling in a quiet wooded area between rolling hills, and with a river bending round its far end where a number of tents were already in place. It was a small site and peaceful as a result, but it still sported all the facilities that we were in dire need of – a toilet/shower block, launderette and a little shop. We bumped across the field to a spot by the river and enjoyed to the full the feeling of coming to rest after a long day's wandering. Chris wandered down to the river and I laid back on the warm grass, arms spread wide and thought lazily about how the rest of the day would go. Putting the kettle on seemed to be the way to start, followed by an unhurried erection of the tent. That done, I'd discuss with Chris whether to bother with cooking that night, or should we walk down to an inn which we saw not far along the road? We had surely earned a slap up feed and a pint or two of something this evening. Daisy would need some fettling too, as I realised guiltily that I hadn't paid much attention to her nuts bolts or fluids, and this I decided could be done before taking a shower, changing clothes and finally visiting shop and laundry.

Chris returned to interrupt my daydreaming, readily voted for the inn option when asked and also agreed on the rest of the plan. Tea, tent, Daisy, shower, shop, launderette and pub – in that order, and we had a couple of hours to do the first six, with all evening to enjoy the last one. A plan with no downsides, I declared, and stirred myself to dig out the stove and kettle. Fiddling with Daisy an hour later, it was pleasing to find almost nothing amiss. She had used some oil again, as usual, and her gearbox and rear wheel needed adjusting to take up a slight slackness in the primary and rear chains. A couple of nuts were slightly loose here and there and she was weeping some oil from that dynamo housing again, but apart from that I could find no real work for the spanners.

As I worked my way from front to rear, I realised that the vibration which had set in and so worried me on the way up the A1, had not got any worse. At least, I hadn't noticed it getting worse, which was tantamount to the same thing, and I started to wonder again what had caused it to appear in the first place. That led me to fretting for a few minutes about the meaning of it's sudden presence. No good could possibly come from that line of thinking, I told myself, and remembered instead the frightful bodge that had been carried out on the ignition in Coldstream. With all thoughts of mysterious vibrations banished in favour of a far more tangible and obvious thing to fret about, I removed the end-cap from the magneto and had a peer inside at the points. It all looked as it should, which was most gratifying, but with an almost morbid curiosity I gave the little screw that retains the points a prod. This was stupid because I immediately became deeply alarmed when the whole assembly wobbled before my eyes. Magneto points should not wobble because the little screw that I had just prodded is there to hold the entire assembly tight, in an exact relation with the cam ring which opens the points at something like the correct moment as the whole assembly spins round. I tried to tighten the little screw, but it was already tight and I couldn't see how the very critical arrangement could possibly be working properly – or at all in fact.

If it ain't broke, don't try to fix it. That old saying has served us classic motorcyclists well, and I had just fallen foul of it. I knew this was true, because having finished fiddling, I found that Daisy wouldn't start anymore and, after expending numerous kicks and even more curses, I was left sitting on a non functioning motorcycle which had been running perfectly before I had touched it. My mood was not helped by Chris, who having watched the entire sorry episode, pointed this out to me, rather unnecessarily I thought. I climbed off and reached for the magneto again, although I didn't really know what I was going to do. After taking out the spark plugs to ease turning the engine over I asked Chris to come and do the honours with the kick-start, so that I could watch what was happening to the points. And there it was; plain as day - as the points rotated and the little arm pushed against the cam, the whole assembly moved sideways from the pressure and the points were not opening at all. If they don't open and close, no spark is generated, no fuel is ignited and the engine won't run. I didn't understand how this state of affairs could suddenly be, or why my simple act of prodding the thing could have suddenly caused the problem.

Confused, I sat back and wondered out loud "How the bloody hell has she been running so well since Coldstream?" Chris grunted something that I suspected to be immensely unhelpful, but I was already descending into self-pity and ignored him as I continued my own rant "I mean, all those miles, all that vibration and the bloody thing's solid all the way, then breaks just because I touch it? – It doesn't make any sense!" and it *didn't* make sense, not at all. I reached for the screwdriver and set to work removing the contact breaker assembly and back-plate for a closer inspection, but with the bits spread out in my hand I could see nothing wrong at all. I tried fitting the thing on it's shaft and wobbling it and suddenly, in a blinding flash of enlightenment I could see the problem and I understood what had occurred. The back-plate, upon which the points are mounted, fits onto a taper. That wholly remarkable design is meant to keep objects such as sprockets, pinions and, as in this case, contact breaker assemblies firmly anchored to their rotating shafts. It is, in theory, impossible to achieve a wobbly assembly that is pressed onto a taper. That is only true of course, if the screw that is meant to push the thing firmly *onto* the taper is actually *doing* so.

With a little experimentation it became abundantly clear that Daisy's vital little retaining screw was doing no such thing because incredibly it was just a fraction too long, the net effect of which was that when screwed all the way up it was reaching the end of its threaded hole just a fraction before actually pressing the assembly onto its taper. In short, the screw was done up tight but was doing nothing at all in the holding things together stakes. I double checked my findings, and confirmed without any doubt that this was the case. I wondered how on earth the thing had managed to stay in one piece for the hundreds of miles that we had covered since stripping it apart on the Scottish border. That thought set me to wondering how it had stayed together *prior* to this trip, when we had gaily bowled around Cornwall, Norfolk, Wiltshire and the main leg up the A1 on this one a few days ago. Surely the same problem must have existed all along? It was a mystery and I could only surmise that by sheer luck the thing must have been pressed onto it's taper just hard enough to get a grip after being put on by hand, each time it had been assembled.

But as I sat there I had a flash of inspiration, suddenly seeing the simple cause of our problem. It was suddenly astoundingly obvious that there was a washer missing, which, if fitted, would allow the screw to do its job by taking up that fraction of length. I cursed silently. I must have dropped the thing into the long grass back there in Coldstream as I had struggled to fix it on that cold damp morning, after Daisy had made her unscheduled and unexpected stop. The discovery presented an immediate problem in that the missing washer was very small, meaning that it was highly unlikely that I had any that would fit. After a quick search of jacket pockets, I was amazed to actually find a few that looked like they might do the job. It was but a minute's work to match one to the screw, fit the assembly back together and note with satisfaction that everything was now good – the plate pushed down good and tight on it's taper, and the points now opened and closed as they should. I climbed back onto Daisy, tried a good kick, and was rewarded as she responded immediately with her throaty bark. "Waheey!" I exclaimed with relief, and even Chris looked suitably impressed as the engine settled down to a steady even tick-over. Time for the pub, we agreed.

We both overslept the next morning and by the time we had breakfast underway it was nearly half-past ten. It didn't seem to matter at all and we took our time, sitting by the river in the morning sunshine. The previous evening, we had managed to get a good shower and had got our laundry and shopping done and in fact, the rest of the evening had been passed very pleasantly in the local inn where, after dining on a superb home cooked meal, we had stayed for the duration of the session chatting to some of the locals. Our southern accents had been met with the inevitable questions about where we came from, what had brought us this far north and pretty soon the story of Daisy and the landmark was being told once again by Chris. By the time the last bell had rung, we had found ourselves amidst a happy group whom it had felt like we had known for years and I had ended up feeling guilty because I had not been allowed to buy a single drink all evening!

The icing on the cake of northern hospitality was the landlord's insistence on a "little nightcap lad, to keep t' cold out" and I had found a seemingly impossibly large brandy in my hand "On the house!" It had been an unsteady return to our tent, at least for me, and it had seemed a good idea to brew up some coffee to assist in warding off the ill effects of so much hospitality, so we had sat ourselves down with the stove outside the tent, listening to the river gurgling along close by, whilst we chatted idly about the day that had begun, what seemed to be an aeon ago. It had been well past midnight when we had finally turned in but I was extremely contented as I lay there in the dark waiting for sleep to overtake me. No surprise that we had awoken late then but it felt good to have no pressing tasks to do other than eat, pack up, fire Daisy up and hit the road. We took our time over the food before turning our attention to preparing for the day's ride.

Eventually everything was packed and loaded and we were ready to go, but right there, as we checked the maps and studied the route to our first target of the day, I realised that this was actually partly the reason I had taken so much time that morning - we were about to swap the idyllic surroundings of that campsite and its wonderful surroundings for a morning of choked motorway, urban sprawl and traffic. The M6 gave us no quarter, with a seemingly endless stream of fast moving trucks in the inside lanes and much faster traffic hurtling past them and it felt like we had just threaded our way onto a free-for-all racetrack. Daisy can hold her own at seventy plus, but amidst such fast moving, and more to the point *heavy* traffic I considered it stupid and potentially suicidal to try to compete. She is after all an old motorcycle, with a far higher percentage likelihood of a mechanical failure of some sort, the consequences of which, should they have occured in the middle of that rat race, were scary to say the least. With this in mind I tucked us in behind a coach travelling at fifty, kept as close as possible to the hard shoulder and simply let the speeding world go by. Easier said than done though, was that, because most of what sped past us was large and carried with it a vicious wind blast that continuously buffeted us. That made the going pretty hard work.

After a while, the built up areas of Wigan and St Helens sprawled either side of the snaking road and even more traffic came flying up the slip roads to our left to join the lemming-rush. It was a huge relief to be through it, after forty unpleasant miles and with a need to get our bearings we began to look for a suitable place to peel off onto smaller, hopefully less hectic roads. The A50 presented itself in due course, and with Knutsford on the signs, a name that rang a bell from earlier perusal of the maps, I pointed Daisy up the slip road. We had a quandary then, I thought, as we consulted the map. The two nearest landmarks on the remainder of that trek were equidistant from our current spot, one to the east and one to the west, effectively halting any Southern progress. It didn't seem to matter which way we went first because neither of them gave a particularly better route to the next batch further South and whichever one we chose first we'd still have to double back to get the other one. I estimated that they were about twenty miles apart, so in truth we'd have to go ten miles or so one way then the full twenty back on ourselves, whilst making no progress whatsoever down-country. I consoled myself that at least we were off the motorway and the weather was still good, so we could at least look forward to far better motorcycling if nothing else.

I checked my watch and did some mental calculations – it was just gone two o'clock and whichever way we went it would be twenty past by the time the first landmark was reached then another forty minutes or so back again. I got to thinking that if we went East first, then doubled-back, that would dump us fairly close to Chester, a town that I had visited a number of times in my working life but, as is often the way, never actually *seen* at all. I remembered being told that the place was well worth a wander round, being steeped in history and still possessing a lot of it to see. The way we had done things the previous day was spot on, camping early and taking our time, so why not do that again and visit Chester? I suggested the plan to Chris, and he seemed quite happy to go along with whatever I wanted, agreeing that the previous evening had certainly been amongst the better ones. So the plan was good, and we set off along the A50 towards Knutsford where we turned East and went in search of what I believed to be the Quarry Bank Mill Museum, which was confirmed on arrival at the map-point.

It was a big place was that. I had always harboured a rather dismal mental image of these huge cotton mills, right from from my schooldays, but to see the reality of the great oblong brick building with it's row upon row of high windows and the inevitable tall chimney, so representative of the times, was something else. We had time on our hands, so it seemed silly not to go in and have a look around and with that decided, we parked Daisy up as close as we could and headed off to the entrance to the museum. An hour later, which could have easily been stretched into two or three if we had more time, we came away shocked at the incredibly harsh life-style of the late eighteenth century mill worker, including the urchins or 'pauper children' and we had marvelled at what passed for technology and raw industrial power back in those ground-breaking years of our history. There were examples of an impressive beam engine as well as a working horizontal steam engine, coupled with various galleries with all manner of widgets and gadgets based around the general theme of water and steam power. We could easily have bimbled around in there for hours, but we both wanted to follow the plan of an early camp and a visit to Chester so we dragged ourselves reluctantly back outside at just after half past four.

We were soon back on the route we had come in on, going West once more, in search of the next landmark, which was a water mill just to the East of Runcorn if my research was to prove correct. Daisy burbled along underneath us, totally happy at the leisurely cruising speed of fifty, untroubled by vibrations, disintegrating points, sudden deflations or moisture of any kind. She was completely in her element right then, performing exactly the kind of duty that her makers had envisaged and delivering exactly that which was asked of her. She did it with such ease that I had no doubt whatsoever that if I chose to, we could keep that up all day long, into the night, and all the way home. We arrived at the mill, and I was still lost in these happy thoughts, thinking that although Daisy may well take such a demand in her stride, Chris and myself could probably not do the same.

It's strange, the way the mind can work, because with those thoughts came a sudden yearning for home. To be with Diane my wife, Chloe, the dog, the luxury of a long hot bath and a real bed. I was startled by the power of the feeling which had sprung up from nowhere, after all we had only been away for six days and although we'd certainly had some challenges, the past two had been a breeze really. Nothing had occurred that would stimulate an emotional pang for the homestead. I managed to shrug off the feeling, but as we threaded our way back onto the road that would take us to Chester I found myself looking forward to the call I'd make that evening, as I had every evening, to check in, let everyone know we were fine, where we were and what we'd been up to. I suddenly wondered if Chris felt the same and half shouting over my shoulder I asked him the question, surprised by the answer that yes, getting home was quite a priority in his mind, but typically for a teenager he confessed that that was because he was missing his computer and the dog! No mention of mum or sister and certainly not the bath. The conversation faltered somewhat, because we were riding a 'B' road at fifty or so and I had to keep my eyes front which made it hard to converse. We settled back into our own little worlds for the remainder of the run, which ended easily when we found a campsite just on the eastern edge of Chester itself. But I had been thinking about things in the past few miles, and had come to a decision that I wa sure Chris would go along with. I'd will wait until we'd set up camp and sorted out the evening meal before broaching it with him though.

We'd gone overboard with the food, I reckoned, as we sat watching three pots bubbling away in front of us. We had potatoes boiling in one, peas and carrots in another and a mass of mince in gravy in the third. All bought at the little shop on site and smelling lovely as I realised just how hungry I'd become through the afternoon. But my mind had wandered again to thoughts of home. I decided that it was as good a time as any to ask Chris what he thought of the plan that had formed during the last miles of the afternoon, and so I floated the idea while we waited.

"How do you fancy making a run for home tomorrow?" I asked "If we drop one of the landmarks, which I can get with Chloe when we do Wales, then I reckon we could do it". He looked at me owlishly, and I could see he liked the idea, but he posed a good question before answering. "It's too far to go isn't it? How many miles is it to home from here?" I had to confess that I hadn't actually got that far, but I was convinced it was achievable so I answered quickly "I don't know exactly, it's probably three hundred or so miles without the other landmark, but I tell you what we'll do – finish dinner, take a ride into Chester for a wander around, find a pub where we can sit down with the maps and we'll work it out and see what we reckon." That met with agreement and we set about dishing out the food without further discussion. By then, I was determined to make the run and I knew that Chris would take little persuading.

Evening found us ensconced in a marvellous pub right next to the Shropshire Union canal, me with a pint of Dogbolter and Chris with a coke, maps spread out in front of us. We had spent the past hour wandering around Chester's fascinating centre, with its ancient walls, castle and shopping rows from another age and then we had settled down to decide on our plan for the following morning. I explained to Chris that we were due to head SouthWest from there into

Shropshire and to the Welsh border, which would have taken quite a time due to the nature of the roads, but I could easily reschedule that for later when doing the Welsh leg with Chloe. The change would allow us to take a more direct route, starting with what would have been the second of our three remaining targets, some thirty miles to the South East. From there, we'd have to jink about a bit to travel a further thirty five miles east, because there was no direct route that we could identify. We'd need to go South to Stoke-on-Trent and then zigzag across to the Derbyshire Dales and finally, hopefully, rock up at the Carsington Reservoir, our final landmark of the foray. Things would be far more straightforward thereafter. With no more distractions, we'd be able to cut across the Northern boundary of Nottingham for forty miles or so until we hit Newark, turn South onto the A1 once more and commence the long, but pretty easy haul home.

"So how many miles is it?" Chris wanted to know, and I traced along the route, estimating the distance as I went until my finger finally came to rest on Ramsgate and home. The number in my head was three hundred and twenty, which is a lot to ask of Daisy, and indeed the pair of us, if we took into account the search for landmarks on the way, and in the latter stages, fatigue. I told him the news and got no reaction at first, as he sat and did some internal calculations of his own, but suddenly he came over all positive, exclaiming "That's about the same as we did the other day, you know, from Loch Ness to that fort." He barely paused before continuing "This'll be easier because there won't be all those mountains and little tiny roads" his last statement however, was startling "We could get home by lunch time!"

Whilst I was delighted to realise that he'd been paying more attention than I thought to our route if he knows the mileage we covered two days ago, I couldn't leave him thinking that this leg would be so much easier that we'd be home for lunch. There was absolutely no chance of us, let alone Daisy, achieving that and I had to tell him so. Not to be put off, he argued the point and we spent the remainder of the evening in Chester in good natured disagreement until I ended up explaining to him how to work out average speed, including stops and landmark-hunting wastage. We finally settled on an agreed average of thirty-five miles per hour, with all things considered, although Chris was convinced it worked out at forty-five. We divided the mileage by the lower number to get a projected time on the road of something like nine and a half hours barring mishaps, and agreed to get an early morning start at six o'clock or so and go for it. I telephoned Diane to tell her the good news and then, eager to get the night over and hit the road, we headed back to the campsite and turned in. I was just dozing off when a voice piped up from the darkness;"You're wrong about the average speed, we'll be home by lunch time!"

We woke up to the sound of drizzle hitting the tent, which was just about the last thing we want to hear. I Manoeuvred myself to the door and peered out at a grey, overcast sky and a very damp landscape, but there's little to be done about it so I closed the flap, reached for the kettle and got the morning brew underway. It was half past five by my watch, and we had agreed to skip the breakfast routine, in favour of getting early miles under our wheels, but not until after a cup of coffee to jumpstart the old metabolisms. By six o'clock we were shivering in the early chill air as we folded up the soggy tent, and shortly afterwards Daisy was warming up as I strapped the thing onto her panniers. We had donned our ridiculously inadequate waterproof trousers once more, and neither of us felt much like talking as we contemplated the soggy ride ahead. But we were going home, that was the main focus of my attention, and I could console myself that at least there would be a hot bath, a homecooked meal and a real bed at the other end of the long ride. I turned to Chris, who was just doing up his helmet,"Ready then?" I asked. "We're late," he said, but then a shy grin appeared as he added "We might be late for lunch now!"

Thirty miles or so to the East, we pulled up damply at our first and penultimate landmark of the day, Little Moreton Hall - quite the most wondrous piece of preserved history nestling damply in the Cheshire countryside. It was truly an amazing sight even in this Country of historic depth. A Tudor manor house, in all its timber glory, the classic, albeit now twisted white walled black-timbered structure bearing it's age superbly in ideal surroundings. What a grand place it must have been all those hundreds of years ago, as even by modern building standards it's fairly big. Clearly a seat of power was this, and I couldn't help wondering what tumultuous events had passed under its very eaves as the centuries slowly passed it by. We couldn't take Daisy close enough for the photograph, so we had to leave her in the car park and walk the rest of the way to have a wander around.

The devil in me struck again. I asked Chris if he could believe for one second that the place isn't haunted. He bit, as I knew he would and we were soon deep in discussion regarding the likely hauntees. A Cavalier, Roundhead, grey lady or a mad monk? Who knows? I suggested he looked the place up on the Internet once we got back home and I could see from his face that this was almost certainly something he'd do. In the mean time we had a challenge to complete and it was time to move on once more, on our zigzag course East to our next appointment in the Derbyshire Dales. The drizzle continued to hang in the air, and Daisy was covered with a film of moisture from the morning's miles, but our spirits were high as we began the countdown to home "Only two hundred and ninety to go!" I enthused, and with that we set off once more.

Just outside Stoke-on-Trent we had to turn almost back on ourselves towards Leek in order to avoid being sucked into the town itself and certain chaos on yet another town planner's one-way nightmare. But then we were forced to turn right back round and head for the place anyway when Daisy sputtered to a stop and I discovered that we'd out of petrol.

The reserve tap, I knew from experience, would only give us between five and ten miles, and it was unlikely that we'd find fuel on that little road so there was no choice. We were soon swallowed by the feared traffic system and although we found fuel easily I couldn't find my way back to where we wanted to be. Round and round we went, wasting about twenty minutes, before finally exiting nowhere near where I had wanted. I had hoped to stay much further North, which would have taken us to our next target via the edge of the Dales, but it was not to be. We stopped to check maps and get our bearings once more and after a few false starts we eventually managed to connect with the A50, which, with it's Southeasterly direction was not ideal but at least identifiable. It meant we were no longer lost.

Down to Sudbury we went, turned North just before the village and headed straight for the landmark, a reservoir. We had wasted a good three quarters of an hour and added probably ten miles to that leg as a result of my stupidity. Chris was a bit fractious about it when we finally arrived at Carsington Water some two hours and forty minutes after setting out that morning. It should have taken two hours maximum or, by Chris's more optimistic calculations an hour and forty minutes. But it was progress of a sort, still only nine o'clock in the morning, I reminded him, and we had all day to complete the remaining two hundred and fifty miles without any further distractions, always assuming that Daisy didn't throw any tantrums.

We pulled into the lay-by near Cambridge that evening, tired, but elated with the knowledge that we had put a huge dent in the landmark challenge. Chris probably thought that I had lost the plot completely as I killed the engine, leaned forwards, gave her tank a big pat and exclaimed "Good girl Daisy, well done!" But we both wanted to get home and wasted no more time. In short order we'd ditched our riding gear, opened up the rear door of the car, and loaded the bike and all our gear into the back. I divested myself of boots, changing into comfortable shoes, turned out the pockets of my jacket for the car keys and settled into the relative luxury of the Espace's soft driving seat. Inserting the key, I turned on the ignition and for a few seconds I gazed in confusion as nothing happened. No dash lights, no fan and no radio responded and as I turned the key further to crank the engine I was met with a dull 'click' and nothing else.

I looked at Chris, muttering "I don't believe this" tried again, but nothing. I stared stupidly at the dashboard as nothing continued to happen and Chris, understanding the situation now exclaimed "Oh just great!" I had to agree, and in sheer frustration that the car, of all things, could do this to us I banged the steering wheel and cursed. Of all the things I had imagined could happen to us on this trip, the car letting us down certainly wasn't one of them and I felt a sense of outrage that it should be the case. We had no choice but to call recovery, wait the hour it took them to show up and then feel foolish when, after the twenty seconds it took the driver to give us a jump start, he pointed in through the back window and suggested that I turn off the rear internal light that had obviously been left on, slowly draining the battery whilst we'd been away. I curse again at such stupidity, but ended up having a bit of a laugh with the guy as we confessed that we had in fact just toured a large part of Britain on the old clunker in the back only to have to call the cavalry to rescue our reasonably modern car. Even Chris couldn't help but see the funny side as the driver bade us farewell and left with a final flippant remark; "Next time mate, leave the bleedin' car at 'ome eh?"

It was nine thirty by the time we got home, but as I asked Chris to grab our jackets and helmets from the back whilst I manoeuvred Daisy out, my own voice was overpowered by a louder exclamation. Chloe exploded from the house and came charging towards us, battling for pole position with the Sheba the dog and yelling "Daaadeeee!" The pair arrived simultaneously, all but knocking me off my feet as Chloe flung her arms around my middle and Sheba scrabbled desperately to climb over her in an effort to lick my face. Chris eyed the whole ceremony with one of those teenage looks, but his facade was shattered when Sheba, abandoning the unequal struggle with Chloe launched herself at him instead, succeeding in planting the slobbery tongue right on the button as Chris tried in vain to fend off her attentions. With my arm around Chloe, who was holding on tight firing questions at me in rapid succession about the latest adventure, as well as demanding to know when the next one, involving her, would take place, I opened the garage door ready to put Daisy inside. I could see through to the rear garden and there was my wife, Diane, hanging out washing. It was a relief when she didn't come charging up the path and jump on me, settling for a good old fashioned hug in a more sedate fashion.

"You made it then? Amazing" she ribbed me "and now I suppose you're hungry? Well it's on but you've got time for a bath first". With that she detailed Chloe to go upstairs and start the thing running whilst I brought Daisy in. I suddenly realised just how hungry I was, but more to the point it was great to be home and yes, I reckoned I really could use a bath. Dinner was a lively affair, with Chris eagerly telling our war stories to his sister as his mum and I shared a conspiratorial look. He had really come out of himself since that first foray into Norfolk and it was fantastic to see him so animated, so enthusiastic. Only the previous year, he would almost certainly have struggled with the challenges we had just come through, would have been quite stressed by it all and certainly would never have been the lively centre of conversation that I saw before me that evening.

He told his stories in a jumble of mis-order, of the puncture, the points falling apart, the appalling weather we had endured early on. A look of awe and wonder settled on Chloe's face as he talked of the ride through the mountains, looking down on clouds and sleeping under the stars in Cumbria. He described the 'race' with the steam train and had the whole table in stitches as he told of the 'mad old woman' at the Shin Falls, even making a fair attempt to mimic that lady's Scottish accent and pronunciation. Chloe tried out the word 'fush' and then the phrase 'D'jyaseeum?' and before we knew it she and Chris were conversing in their own version of pseudo Scots. Suddenly Chris changed tack completely; "When can I get a bike?" he asked and Diane gave me *that* look again. Dinner lasted quite a long time that evening, and we were still sitting round the table an hour later. I was totally content, feeling deeply satisfied and even the ritual of clearing up afterwards, a task that I was left to do as the rest of the family retired to the living room, had the pleasant ring of home about it. I pottered about doing the mundane things but before too long my mind was drifting back out there on the road, in the mountains, valleys and dales and I realised that already, I was eager to go and do it all again, in Wales.

The next morning I had a long lay in, not even waking up until gone eleven and when I eventually came downstairs I found that Chris still hadn't surfaced either. Breakfast was a leisurely affair as I wallowed in the luxury of not having to do anything in particular, other than unpack Daisy. She had simply been parked and left fully loaded the previous evening, and rembering that I wandered out after a while and began to un-strap and remove the various bits that made up our touring kit. She looked like an old pack-mule festooned as she was with tank bag, throw-over panniers, tent and bedrolls. It all came off within a few minutes and she looked strangely bare without them, I thought. I sorted through the stuff, hanging the camping gear up in the garage, ferrying the laundry into the house, stowing bag and panniers away ready for next time and finally I could wheel Daisy out into the sunshine for a post campaign check-up.

The first obvious thing to do was give her a good wash, because she was looking very grubby, with a layer of light brown grime covering all of the forward facing surfaces, particularly those closer to the road. Most of her chrome was a dull grey colour. I noticed also that where the tank bag and panniers had rested, collecting water under them, there was a smudgy pink residue smeared all over, the remnants of her previously polished wax finish which had been eroded and emulsified. She was certainly not the gleaming machine upon which we had set out a week ago. A good wash transformed her but as I scrubbed and polished each area, including all the nooks and crannies I was building a little catalogue of things that had come loose or in some circumstances, come off altogether!. A session with the spanners seemed in order and while I was at it do some basic maintenance, an oil change and finally a good polish and wax would not go amiss. But first, realising that a certain degree of attention must be directed at other matters, I took Diane out for a late lunch!

I was surprised in the late afternoon, as I prepared to set about Daisy with the sockets. Chris had surfaced from his pit and had joined me in the garage, showing an interest for the first time in Daisy as a mechanical object rather than just the source of high adventure. I do believe he's getting the bug, I smiled to myself, as he asked what he could do to help and reached for the spanners. Happy to encourage him, I talked through the list of things we had to do and decided to give him the job of changing Daisy's oil. I explained what needed to be done and pointed to the nice fresh can of lubricant waiting to go in. As we worked and chatted we were soon back onto the subject of a bike of his own; how long must he wait, what can he get and how much would it cost? - and I had a sudden memory of myself at his age, helping my own father with his BSA A10, a deep longing growing within me to own a machine of my own but knowing that I'd have to wait several years.

I remembered clearly that it seemed an impossibly long wait and that I would have given anything in the world right then to own a motorcycle of my own. I remembered also the great day, shortly after my seventeenth birthday, when my father told me of a machine that was for sale for a reasonable sum, a suitable machine to learn on he suggested and a British one at that. I was in my first job at the time, earning the princely sum of thirty pounds a week and the bike would set me back some three months pay if I saved every penny after tax and keep were deducted, but my father had thought of that. He offered a loan of the two hundred pounds asking price. Within a week I was the proud owner of a 200cc Triumph Tiger Cub and had my first accident the very next day.

I found myself telling Chris the story as he struggled to complete the oil change. He had no previous mechanical experience and was not a natural hands-on type at all, so he struggled a bit with this, his first spannering job and quickly became frustrated. I had to calm him down as I tried to help, but it was uphill work so in an effort to explain that all new things take some mastering, I got us back onto the subject of the great moment when I sat astride that little cub for the first time all those years ago. I had no concept whatsoever of clutch, gears and a footbrake.The controls had felt alien to me as my father explained how things worked. Finally, with the engine running, first gear selected and the clutch held in, I had revved the engine far too much, let go of the clutchfar too quickly and we were suddenly off up the garden, completely out of control. I couldn't get my head round the controls, forgot to pull in the clutch, forgot about the brake pedal and rode in glorious disarray straight into the pear tree fifty feet up the garden. It was a complete shock and I had felt utterly stupid, but I was also drunk from my first experience of engine power mixed with adrenalin. As i picked myself, and the bike up with trembling hands there was only one thought in my mind; "Wow!" I was hooked, plain and simple, and the only thing to do was get right back on and try again, as many times as it took, until I had mastered the basics and would dare to venture out onto the roads.

The story did the trick with Chris and we began comparing the ease with which I had been able to take up bikes with the much harder and more restricted task presented to young riders nowadays. For me it had been insanely easy, for the law back then was far more liberal and prospective young riders could choose anything under 250cc, slap on 'L' plates, get insured with relative ease and launch themselves into an unsuspecting world with no formal training whatsoever. They could ride like that as long as they liked with no pressure to take the comparatively simple test at all. Life used to be so simple. Chris stuck around for the duration of the afternoon's tasks, but I couldn't help but notice that he didn't reach for any more spanners once the oil had been changed. But he certainly was keen to talk about bikes, biking, camping and adventure.

As I worked, we talked some more. I suggested he might consider the merits of a BSA Bantam for his first bike and he went quite quiet for a while but when he next piped up, I was amused to discover that his imagination had been working overtime.He suddenly, and enthusiastically stated that once he was seventeen, he'd get the bike, pass the test, and then he would ride it to Le Mans just like we had done on Daisy. A bit ambitious was that, I suggested, but he clearly had the wanderlust and dismissed my observation with the comment "It'll just take longer is all!" He went quiet again, and I just knew that he was suffering that same deep yearning that I had suffered all those years ago and just like I did he was probably thinking that his seventeenth birthday was an impossibly long way away. After a while, he wandered off into the house and I felt truly sorry for the lad. Still, when you wait that long for something, it's all the more satisfying when you finally get it, although I found myself wondering what the current going rate for a Bantam was, and with Christmas only a few months away, I might just have a word with the management (Diane) before the summer's out.

In the mean time, I reviewed the progress on Daisy's list. She had lost a bolt from the right hand exhaust, a nut from her front number plate, a nut from the speedometer mounting, one from her chain-guard and finally the retaining screw had gone from the dynamo cap. All of these had now been replaced, pausing only to marvel at the fact that the dynamo cap had actually stayed in place. I had checked all other mountings and found a few loose, including of course the big horn. Her oil had been changed for fresh new gloop; I had adjusted her tappets and even checked and adjusted her tyre pressures. Time for a test ride in the late afternoon sun then, and I went indoors to retrieve my jacket and report to she who commands that I won't be long. Both Chris and Chloe declined the offer of a ride, having just attached a lead to the dog in order to head for the local park.

Two immediate things impressed themselves on me as I pulled away and accelerated up the road. Firstly, after a week of all day riding two-up and loaded for camping, the now unburdened Daisy felt incredibly light and very lively, but secondly my afternoon's efforts at servicing and maintenance, far from making her all tickety-boo, appeared to have done something alarming at the back end. Within fifty yards I had pulled over urgently to investigate the harsh clanking noise that had sprung up from nowhere and was ringing out with every bump. Also, I couldn't help but notice that she felt remarkably skittish at the back there as well. I crouched down and inspected her rear section, the mudguard stays, the wheel mountings, chain guard and the chain itself but I could see nothing wrong and nothing seemed to be loose or misplaced. Strange, had I imagined it? No, definitely not. I sat astride her, wobbled my backside from side to side and bounced up and down a bit but to no avail. Stranger still, and definitely worrying I thought, as I pulled on my gloves again, selected first gear and pulled away once more, gently this time and with my head cocked, listening for any untoward noises.

There it was again, a harsh metallic clonk coupled with a definite feeling that all was not well back there. Without further ado, I executed a 'U' turn and rode slowly back to the house, ears straining and head swivelling from side to side as I tried look down and backwards for a glimpse of anything doing something interesting. Outside the house once more I parked by the curb and started a manic inspection of the rear end, but there was nothing to see, the cause of the startling noise and the very disconcerting skittishness remained a complete mystery. I pulled things, pushed bits and generally prodded around. I spun the wheel, which taunted me as it spun silently and steadily on it's bearings, refusing to do anything nasty and so I gripped the thing and heaved from side to side but it was solid. I climbed back on, bounced around and generally shook the poor bike all over the place but worrying noises continue not to happen - nothing. I considered that I must be going mad and I decided that what I should do is go indoors for a cup of tea and a bit of a fret, but half way up the drive I had a sudden thought which was startlingly, obviously the answer and would have been plain to anyone other than me in idiot mode. Something was loose in the toolbox! I did a sharp about turn and opened the thing with a coin, anticipating the sight of a loose spanner or screwdriver and that only added to the sense that I was going mad because the thing was empty. Back to plan 'A' then, I went indoors and made tea, retiring to the sun lounge where I did indeed fret about phantom noises and more specifically, my total inability to identify the probably obvious source. Diane didn't help much as she popped her head through the door and teased me "broken it then have we?" She asks unkindly.

The kids arrived back from the park to find me sat cross-legged next to Daisy and in a fractious mood. I had been up and down the road numerous times by then, clanking and skitting each time but failing miserably to make any progress in identifying the cause. To help matters along, my imagination had furnished me with various nightmare scenarios involving the inner gubbins of the dread sprung hub and I was, not to put too fine a point on things, officially worried. I was also struggling to understand the apparent suddenness of the symptoms and just to satisfy myself that I hadn't imagined it I grilled Chris about the final long ride yesterday. Had he noticed a noise, or anything like that? He had not.

"Right" I declared, "I need your help with this!" He eyed me suspiciously, looked at Daisy and then back at me, confusion on his face as he blurted, "I don't know what's wrong! How would I know what's wrong?" I had to quickly explain; "I didn't say you did, but you can help by riding with me and seeing if you can pinpoint where the noise is coming from. I can't do that and ride at the same time, but you probably can" He looked appalled at the suggestion, rapidly backing away and forcefully declaring "I'm not going on that if it's broken! It's dangerous!" and just in case I tried to persuade him, he turned on his heel and strode off up the drive. Conversation over it seemed. "Well thanks a lot mate!" I shouted after him, but he was already in the porch and not about to come back for more.

"Bloody marvellous", I raged and decided that he really can't be allowed to get away with that attitude, not after all we've just been through, and certainly not if he had aspirations to become a classic motorcyclist himself. I pursued him into the house where I made that feeling known and we were just getting into a lively argument when Chloe piped up in the middle with "I'll go Dad" and I realised that there was no mileage in continuing to argue with Chris, even though I was deeply disappointed with his attitude. I grabbed Chloe by the hand, exclaiming "Marvellous, thanks Chloe" and we headed straight out to Daisy leaving Chris, hopefully, feeling a little bit ashamed. I had second thoughts almost immediately however. Perhaps he had a point and in fact I'm being a bit gung-ho regarding the safety of what I'm proposing. What if it was something nasty? Something that *was* about to break imminently? Chris was right to be concerned, particularly if the problem turned out to be inside that hub. Was I being irrational and, when all's said and done a tad reckless? I was gripped with indecision suddenly but Chloe had no inhibitions

"What do I have to do again?" she asked, doing up the strap on her helmet and pulling on gloves. I made my mind up there and then to take it very slowly and tell Chloe to hold on tight, but I simply had to find out what's making that bloody noise! Up the road we went, slowly at first and I was amazed to note that both noise and the skittishness had vanished. We stopped and I asked Chloe if she had heard any noises at all. She hadn't apparently so I turned us around to go back down the road, a little faster this time. No noises, and no skits. Unbelievable. "We'll go a bit further" I declared, "You keep you ears skinned and yell the minute you hear anything OK?" and with that we set off again. A ten-mile round trip later, I was thoroughly confused by Daisy's refusal to misbehave in any way. No dread clanks, no skits and in fact she felt wonderful in every way. Back at home I put her away somewhat bemused, and I began to fret about the now mysteriously absent symptoms of doom. I had definitely not imagined it. Something had been sounding decidedly horrible, coupled with a distinctly physical change to her feel on the road, which was enough to scare any motorcyclist.

With another long adventure awaiting us, for which Chloe would occupy the pillion, I couldn't shake the niggling worry that imminent disaster was waiting to strike. I discussed my fears that evening with Diane and both kids, and the general consensus was that we should not embark on the Welsh trip until I could satisfy myself that there was definitely nothing wrong. Chris had not changed his earlier stance at all, and if anything was even more adamant that he was not going back on the bike until we could be absolutely sure. I was left with no real choice but to investigate further, but that meant removing the rear wheel again and investigating the scary innards of the hub. So be it, I assured everyone that I'd set about the job first thing the next day and Chris offered assistance – after all, he'd had experience of that back wheel and was happy to perform the role of chief mudguard remover once again.

Early morning found me wheeling Daisy out for another ride around before I did battle with the hub. The noise was back with a vengeance and I suddenly realised that it was only occurring when there was no load on the back. I returnede and press-ganged Chloe into a test ride once more and sure enough it was gone again. Off she got, I rode twenty yards without her and there it was again. Back home I puzzled over this strange phenomenon but could not for the life of me fathom it out. It simply had to be something to do with the rudimentary suspension in the hub, so I headed indoors to peruse the original manual and gaze in wonder and fear at the exploded diagram of the nightmare thing. I read the description of servicing, with it's dire warnings that on no account should the thing be tampered with unless the tamperer is:

a) Properly equipped with the special Triumph jig for the job and

b) Mildly insane.

Clearly, this was no job for the faint hearted! A bit of research followed, by way of telephoning a couple of highly knowledgeable suppliers and the message was clear: unless I wished to end my life prematurely or risk serious injury, on no account should I attempt to dismantle the insides of a sprung-hub! I listened in awe to one fellow who told the story of a chap who had decided to ignore such good advice, going ahead to pull his own hub apart in his shed. The resultant injuries had left him in hospital for several weeks with a broken jaw and when he finally came home he had been amazed to find a hole in his shed roof measuring nearly a foot across, presumably the exit point of the main spring. That was enough for me, and I had to accept that there were only three options available to me. Send the wheel off to an appropriately equipped expert, find another wheel in good order or find a rigid wheel without the hub design (Daisy's original specification in 1948 was actually a rigid wheel, with the sprung hub being an 'option' for an extra few quid). None of these options would be cheap. More to the point, none of them would be *quick*.

Thoroughly depressed, but realising that action was the only way forward if we were to have any hope of completing the challenge with Daisy, I spent the following morning making more calls and reached an agreement with one of the dealers that if I send or take the wheel to him he'd at least give me a free estimate for repairs. In the mean time, there was an auto jumble coming up that very weekend and I could go to that in the hope of finding something there, even if it was unlikely. I returned to the garage to set about getting the wheel out and decided that I'd take the thing down to Hastings for the estimate straight away, but as I slotted the large spanner onto the first of the big wheel nuts I stopped absolutely dead in my tracks. I had just noticed something that was so ridiculously obvious that at first I thought I must be mistaken. I stared at the thing in bewildered incomprehension for a minute, and yes, there was no doubt at all. The sprung centre of the hub was upside-down! I grabbed hold of the rear mudguard and tried to bounce the back end to check my suspicions, and it was so blatantly obvious that I almost laughed out loud at the ridiculous reality.

The whole concept of the sprung hub is to mount the wheel spindle between two mighty springs, with the whole lot locked in place within a steel spring box. The spindle is effectively offset to allow the wheel to move against the stronger spring over bumps, providing an effective two inches or so of movement. This is all fine and dandy, but relies on the spindle being at the top of the slot, and mine was clearly at the bottom, effectively preventing any wheel movement and obviously causing some kind of jarring reaction with every bump. That certainly explained the clank, and with the wheel effectively rigid as it stood it would also explain the skittishness. Surely the designers would have thought of this and made it impossible to fit incorrectly? Apparently not.

Eager to pull the thing off and get the centre hub inverted, I summoned Chris to help and in short order we had discovered that there was a design feature that supposedly prevented incorrect insertion of the wheel.It was so obscure and vague that it was entirely easy to miss and we discovered that with a bit of brute force it would go in upside down. Whilst struggling in that field near Newcastle, I had obviously failed to notice the slight offset of the locating arm and had clearly forced it incorrectly into the already worn slot without noticing my error. Now that we had it the right way round, it positively glided into position with no resistance at all and I felt utterly stupid to have not noticed the arrangement before. I grasped the mudguard once more, bounced up and down, and glory be we had suspension, of a sort, once more. Now for the real acid test, I hurried indoors to retrieve jacket, helmet and gloves, wheeled Daisy once more to the road for yet another test ride and I nearly cheered out loud as she smoothly ate up the bumps in wonderful silence. The back end was once again behaving itself and I returned home with a mixture of delight and relief that the obscure problem has been overcome without either a lengthy wait or just as importantly the need for startling expenditure.

I could now get right back on with planning the final stages of our campaign, which only that morning had been looking in serious jeopardy. At dinner, I couldn't suppress my rediscovered happiness and monopolised the conversation, raving about the design of that hub, my own stupidity, the fears I had suffered that our landmark challenge had hit the rocks, the subsequent delight that it hadn't and I realised, as I babbled away, that the whole thing had become bizarrely important to me. I was more determined than ever that we should win that trophy and after we'd cleared away the plates, I spread the maps out once more to take a squint at Wales. Chloe joined me eagerly and we were soon happily lost in deep contemplation of what should, we hoped, prove to be our final, successful foray.

10. The World Strikes Back!

The plan emerged and it seemed that fate had thrown the dice on our behalf and come up with a double six. The landmarks that remained are in fact arrayed in beautifully logical order from the Cambridge base that had become so familiar. From there we can see a clear anti-clockwise route that starts at Santa Pod, from where we'd loop to the North of Birmingham, up to Chester once more, circumnavigate Wales in a big loop, to arrive eight hundred miles later at the very last target, Draycote Water, not fifty miles from our start point. The large natural reservoir would be the final triumphant stop and our fiftieth landmark, so we circled it several times in thick red marker.

But an awkward moment beckoned, something I had not really considered at any point when I had coerced the kids into joining me on the adventure. It was simply that the great moment of completion could only be shared by one of them, Chloe as it turns out, and plainly Chris was feeling left out because I come to realise that he'd been hanging around on the periphery of this final evening of planning, but hadn't joined in or said a word. He was looking a bit sullen and and a bit upset. He'd been involved in more of the actual riding, and had endured some pretty tough conditions along the way, but he wouldn't be there at the finish to share the moment. It was a bit of an emotional moment for me as I locked eyes with him for a fleeting second, the unsaid disappointment was communicated silently before he looked away quickly and exited towards his room. Chloe stares after him and asked "What's up with Chris?" but before I could formulate an answer she'd clicked. "Oh" she added, which just about said it all. We stared glumly at the route which we had been discussing with such enthusiasm just moments before, as I tried to think how to handle the situation, but no inspiration came so I decided to leave it be for the moment. I'd see if his mother could come up with any bright ideas, but right then it was time to call it a night.

Diane's suggestion was that I should try to include Chris by way of telling him that we couldn't celebrate the great moment without him, and therefore he would need to be waiting near the telephone at around the right time on the great day, when he'd find that there is something special in the 'fridge, such as a bottle of beer, a rare treat indeed.He could use that as a toast to our success. Of course, that would require that we stay in touch so that he could track our progress and by doing that we'd be able to remind him of his own involvement and allow him to be at least loosely part of the final foray. I'd have to sell this whole idea to him carefully, but it seemed to be an almost perfect answer to an otherwise unsatisfactory situation. I slept on it and the next morning the idea was every bit as good, although I realised that at the hormone-bouncing age of fourteen, Chris would probably still see it as a less than satisfactory conclusion. All such thoughts were pushed to the back of my mind by the intrusion of the telephone however and within a few short minutes everything had changed.

The real world had just woken up, eyed me lazily, found me wanting and decided to intrude on my recently acquired utopian lifestyle with a sudden opportunity to get stressed, be put upon and generally have no fun whatsoever. An issue had arisen within the business, involving one of the sites for which I had promised I would always be available when I stepped back from my Director's role. Steve needed me back on the case. It was urgent, would require my complete and immediate dedication and would take me eight thousand miles away from home before it was done. Would I please attend the offices the next day for a full briefing? Fate it seemed, had decided to take her dice back and call 'foul' and suddenly my dream of completing the landmark was once again under serious threat.

The next morning found me sitting in my old office suffering an overwhelming feeling of déjà vu and cursing at the unbelievable timing of the project that had just landed unavoidably in my lap. When I had stepped back from the Company, I had promised to maintain involvement and be available for any serious issues or projects involving two of the firm's long standing customers. One in particular had been so completely 'my baby' over the years that it was almost impossible for me not to be intricately involved in anything that should arise. The site that now required me to honour this promise was in the Falkland Islands in the South Atlantic, where any project timing was dictated by the seasons, not to mention the fact that preparation of equipment, supplies and logistics had to take place a full six weeks before the actual job (it takes that long to ship the stuff down there). Of course as usual everything had been left to the last minute which meant that there was a blind panic going on that was suddenly, exclusively mine. It was no wonder I was feeling put upon!

I desperately took stock of my options, but it seemed that whatever way I looked at it there weren't any that would allow me to complete the challenge during what little remained of the summer holiday. I cursed again at the unfairness of life, particularly the ironic fact that I had walked away from my career for exactly this reason - it was intruding unacceptably on my family life. How on earth could I tell Chris and Chloe that everything we had set out to achieve on the challenge was now dashed by the very pressures of business that had spawned the whole thing to start with?

The next few days whistled by as I found myself right back in the cut and thrust that is modern business, and reluctantly I had to be fully focused on my new project. By the end of the week however, I had the shape of the thing, had identified the exact requirements and knew the schedule to which I must work. I had deliberately not mentioned to the kids the potential disruption this project could bring, and now that I knew what was required of me a glimmer of hope had emerged from the chaos.

There were two full weeks of the summer holiday left, and I had estimated that Chloe and I could complete the last leg of the challenge comfortably in three days. Most of the next week would be taken up with specification and ordering of computers, software and peripherals for the Falklands, followed by the completion of the full project plan and finally the internal paperwork that is the bane of every office nowadays. Crucially, I would then have a whole week free whilst awaiting delivery of all the project components, after which I would be fully occupied with the preparations for the trip to the Falklands. It was clear then, that if Chloe was to join me on the last foray, it would have to be in that second week, just before school started again. I'd just have to hope that Daisy didn't decide to do anything interesting to us that would prevent completion, and that got me thinking.

First, I made a mental note to make sure we were properly equipped to deal with a puncture next time and that led me to remember that I also needed to get a new set of points, rather urgently! There are times when I can be astoundingly idiotic, I chided myself, as I realised that during the so-called complete check over and maintenance I had performed after the Scottish leg, I had utterly failed to even look at that bodge repair to the magneto. The thing must have been all but falling apart by then and it would be foolish indeed to set off on another eight hundred mile trek without replacing it. It was too late to do anything right at that moment, being past five thirty on a Friday evening, so I scribbled a note for myself for the next week and placed it squarely in the middle of the desk. As I got up to go home, I stopped and wrote 'urgent' in big letters at the top just in case.

A free weekend at home then, but I couldn't relax because I had yet to get any of our photographs developed and of course without them we would have no claim to the challenge at all. For some reason I had been feeling increasingly paranoid about that. What if the cameras had been shaken about too much, or worse, got too wet and the precious film ruined? It was unthinkable, but I couldn't shake the growing doubt that perhaps the cheap disposable units I had used were not the best of ideas. I had been sensible enough to carry two and record the Landmarks on both, but until I was actually in possession of the final prints from at least one of them there was much to worry about. Selecting the primary three cameras containing the vital evidence then, I headed off on Daisy to the local supermarket where there was a fast print shop, handed them over to an attendant who didn't look a day over twelve and therefore worried me even more, collected my one hour service receipt and then wandered off to wait anxiously for the results.

I managed to find a small cafeteria to sit in whilst I sipped possibly the most foul cup of coffee I'd ever experienced and I festered nervously as I convinced myself that at least one of the cameras would turn out to be useless and all our efforts will have been in vain. Of course, I told myself, the one that was most likely to have been ruined would be the one from the Scottish leg, and with no chance whatsoever of a repeat trip if necessary, that would sound the death-knell of our attempt at the trophy. The hour seemed to drag past at half speed, but eventually it was time and I returned to the print shop with butterflies in my stomach. I nearly died on the spot when the acne'd young man got the three packages but rather than just handing them over, he opened one, frowned, stated "One of your cameras had water in it I'm afraid" and pulled out a print to show me the worst.

My heart gave a flutter, but then relief flooded through me because the print he was showing me was actually a clear photograph of Daisy in Scotland. There was a horrible pink smudge across the top left corner, which effectively ruined the thing in terms of being a happy holiday snap, but for my purposes it was absolutely fine. I took the package and riffed through the rest and although nearly all of the prints had at least a small pink smudge along the top somewhere, they all showed what they needed to show. I was massively relieved. The attendant eyed me with deep incomprehension as I looked at him with a huge grin and assured him that these were just fine. Abso-bloody-lutely marvellous in fact!

Delight to deep concern in two minutes. That is what happened as I hurried from the supermarket only to find a police officer standing next to Daisy, clearly waiting for her owner and looking distinctly un-amused. I had the usual quick pang of worry as I approached, but then I assured myself that this was stupid for there was nothing, surely, that can put me on the wrong side of the law? She was MoT'd, taxed, insured and in good fettle, but the the look on the constable's face seemed to suggest a different story. Oh Gawd. I approached nervously and having established without doubt that I was the guilty party the officer addressed me. "Is this your motorcycle then Sir?" Here we go then, I was about to find out what heinous crime I had unwittingly committed and experience told me to adopt a polite and respectful demeanour in my responses "Yes she is" pause, then "Isn't she pretty?"

My tormentor studied me for a few seconds before turning to Daisy with exaggerated slowness, inspecting the clearly disgraceful object in front of him. "That's as well may be Sir, but right now I would suggest to you that it's only 'pretty' as in 'pretty dangerous!" he paused, switched his gaze back to me and added "Do you know why it's 'pretty dangerous' Sir?" Some coppers just have a knack of getting right up my hooter, and this was one of them. I have often wondered if they have extra evening classes at training college on patronising sarcasm and how to deliver it. I was not about to rise to the bait, but neither was I going to take it lying down. "Well, obviously I don't because I wouldn't be riding it if I did now would I?" was the best I could come with. I had no idea what it was that had given him cause to pull me, and I suspected that he knew it. We studied each other for a moment and then, adopting the air of a headmaster addressing a particularly errant scamp of a pupil, he crouched down, indicated that I should join him, stabbed a finger towards at Daisy's rear tyre and raised an eyebrow in anticipation of my response.

"Bloody hell" is what sprang to mind, and in fact is what I exclaimed, as I could now clearly see the two inch ragged tear in the sidewall and the strangely shredded bald patch in the tread adjacent to it. There was no denying it; no excuse for it and indeed it did look in a dangerous state. Clearly I was nicked, as they say. The rozzer stood up and we went through the usual rigmarole of license, insurance, MOT the latter two of which he handed back after a cursory inspection before instructing me to stay where I was as he headed purposefully to his car with the license. He talked for a minute or so into the radio, then returned and handed it back. He sighed, studied me for a moment, and then started to speak. "We seem to have little problem here don't we?" he pointed at the bike and raised that eyebrow again. I decided that a non-committal shrug was the best response. I couldn't help noticing that the 'Sir' was no longer part of his repartee, either. He was holding all the cards and he knew it, I was just going to have to put up with his razor sharp wit while I waited for him to spell it out. "Right, I'm going to talk for a minute and you are going to listen carefully, agreed?" we looked at each other, but I was careful to try and look neutral because this was beginning to sound promising. What came next was almost unbearable and clearly set out the way the interview was about to go. "The answer I was looking for there was 'Yes officer' - do you see where I'm coming from?" at that moment I wanted to poke him in the eye, the one with the raised eyebrow, but I found myself mumbling "Yes officer" whilst thinking 'Insufferable git'.

He relaxed, having established control of things, and launched into a little speech about road safety, the important role that a good set of tyres, for example, might play in achieving it and in conclusion he spelled out what he expected me to now do. "You take this motorcycle straight home, slowly, and before it sees the road again you will replace the tyre." He pauses and the eyebrow does it's party piece again, "Yes officer" he suggests patiently. "Yes officer" I parroted. "Good, and in future you will be sure to check the condition of those tyres regularly won't you? - Say 'yes officer' once more". He'd had his fun and I had played my part, so with that he turned on his heel and headed for his car, leaving me steaming gently behind him. As he pulled away, he slowed down and wound down his window, and I steeled myself for one more intensely annoying comment. But with a genuine tone in his voice he said, "One thing Sir, I do have to agree she is *very* pretty!"

At home I dumped the photographs in the dining room and headed straight back out to the garage to inspect that tyre. As I stared once more at the angry welt in its surface I wondered how on earth I had missed it when we were mucking about with the wheel recently. It was undeniably knackered which was just about the last thing I needed on top of the other distractions and it also meant that the sodding back wheel would have to come off *again*. I was initially at a complete loss as to how this could have happened but thinking back over the events of the Challenge to date I realised that there had been a number of incidents that could have caused the damage. There was that horrible sliding skid at the edge of the river in Devon, the puncture in Newcastle of course and then the out of control descent of that scary drop on the Hardknott pass. I'd never know which one of those hairy experiences had delivered the fatal wound and it wouldn't change anything anyway, so I focused my attention, got right down to removing the rear wheel yet again and then set to with the tyre levers for the second time in three weeks. I left Daisy resting on her rear stand, so useful at times like that, threw the old tyre into the corner and headed back indoors reminding myself that there was now an extra item to be sourced urgently before we could set out on what was trying its hardest to be an ever more elusive last leg.

The week didn't start well, with complications and difficulties on the Falklands project distracting me to the point that by Tuesday evening I had still completely failed to source or order anything for Daisy and only realised that when I rediscovered the note to myself buried under some other papers that had been given to me first thing on the Monday. Someone had also pulled a flanker, for I had inexplicably found myself dealing with another project alongside the Falklands one, on the grounds that it required kit ordering from the same suppliers that I was already dealing with as well as apparently benefiting from my experience in its planning. From my perspective it had all gone horribly wrong all of a sudden. My break from that business, working as a free agent, my new life-style, the challenge - everything. I was utterly hacked off and as I slumped in my chair, staring at the note, cursing inwardly, I realised that drastic action was required if I was to get things back on track again and prevent the inevitable black-hole type attraction that was sucking me right back into the old ways.

Over my dead body. I decided it had to stop right there. I scooped up the additional, non-Falklands paperwork that had found it's way onto my desk (and the irony that it was this stuff that had obscured my note had not escaped me) and on my way out to go home I shoved it back under the door from whence it came. I would deal with the questions later, the word 'no' would be prevalent in my answers and Daisy and her needs would take priority over everything else. I felt better already. The evening was spent finalising the route plan for the Welsh leg the following week, with Chloe and Chris joining in. I had sat Chris down before starting, in order to unveil his mum's plan for the big moment of completion, showing him the bottle of Newcastle Ale reserved for him in the 'fridge and promising that we'd be reporting in so that he could track our progress. On arrival at the final Landmark, we'd 'phone in and he could crack the bottle and share the moment with us. It wouldn't be right otherwise, I assured him and to my relief he accepted that philosophically and was soon burbling of his own involvement, reminiscing about some of the high points and low points, comparing experiences with Chloe and enthusiastically describing for her the splendour of motorcycling through mountains, a pleasure she was yet to experience, but one that is waiting for her in the Snowdonia National Park.

We find it on the map and Chloe traced her finger from our start point, wanting to know how far we'd get on day one, how long it would take from our camp to Snowdonia on day two, how long we'd be in the mountain region and the time flew by as we discussed it all with enthusiasm. By bed time I was well on the way to being fully content once more, happy in the knowledge that we were getting back on track and all I had to do was make some calls the next morning, secure Daisy's vital bits, get them, fit them and head off into yet another glorious bimble, free of pressures, deadlines, schedules and most importantly responsibilities. This was how it was going to be, there was no possibility of it being any other way and for once in my life, things really would go exactly as planned. By lunchtime the next day I have indeed sourced and ordered Daisy's bits, said 'no' to a whole host of wheedling persuasion with regard to the additional project, dealt with the few remaining issues that had arisen with the Falklands, and completed most of the paperwork expected of me. I was determined that Friday would find me waiting at home for the deliveries, the immediate fitting of which would be my only priority of the day and that we would be ready for our final foray starting Sunday.

On the day, I prepared our computer strip maps and then topped up supplies such as coffee, tea and sugar whilst I waited for the courier. Chloe had the wanderlust on her and buzzed around helping, her excitement showing as we packed the maps into their place in the see-through panel on the tank bag. She talked incessantly about the adventure to come, the mountains, Wales and the Welsh and this led her to another thread; "Do they speak English?" she asked. I never got to answer that one because at that moment the arrival of Daisy's tyre was announced by the dog exploding into a frenzy at the front door in her normal manic postman routine. Only the tyre had arrived though, there were no points for her magneto - yet. At least I could get her ready to roll and after a relatively painless fitting of the new rubber, taking care that time to get the sprung hub the right way up, she was all set and waiting to be loaded up for wild adventures in the valleys. Chloe helped with the familiar routine and we couldn't help but notice that the dog had cottoned on as well, as it slunk around us looking sorry for itself, ears down and tail low. She had spent almost the entire week in the garage while Chris and I were touring Scotland, her nose pressed to the crack where the doors meet. According to the girls nothing could keep her in the house and it had even taken some considerable coaxing to get her to come for her dinner. Clearly we are about to abandon her again, and she was not at all happy about it.

Saturday evening, Chloe had happily gone off to bed before her usual time ready for an early start, an unheard of event in any other circumstances. She had left me fretting however, because the new points for Daisy's magneto, when they had finally arrived earlier in the day, didn't fit. More buffoonery on my part, it must be said, because when ordering the things I had neglected to tell the supplier that Daisy's magneto was not the Lucas item that one normally associates with Triumphs of this era, but the less common BTH. I believe that this was an option just like the sprung hub at the time Daisy rolled out of the factory and I had overlooked the necessity to inform the guy. Strictly speaking I should do something about it, but I was lost as to what exactly I *could* do. The last time I had fiddled with the things I had only managed to stop them working at all but on the other hand would they last another eight hundred miles? I decided to leave well alone and trusted the great God of Triumph sparkery-things to look after us.

Time for bed then, pausing only to trip over the dog, who had taken to following me around all day, absolutely everywhere, inches from my heels, lest I suddenly disappear for another week and leave her to that lonely vigil in the garage once more. I sat and took her head in my hands, rubbed her ears and talked softly to her, but I couldn't get the usual waggy-tailed response and I could see that she was deeply unhappy – she just knew, and there was no consoling her. Perhaps when I phoned in to give Chris our progress reports, I'd get him to hold the telephone to Sheba's ear so I could talk to her. That way she'd at least know we were still around, somewhere. I stopped that thought dead in its tracks as I headed for bed – what on earth was I thinking about? Surely that way lies madness – attempting a meaningful conversation with a dog over the telephone!

11. Wales, Sheep and More Trouble with Landmarks

I was yanked awake by the alarm clock at six o'clock and stumbled downstairs to find Chloe already up, dressed and eager for the off. I used her enthusiasm to leave as a bargaining chip to con coffee out of her, and once that had helped to kick-start my heart I agreed that it was time to go. This was it then, we were on the road for the final leg and we were blessed with a glorious sunrise as we thread our way through the sleepy outskirts of Ramsgate and hit the open road towards Cambridge. We were giggling like school kids (which was fine for Chloe, she was one after all) because Chloe had coined a little saying adapted from the Star Trek series and had just announced, in an attempt to mimic the voice-over that accompanies the beginning of each episode. "Wales," she said "The Final Frontier" and continues to rattle out a version of the rest suggesting that Daisy was about to boldly go where no 'old heap' had gone before. It was silly stuff, but had us sniggering all the same as I accepted the well meaning insult to Daisy and interrupted her with the odd "Oi – careful, She'll hear you!"

By the time we had arrived and commenced unloading in our lay-by, it had become a warm, balmy day and we just couldn't wait to put the big roads behind us once more and start the final landmark countdown, from the ten remaining to the last one, only thirty miles away. Before we went however, we made the first call to Chris, as promised, and as I talked to him I could picture him studying the map that we'd left at home for him. It showed the route we'd be taking over the next three days and he'd be ticking off each target as we reached it, counting down with us to the moment when he could get that beer from the 'fridge and join us in a toast to success. Chloe was peering over my shoulder as I bent down to look at our own map, tracing a finger from our current position to our first stop, the Santa Pod raceway and drag strip. Forty miles or so, a nice little first hop before the longer haul around the north side of Birmingham. Promising Chris we'd check in later, it was time to get going.

Daisy had never felt better as we cruised along in the sunshine, heading directly west on the A428. I was not going to take any risks on this, our last foray, especially with the knowledge that those bodged points were still providing the sparks! We settled down to a leisurely fifty-five. I reveled in the feeling of freedom once more as the pressures and trials of the past few weeks dissolved into insignificance. We were back doing what we wanted to do, success was within our grasp and everything that could be good in the world was, indeed, good. Being relatively early on a Sunday morning, there was very little traffic about to spoil the ride and it was at times like that, I pondered, that the English countryside is at it's most enjoyable. Of course, that was nothing compared to the geography that awaited us, where we'd hopefully enjoy yet more unfenced roads meandering through the splendour of the Snowdonia National Park, but it was relaxing and enjoyable just the same. It was also true that with the long and eventful Scottish leg completed, a new-found confidence in Daisy, and my own ability to handle her few foibles had buoyed my spirits to the point that I was viewing that last foray as virtually a formality. Nothing could, or would, stop us now.

I was still pondering such thoughts as we left the larger roads and dived into the green lanes just to the west of Northampton, in search of Santa Pod. It proved to be a tricky place to find, with the poor detail of maps that we had coupled with a surprising lack of clear signposts that I had expected to find. Indeed, when we did finally stumble across it, more by luck than any feat of navigation, I commented to Chloe that for a famous site so popular amongst petrol-heads, its most notable feature was the fact that it was surrounded by nothing more than trees and fields. It was also shut, so after a short break and the by then familiar routine of positioning Daisy for photographs, we wasted no more time other than to report in for Chris. Inexplicably, I managed to lose the road that had brought us from the A428. After a while we were completely lost in the green lanes and almost certainly going in the wrong direction. As usual, the little villages that appeared from time to time on the very few signposts could not be found on any of our maps. I attempted to follow the compass instead, a tried and tested navigation method previously.

I knew that as long as we maintained a vague northwesterly direction we wouldn't go too far wrong, but even that proved impossible because the roads simply wouldn't behave and kept heading off in anything but the direction that we wanted. No sooner did we find a junction that offered a route that seemed to go in our required direction, we then found that it was a false hope yet again and the thing invariably bent round to the east, as if to deliberately taunt us. At one point, rising through a wooded area to burst into the sunshine on what seemed to be a plateau, we stopped and I gazed at the horizon all around, straining to see anything in any direction that looked like civilisation. A place we could use pinpoint our location on the maps, find a bigger road that would lead us somewhere meaningful, or, at the very least contain a café! But I could see no such place, and whilst it must be confessed that what I could see was undeniably peaceful and certainly pretty, I would rather be enjoying it whilst at the same time making progress towards Wales instead of Germany, via the North Sea. There was nothing for it but to keep trying really, but to negate the need to keep stopping and scrabbling around in pockets, I taped the little compass onto Daisy's steering damper knob.

Half an hour later, we finally connected with a bigger road, and even better found a sign to a place that was actually on our maps. We had managed it seemed, to spend the last half an hour going in circles to the southeast of our last stop, but more to the point we had also managed to go about ten miles in the wrong direction. However, this was the A6 according to the sign in front of us, which promised to at least lead us north towards Wellingborough, which was the only recognizable place on our maps. From there we could jink west on the A45 and with a fair wind or whatever, we'd get onto a proper Daisy road, the B573, that would shoot us between Northampton and Wellingborough. And so it went, with almost no clownery at all, until we were once again bowling along in open country, not a care in the world.

We passed under the M1 after a while, got sucked into Rugby town centre somehow, emerged, against all the odds, heading north on the right road and began the circumnavigation of the huge sprawl that is Coventry and Birmingham. Strangely that was not a chore at all. The countryside and general geography around Brum is actually very satisfying as a motorcycling experience. For large stretches, where the view was obscured either by hills or trees, it was near impossible to believe that a sizeable metropolis was but a few miles away, but studying the map it was clear that we were on the very edge of the suburbs and should, by rights, have been threading our way through built up areas, fighting with bus lanes, traffic lights and endless mini-roundabouts. We saw none of those things at all until suddenly, almost out of the blue, Stafford hoved into view and we were drawn like the proverbial moth to a flame. It was a good place to stop and Chloe agreed. She was hungry, she informed me, and wasn't it time for lunch? I had to agree – the day had flown by and it was already half past one. Lunch was clearly the thing to do.

I like Stafford. Always have, because it's the quintessential Olde English town packed to the hilt with history. Some of the buildings, which as a rule have survived remarkably well, date from the eleven hundreds and the place possesses what's believed to be the largest standing authentic timber framed house in England, dating from the sixteenth century or so. As fine a place as any for lunch, we reckoned and we set about finding a suitably patina'd pub to do the honours. The Swan hotel was just the ticket, with it's little tables outside on the pleasantly landscaped street, and we settled for a ploughman's apiece then just relaxed in the sunshine, watching the world go by. The grub, and a pint of rather murky real ale, was consumed in a leisurely fashion and then it was time to press on towards North Wales where one of my all time favourite roads awaited us.

We checked our proposed route which would take us directly west, through Shrewsbury, Oswestry and then turn north up towards Wrexham. We would cut across country at Llangollan, through the mountains, in order to join up with the north coast road, the A55, and the reason that this road was a favourite is the string of tunnels that claw through the rocky coastal headlands as it passes through Conwy on it's way to Anglesey – a good road to drive or ride but especially good on an old twin like Daisy. I estimated that it was approximately a hundred miles to the point we'd join it, and I told Chloe that if all went well we would get to it some time around six o'clock and could then look for camping. I hadn't got her full attention however, because she'd spotted the word 'mountains' on the map and was far more interested in what time we'd be getting to *them*. We'd get to the mountains at five o'clock, I declared, unaware that the dark force of Sod was gathering to practice his Law, and in fact we were in for a bit of a shock.

I had forgotten about the roads in Wales. On the face of it, they're no worse than any other rural roads, but there seems to be a break in the very fabric of the space-time continuum that causes a normal rate of progress to be absolutely impossible. If you take any given ten mile stretch of rural road, anywhere else in the United Kingdom, you can ride it's length, stop, have a picnic and probably a short snooze and maybe even wash the bike before you'll complete the same distance in Wales. Strange, but true. I have a theory that some ancient, mystical power interferes with modern instruments and causes them to misrepresent true speed. When the needle says fifty, the actual rate of progress is in fact thirty-five. Of course, the locals know about this, but aren't about to let on to us lot, preferring to save the pleasure of doing an indicated eighty on a minor public road all for themselves. Certain parts of Ireland are obviously on the same ley-line. This also explains why North Wales Constabulary have such a good track record for catching speeding drivers – their equipment tells them, as you bimble sedately along at fifty-five, that in fact you're doing seventy and being 'locals' themselves, they use this quirk of physics to great advantage.

I could, of course, be entirely wrong, but as we sat in a lay-by that afternoon, eyeing the silhouette of the distant peaks, I enjoyed explaining my reasoning to Chloe. "You're mad" was the rather unsatisfactory counter argument. Nevertheless, since passing Shrewsbury, progress had been inordinately, undeniably slow, and although the view on the horizon was highly suggestive of a great ride ahead, it seemed to be taking forever to get there. Then of course, there was the peculiarly Welsh double-whammy of caravans and tractors. We were forcibly reminded of their ability to turn any given planned journey into a frustrating and stressful experience, when we came across an example of each engaged in a face-off. The particular road we were travelling should, along most of its length, allow all vehicles, of any size, to pass without much trouble. But as is the way of things, the tractor we could now see in front of us, with it's large trailer full of hay and the Volvo estate coming the other way, with it's ridiculously large caravan, had met on one of the very few stretches of road that would not. Not only could they not pass, but in trying to do so they seemed to have become jammed, like corks in a bottle. Both vehicles had pushed as far into the hedgerow as they could and unsuccessfully tried to edge past each other, and the Volvo had found a ditch by the looks of things. There is no way past.

We pulled up a little way down the road and watched for a minute or two before I decided that nothing was going to change in a hurry, reached out, killed Daisy's engine and told Chloe that she could get off. As we sat by the hedgerow watching, another car towing an equally huge caravan cames round the far bend and very nearly ploughed into the Volvo. By that time, both the tractor driver and the Volvo driver were engaged in a heated discussion, presumably about who should reverse. This was made laughable by the fact that the Volvo driver couldn't actually get out of his car because the tractor's huge rear wheel was preventing him from opening his door and the hedgerow was preventing him opening the passenger door. I could see his wife giving him grief in the other ear, and the whole situation showed a promising likelihood that it would become highly amusing when he broke off the argument with the tractor driver to start one with her instead. I can't lip read too well, but the expletives exchanged were so very obvious that I didn't really need to! We settled down to waiting.

I considered the phenomenon of caravans and tractors. I'm sure that if a statistical analysis were to be carried out, Wales in mid-summer would be found to posses a far and disproportionately higher concentration of the things per square mile than almost any other place in Europe. With the possible exception, when it comes to caravans, of Cornwall. But that train of thought was interrupted as the main matinee performance got underway down the road. The tractor driver, obviously growing weary of the verbal haranguing from Mr Volvo, had decided to act. He revved the tractor and slowly began to move forward, despite the fact that the only way he could do this was by dragging his trailer along the side of both Volvo and caravan. There was a horrible wrenching and scraping noise, but that was immediately drowned by the maniacal gargled scream from Mrs Volvo and a hysterical barrage of vitriolic babble from Mr Volvo. Chloe and I watched the unfolding drama, absolutely agog, as the big trailer inched forwards, wreaking a terrible havoc on the shiny, expensive car and finally met the leading edge of the caravan. The tractor's irresistible pull dragged it through the initial resistance and I stared in wonder, my heart in my mouth, as the big white home on wheels seemed to buckle slightly and rear up before giving way with an ear shattering splintering noise. Mr Volvo looked as though he'd had a coronary, because nobody should ever be that shade of red and stay healthy, but I think Mrs Volvo had actually passed out. Mr Volvo revived impressively quickly, launching into an unspeakable tirade through his open window and as the trailer's rear-end finally cleared his door, continuing it's inexorable progress along the side of his caravan, he was out like an Exocet missile and doing a little dance in the road as he watched the final cataclysmic raking of his pride and joy.

The driver in the car behind the Volvo had recognised that there, but for the imminent grace of God, might go his own caravan and had already taken urgent evasive action, reversing back up the road to where it widened, and to my amazement the tractor driver, free of the dragging effect of the once plush but now wrecked conveyance behind him, made a break for it, simply carrying on up the road with Mr. Volvo in hot pursuit on foot. They disappeared round the far bend, the tractor clearly opening a big lead and an eerie quiet descended on the lane. We decided not to hang around, because there was no telling when Mr Volvo would come back and we'd be pretty useless as material witnesses anyway. All we'd seen was a large trailer full of hay and glimpses of a tractor from our vantage point, we hadn't got a look at the driver and there was no number plate to be seen. I couldn't even reliably state what colour the tractor was. In short, I was busily convincing myself that we wouldn't be much use to anyone and I suspected that Mr Volvo, when

he returned, would be very tiresome anyway. There was also the small fact that we'd lost nearly an hour sat there watching the pantomime being played out. Certainly not a wasted hour, I felt, because being a life long fan of Laurel and Hardy I was in fact highly appreciative of the great piece of free slapstick comedy. Nevertheless time was pressing by and we really did need to get a move on.

We passed the Volvo and caravan slowly and Mrs Volvo, her pride and ego already fatally wounded, simply stared straight ahead through the windscreen, showing no sign that she'd even seen us. The great gouges along the side of both car and caravan were bad enough, but the offside front corner of the caravan had the entire top two feet of it's side panel neatly rolled back exposing the inside, reminding me of the old fashioned cornedbeefntins that you had to open with that little key to turn back the lid. I mustn't laugh, I chided myself as we passed but Chloe had no such inhibitions, and I heard the barely suppressed giggle escape her as I selected second gear and accelerated away. Bizarrely, we passed the tractor some few miles on, but there was no sign of Mr Volvo. Perhaps he'd done a Reginald Perrin and simply walked away from it all, across the fields!

Time was really getting on by then, but we eventually joined the A55 just south of Rhyl at a little before seven o'clock, and we set about looking for a campsite. We stopped for a rest in the first lay-by we found, I showed Chloe where we'd got to and pointed out the Colwyn Bay area, fifteen miles or so to the west, suggesting that it would be a sure fire camping area. We'd head that way and camp at the first site that presented itself, I suggested. Half an hour later I was cursing, because as the sun began to set, and I pulled over to lift the tank bag to turn on Daisy's lights, nothing happened. No lights. Not even a faint glimmer. A quick check confirmed that the battery was absolutely dead, and I found there was nothing registering on the ammeter when the engine was run. I hadn't noticed this earlier, as the instruments are tank mounted on Daisy so the tank bag covers them up, and of course being magneto ignition the small detail of a flat battery has no effect on her ability to start and run. Bugger.

The thought of riding in bad light on that fairly fast stretch of road was, to say the least, unacceptable. Clearly the need to find a camp site had suddenly become fairly urgent and with that thought burning bright, we pressed on with all haste lest we end up stranded. We carried on west, with Daisy cranked up to nearly eighty in order to make better progress, but as the light steadily failed I was getting increasingly uncomfortable with the situation. I finally conceded that we were fighting a losing battle, which was now becoming a potentially dangerous one and so I decided that we had no other choice but to take the first available turning off the main road, where at least we'd be out of the danger of a tail-ender from fast approaching traffic. I hoped to hell that we could get directions in the nearest village to a camp site somewhere very near.

Before any turnings come along, we found ourselves approaching a service area where I spied a Travelodge sign. I didn't really want the expense, but our predicament was pressing and it was better than risking an accident. As we pulled off onto the slip road however, we saw a little camping sign pointing up a track to the rear of the parking area. Not quite believing our luck we followed it and sure enough there was indeed a campsite at the end, sprawled around a large farmhouse. We were received warmly, allowed to check in and made our way to the tent area, noting as we did that there were not many facilities. Luckily we were armed with food and I also had a couple of tins, coke for Chloe and bitter for me, nestling in the tank bag alongside the bottle of Newcastle Ale and the tin of Red Bull that were reserved for the big moment of completion.

We parked Daisy up and Chloe was an immediate blur of activity as she did the honours with the grub whilst I made camp. Half an hour later we were sitting in the twilight watching a huge yellow full moon rise slowly over the fields while we ate. Chloe was delighted to discover a big local bunny population, appearing from the hedgerows as they do, to sit with their ears standing upright as they contemplate whatever it is that rabbits contemplate of an evening. In the distance, high on a rise, we could see a pub, brightly lit and glowing invitingly, so after dinner we set out to find it on foot. That proved to be harder than it looked, and we had to walk along the edge of the A55, behind the crash barrier, stumbling along in the dark until we reached the turning that we hoped led to the pub. A brisk walk later, we were happily ensconced in the snug little bar and poring over the maps that I had brought along. There was a distinct sense of anticipation radiating from Chloe - we'd be riding through Snowdonia National Park the next day.

Chloe liked to see where we'd been on these forays, and just as she had done in Devon and Cornwall, she wanted to know the route travelled and traced her finger slowly across the map as I described each hop that we had made through the day. But as she moved her digit across Shrewsbury I realized suddenly that buffoonery had occurred again and I stopped her progress across the map by exclaiming "Oh God! I don't believe it!" Chloe looked up, startled by the sudden change in my demeanour, as I continued with "Bloody hell, I am such an idiot!" Having no idea what it was that had suddenly upset me, she asked the inevitable question and I pointed to the map just below Shrewsbury, where there was a landmark point highlighted by one of the computer's virtual push-pin labels. It was the one that Chris and I had decided to leave on our homeward leg from Scotland, the one that I was meant to have scheduled into this foray with Chloe. It is the one that I had in fact completely forgotten about until that moment. I could not believe how stupid I'd been, and the thing taunted me from the page as I confessed the frightful cock-up to Chloe. We had actually passed within ten miles of the thing earlier that day!

We huddled together trying to calculate how far back from our current position it was, but it was not good news because we ended up agreeing that it was a good eighty miles away. To double back would put a huge extra leg on our plan; the best part of a day's riding in fact. I had another idea. "OK, let's follow the route round and see if we get closer at any point" and with this Chloe's finger went into action again whilst I silently cursed myself some more for such blatant clownery. In the end, after trying out various detours from our planned route, we worked out that the least disruptive course of action would be to tack the overlooked landmark onto the very last leg, just before the final stop in the Midlands. Instead of taking a direct cross-country route from the Brecon Beacons via Hereford, we'd have to dogleg north and skirt the southern tip of Birmingham rather closer than we had planned adding a paltry forty miles to the overall distance, as opposed to the next best option of hopping east from Snowdonia and back again, which would add something like eighty miles.

With that decision made, it was time to place our call to Chris, waiting patiently at home for the promised progress report and after a lengthy update during which he helpfully pointed out that I was a twit, Chloe and I returned to our deliberations regarding the next day. We stayed in the little bar until the last bell invited us to make ourselves scarce. I was more than ready for bed anyway, after what had been a long but mostly pleasant not to mention in places amusing day. We wandered happily back down the lane, braved the dark no-man's land behind the crash barrier and found our way back to the farm. It seemed as if the entire rabbit population of Wales had migrated to our field, but as we stumbled out of the trees they took fright and shot off in every conceivable direction, much to Chloe's delight. We decided to brave the very rickety-looking shower block before turning in, which was a decidedly uninspiring experience, and both of us dropped off to sleep almost immediately once we'd snuggled into our sleeping bags.

Chloe was first up in the morning, and when I managed to regain consciousness at seven o'clock, I was surprised to find that she was not in the tent. I poked my head out onto a misty morning, to find that the bunnies had returned in even more numbers than the previous evening and Chloe was stalking them, ever so slowly. I watched fascinated for a few minutes as down on all fours, she inched forward, careful to make no sudden movements that would start the mass stampede that we had witnessed the previous night. Closer and closer she got, when suddenly the nearest rabbit to her took fright and legged it. Chloe broke cover and ran forward but within seconds the whole field had exploded with activity, and in the blink of an eye there was not a bunny to be seen. She ambled back towards the tent, her cheeks glowing red in the early chill and I don't think I've ever seen her look happier than she did right then. She finally saw me watching, ran over to plant a kiss on my nose, harangued me into getting up and we soon had bacon and scrambled eggs on the go, with lashings of hot tea to wash it all down.

Chloe was almost bursting with anticipation, incredibly eager to break camp and set off on our adventures once again, and as she bustled about clearing away the breakfast stuff, firing questions at me about how long it would be to Snowdonia I found her enthusiasm to be infectious enough to get me moving. We were packed up and ready to go within twenty minutes, Daisy fired up first kick, Chloe climbed aboard and gave me a big bear hug from behind and at that moment the sun broke through the mist to bathe us in it's early golden glory. At that moment, I felt like the luckiest man in the world, and congratulated myself for having bought Daisy, taken up the challenge and indeed encouraged the kids to join in. It was time to put more miles under our wheels and enjoy another day of adventure. I pulled in the clutch, selected first gear, looked over my shoulder and asked the unnecessary question; "Ready?" the answer made me laugh as Chloe pointed to the horizon and quoted from another favourite film of hers. "Yep!" she exclaimed "to infinity and beyond!".

We were soon leaving Denbighshire, travelling on the empty road west into Conwy, and before long we were bowling along the coastal stretches watching the sun sparkling on the surface of the open sea. The fresh sea air was invigorating and it was just about the perfect start to the day. I had already described what was coming to Chloe, telling her that Daisy was going to sound tremendous as we passed through the string of little tunnels that pepper that road, but before we reached those we needed to make a brief detour south, to stop at the next landmark, which we had already identified as Bodnant Garden. It wasn't open when we got there, so we only stopped briefly before doubling back up to the A55 once more and proceeding west again along my favourite bit of the road. Half an hour later, we were indeed having a whale of a time, making plenty of noise in those tunnels, accelerating into each as we approach and then letting Daisy drop onto the over-run for maximum effect as her deep exhaust note bounces around in the enclosed pipes of concrete that cut through headland after headland.

Eventually they werre behind us and soon after we crossed the Menai straight, marvelling at the spectacular view afforded by the deep cut between the mainland and the island of Anglesey, which always looks to me like some exotic picture-postcard millionaire's playground, with the yachts parked in a sparkling clear sea against the backdrop of steep wooded coast on which the odd white building can be seen peeking out over the straight. Wonderful, but we continued into Anglesey, heading for our next target area and wondering what we'd find because another landmark that we had been unable to identify from any of our research awaited us. The written clue 'A trough of airmen' gave us a general idea, because the maps clearly showed an airfield at the map reference, but we hadn't worked out the trough bit, or what it may signify. But of course, that's all part of fun.

Everything was going rather swimmingly I reckoned, as we came off the far side of the rather picturesque bridge into Anglesey proper and began the straight trek west. Daisy was lapping it up, as had become expected of her, we'd made good time along the coast road, already had one landmark in the bag and it was still early yet. I was just contemplating the fact that it could only get better, because the day's ride ahead was what we'd both been looking forward to the most, when I was suddenly jerked back to reality with the sound of disaster ringing in my ears. Or rather the sound of disaster *not* ringing in my ears. Daisy's engine, as if she had overheard my thoughts, had just stopped dead without warning, and we endured a horrible moment where we went from the entirely satisfactory growl that she emits when cruising along at fifty-five to the depressing, flat descending drone of a suddenly non-functioning power plant. I blipped the throttle a couple of times without any response and I was forced to simply pull in the clutch, coasting to a halt on the hard shoulder, where it became immediately apparent what was wrong. There was an overpowering smell of petrol and as I looked down in alarm I could see the stuff all over the gearbox and oil tank.

We dismounted, crouched down for a closer inspection and discovered that the petrol pipe from the tank had split just below the tap, allowing the vital liquid to simply ooze away onto the road until Daisy was breathing fresh air. "Bloody marvellous!" I exclaimed, throwing up my hands, but after pulling it off, examining the problem more closely, I could see that all was not lost. There was enough length on the pipe that after a bit of fiddling I managed to cut the thing back and reconnect the unblemished new end to the tap. Daisy has a reserve tap on the other side of the tank which is good for a few miles, but we wewere in the middle of nowhere as far as I could see, with no sign of any civilization particularly close by.

I discussed the options with Chloe, but that didn't take long because there were only two. We could continue on that road and trust that there was a petrol station not too far away, or we could take the first available turning that suggested it actually went somewhere and hope that there was one there. It was not a clear choice at all, so in the end we decided to toss a coin, heads we would keep going, tails we would turn off. Heads it was, and off we went on reserve, accelerating very cautiously and settling at a paltry thirty miles per hour in an effort to preserve every drop of fuel that we could. Eight miles or so later we had neither seen any petrol stations or any attractive looking turn-offs and the inevitable moment arrived when Daisy once more sputtered to a halt. We got off again and surveyed our surroundings, but there was nothing to see but fields and the odd sheep. Neither was there much traffic and really there was nothing for it but to start pushing and hope that salvation came along!

I started the long tedious slog, disheartened even further because the road climbed slowly but surely uphill and made my task even harder. Chloe brought up the rear carrying the helmets and my jacket but before very long, as Daisy got heavier and heavier whilst the sun got hotter and hotter I began to think about parking her up somewhere and trying to hitch a lift to the nearest place that had fuel. This was not an action that I was prepared to take lightly, because if I did do that there was a very real risk that some of our gear or some of Daisy's fittings would be stolen, or worse the whole bike may end up in the back of a van, never to be seen again! Equally, for obvious reasons, it was not an option to leave Chloe with the bike whilst I went swanning off over the horizon, destination unknown. No, on reflection, we'd just have to tough it out.

I needn't have worried as it turned out because before we'd progressed more than two hundred yards up the road, which incidentally was enough to nearly kill me, we found a lay-by into which we trudged to have a rest, and discovered a little side road hidden behind a grassy bank. There was a family with a caravan, having a picnic

lunch, but far more interesting was the bright green petrol can sitting under the caravan's steps! A tentative enquiry revealed that yes, it was half full, and yes the chap was quite happy to sell us a few litres so that we could get to the next town. He followed us over the bank with his can, but he obviously wasn't expecting to find anything like Daisy the other side. "Bloody 'ell" he exclaimsed, "Was petrol invented when that thing was made?" He chuckled to himself as we reached her, but his face turned to respect as he inspected the pillion pad and then turned to Chloe "And this is your seat is it? All day long you say?" he asked. She assured him that in fact itwas very comfortable, not at all as bad as it looked, but he didn't seem convinced.

I had emptied his can into Daisy's tank by that time, and after tickling the float bowl to re-fill it I straddled her once more and tried a kick. She responded immediately and our saviour let out a good humoured cheer. I wondered if, when

we'd arrived, he'd been getting bored back there with his caravan, and perhaps our arrival was equally good for him as it was for us. He didn't seem to be in a hurry to return to his lunch after I handed the can back with some money for the fuel. I felt a little awkward just buggering off, but we needed to get going, and so after explaining that we still had a long way to go, we mounted up, waved goodbye, yelled out a "thank you" and rejoined the main carriageway. I looked round as we reach the top of the distant rise to see him still standing in the lay-by looking our way, one hand raised in distant salute.

The obscure clue to the next landmark turned out to be very easy to solve, once we got there. It was RAF Valley, as proclaimed by a large MOD sign inviting us to not even think about trespassing. We didn't, simply getting our photographs and turning round to make our way back to the mainland. I made a big thing with Chloe that it was "Snowdonia here we come" and the grin on her face said it all. But first we needed to find petrol, which we already thought we had done just up the road, only to find that the forecourt and four pumps we had spied at a junction turned out to belong to an abandoned station that was no longer trading. In fact, no juice had flowed there for years by the look of things. We stopped to ask a local, but the directions she gave us were so complicated and convoluted that we moved on, none the wiser, and tried another local further up the road. If anything, that chap's assistance was even less likely to take us to the much needed juice, and after listening to a seemingly endless set of instructions we carried on the way we were, feeling exasperated. Third time lucky, I suggested to Chloe, as we pulled over towards yet another fount of local wisdom. This guy tried to send us back to the defunct station that we had already been to and I had to resist the urge to gibber as I listened politely to the third lot of useless directions in five minutes.

What we needed to do, I decided, was to study the map and find a bigger town, where surely there would be a plethora of the damned things. Anglesey is only about twelve miles across, I reasoned, and looking at the map we couldn't be too far from Holyhead, where ferries go to and from Ireland. There simply had to be a petrol station there, so that's where we'd go. In the end, it was all academic because we find one on the main road within two miles. Having filled up with juice, and topped Daisy's oil tank off, I turned to Chloe and declared that "Right, *this time* it's *definitely* Snowdonia here we come!" With that we saddled up and got under way once more, heading back to Conwy where, just across the Menai Straight we turned south to follow the deep rift that has been formed by the Irish Sea. We stayed on the A487 until we could peel off east on the A4085, the road that would take us through the heart of Snowdonia and we could almost immediately see the stark peaks looming in the distance, beckoning us onwards.

I was reminded of my first encounter with mountains in Scotland when Chloe, just like Chris before her, tapped urgently on my shoulder and pointed to the horizon. Like her brother, she had been waiting for this above anything else, and the wait was about to be rewarded. I was struck once again by the closeness of the countryside in Wales, compared to the arms length grandeur of Scotland. Here, the tumbledown woods and hills pressed right up to the road, and one could simply pull off in any number of places and walk right into it. The roads themselves were absolutely taylor-made for Daisy, allowing a good cruising speed through their winding length, but restrictive enough that most traffic kept to a sensible speed. We were not jockeying for position, neither did we have anything pressing us from behind and it made for an almost perfect ride.

We finally entered the National Park area and stopped at the first available place we could find, which was a lay-by with a caravan selling teas and snacks. After ordering what turned out to be a surprisingly good mug of tea each, we surveyed our surroundings. The view from our current vantage point was grand indeed, positioned as we were on the upper edge of an escarpment that looked across a lush, green, humpty-bumpty landscape towards mount Snowdon itself. Around it were the lower peaks and the foothills which, I assured Chloe, we were about to ride straight through. We took our time over the next twenty or so miles, because it would have been almost criminal to do anything else. The wide sweeping landscape gave way to rocky outcrops and the road snaked it's way around the base of Snowdon, following the contours of ancient glacial valleys. The views were simply breathtaking and we found ourselves stopping for a few moments, regularly, just to stare in awe at the mighty splendour spreading in every direction.

But as we progressed, we couldn't help but notice that with each hour that passed there was an exponential increase in the number of caravans and campers on the roads, and before long the bloody things were becoming a real pain. No sooner did we manage pass one, having had to sit behind the thing as it lumbered around blind bend after blind bend, than there's another, waiting to take up the duty of seriously aggravating everyone else on the road. By the time we reached the far side of the park I had grown to detest the things with an intensity that was surprising. Certainly for us, they had spoiled what would have been the best ride of the challenge so far. The things should be banned from minor routes during daylight hours, I reckon. Still, we had enjoyed a most satisfactory ride all told, Daisy has taken it all in her stride, and despite the plague of caravans we eventually joined the A487 again on the other side, feeling pretty fresh and deeply contented.

It was well past midday when we finally stopped near the boundary of the park's southern side. We had one of those landmarks to get next that required us to detour sideways and then back on ourselves again, in the process making no actual forward progress. As I showed Chloe the next leg, twenty miles there and twenty back again, I commented on the fact that if we could do all of these 'as the crow flies' it would be no challenge at all. This one had no direct route to it, and in fact our map showed no roads in its immediate vicinity at all. We were going to have to rely on our instincts and the compass again, even though the last attempt to do that had got us well and truly lost around Santa Pod. We did have two clear choices of route. We could drop out of the Snowdonia National Park and pick up the bigger roads that went most of the way to our next target, or we could stay within the boundaries and take a less direct route on much smaller roads.

Chloe wasn't going to hear of leaving the Park until we had no choice, and of course, in the spirit of that whole adventure she was absolutely right. No argument from me then, and it was cross country we meandered on the wonderful unfenced roads, so reminiscent of Cumbria. We wound our way through a number of tiny hamlets and villages, at little more than thirty mile per hour, as the road followed the lazy meanderings of the river Dovey, crossing it in places via typically rustic stone bridges, and we stopped at one of these crossing points to rest. Chloe was able to splash about in the shallows of the pebble-bedded stream as I just relaxed for ten minutes, and the real world might as well have been a million miles away. Inevitably, we had to press on and finally exited the park just to the northwest of lake Vernwy, the visitor centre of which is our target.

We had swapped the splendour of Snowdonia's peaks for a rolling green landscape of valleys and lakes, and this one was a real joy to ride along. The road hugged the western shore of the lake and was an entirely joyful experience, with Daisy humming along at a steady fifty-five, the sun glinting off the deep blue of the lake and in the distance we could see what looked like a dam across the far end of the water. We arrived at the visitor centre, where the first priority for both of us was an ice-cream, which we ate sitting on a grassy bank with the dam-cum-bridge stretching away in all it's splendour, right in front of us. At the visitor centre, we were informed that this beautiful dam was constructed in the late nineteenth century, in order to form a reservoir to feed the growing needs of the population of Liverpool and it's surrounding areas. The original settlement of Llanwddyn was actually submerged by the resulting lake, its inhabitants having been re-housed in a new settlement, of the same name. This all happened in 1881, and was all paid for by the Liverpool Corporation.

Apparently if the water level drops far enough, the ruins of the old village can still be seen. The dam itself is very typical of the Victorian architecture that is to be seen in many a viaduct around Britain, and with the lake stretching away beyond it the effect was quite charming, so we positioned Daisy to ensure that our photographs included it as a backdrop. What then happened was a bit bizzarre. As we finish snapping, I was amazed and quite taken a-back when an American family walking past stopped, removed their young toddler from a push chair, and without so much as a by-your-leave proceeded to plonk the lad in my seat on Daisy! They helped him stretch his arms forward so he could hang on to the handlebars and then started to take photographs. Before I had mustered the wits to object they had whipped him off again and were on their way. Some people have the most unbelievably bad manners!

Before long it was time to get going and set out west again. I was incensed that I have to wipe a set of grubby child-sized fingerprints from Daisy's headlight shell, and I wondered again at the blatant gall of that family. But there was no time to brood over such matters, we had to get going. We took a different route back to the southern tip of Snowdonia and if the road we had come out here on was delightful for it's gentle meandering by the river, this one was exhilarating for the opposite reason. A wide, well kept surface, dipping and rising through the hills and encompassing a long set of sweeping bends with not a caravan in site, or any other traffic for that matter. We were soon having a whale of a time, and it seemed like no time at all that we found ourselves riding down a tremendously long descent, bordered by a sheer rock cliff on one side and heavy woods on the other, to burst out into bright sunshine at the bottom. There we found the little stone hamlet of Corris, where a steam museum, our next landmark, awaited the cameras.

There are museums, and there are museums. This one is brilliant, for the simple fact that it's tiny, quaint and friendly. We took our photographs, but it would have been rude to leave without ducking in through the tiny door and having a look around. I've always found these little pieces of 'living history' fascinating and feel strongly that they should be supported. The best way to do that, of course, is with the wallet, so we did our bit. In the cool interior we discovered that the railway was constructed to run from the quarries at Aberllefenni to the mid-Wales town of Machynlleth and was commissioned in 1858 before opening for goods traffic as well in 1859. By the 1880s passenger traffic had commenced too until the railway was acquired by the GWR in 1930 and closed to passenger traffic soon after. It was a slow decline thereafter and the last train ran in 1948 after which the track was lifted leaving the bed in place. Some of the original Corris locomotives and rolling stock were still running on the Talyllyn railway, but the Corris railway was undergoing restoration by a group of enthusiastic volunteers, drawn from the members of the Corris Railway Society. At the time of our visit they were laying track from Maespoth Junction, a few miles away, going towards Corris itself. Good on 'em, I told Chloe, and I gave her a fiver to shove in the collection box.

With the time pressing on, we had to be off again, heading south for some fifteen miles before another detour inland. But we got tangled up once again with holiday traffic and the going was inordinately slow and congested. It was a huge shame because the delightful road would have been fantastic to ride if I could have just given Daisy her legs, but instead we were forced to trundle along amidst a seemingly endless crocodile of the dread caravans, which were out in force. Finally the road eased it's twisting and turning, allowing us a clear view along the centre and we ended up having quite good fun weaving in and out of the traffic, waiting our chance to hop past yet another carbuncle on wheels and tucking back in to miss the oncoming caravans. We finally reached the front of the queue, and suddenly it was clear why everything had been backed up so badly. We took our chance to hop past the last vehicles where, right at the front, we find a huge, very slow moving tractor pulling the inevitable trailer full of hay.

Now we could let Daisy canter along on the suddenly empty road and it wasn't long before we turned east once more to cover the last ten miles or so to the penultimate stop of the day and a very late lunch. At the next landmark, which turned out to be a silver mine, there was a nice little café and we were grateful for the chance to eat whilst we contemplated the maps again. Chloe chattered away about the things we'd seen and done that day, enthusing mightily over the magnificent presence of mount Snowdon, laughing at the Americans and moaning about the caravans. As she rattled on, I realised that the day's riding had probably been the most pleasant of the whole challenge so far in many ways, and I marvelled that after nearly eight hours in the saddle I was still feeling fresh and relaxed. We wouldn't be sorely pressed for the rest of day either, as it was four thirty and we only had about sixty miles left to do before camping somewhere near the next landmark, already identified as Cilgerran Castle and situated three quarters of the way along the piggie's nose.

I decided to take a bit of time before we left again, checking Daisy over for any obvious problems, loose nuts or missing bits, although I was not about to go anywhere near that magneto. It ain't broke, even if in the back of my mind I was waiting for it to do so, and I wasn't about to make the repeat mistake of 'fixing' it before I had to. I pulled out the spanners and a couple of screwdrivers, but less than ten minutes later I found myself singing the old girl's praises because I couldn't find anything amiss whatsoever. She hadn't even leaked any oil and didn't seem to have used any since the previous day. To Chloe's amusement I patted Daisy's tank and happily told her she was a good girl, before declaring that we were ready for the final hop of the day which would take us to Aberaeron, where Daisy would need a drink and I would look for a cash machine. I'd just spent the last of my ready cash on our late lunch.

As we joined the main coastal road we got tangled up in what must pass for rush-hour in Wales, with the result that the going got very slow and tedious once more. By the time we finally got to the place it was pushing six o'clock but it seemed later, because for the first time in days there was a dark band of cloud climbing slowly in the west, and it had snatched away the sun. Chloe remarked that it seemed to have got awfully chilly all of a sudden, and she was right. The absence of direct sun had without a doubt had a marked effect on the air temperature and the breeze drifting across from the sea had a distinctly less than a warm feel to it. Never mind, I assured her, there were only thirty odd miles left to do that day, although we could actually stop anytime if we felt like it because there was no pressure to get home. We'd see how things went.

Finally pulling up on the outskirts of the town we got our fuel before taking a detour in order to hunt down a cash machine, and we find a delightful town centre brightly decorated with flowers and the like, and remarkably clean looking. This was supposed to be a whistle-stop purely to get cash, before getting straight on down towards Cilgerran, but as I returned from the machine and approached Daisy, I found that somebody else had other ideas about a quick getaway. Waiting for me there was a pedant. A self appointed expert on all things classic bike and dread Custodian of an opinion which, judging by his expression, was the only one that ever counted. He was a little ferret of a man with an air 'of little-man syndrome' about him. The sort of chap that you tend to find in the security hut at the main entrance to any corporation headquarters in the land. He was with two mates, so he had got an audience, and in Daisy he had clearly spotted a perfect opportunity to show off his prowess and expertise and then deliver his opinion and he was not about to pass it up. It would be game set and match.

"Oh dear, oh dear" he chuckled as he darted across to us and effectively stopped me getting on. He crouched down with a theatrical sigh and I studied him for a second, then looked at his mates, who gave me a knowing look. Feeling a bit put out at the sudden intrusion, I returned my stare to the gnome, but his attention was all on Daisy as his gaze swept her entire length in expert judgment. He made a series of little "Tsk Tsk" noises with each detail that failed to meet his exacting standards, whilst his mates adopted an air of expectation. It was obvious that they had seen the performance before and were looking forward to the show. I glanced at Chloe who pulled a face as if to say "Who on earth is this, and what's his problem?" I found myself fascinated by the gnome's mannerisms though, and I was stunned that he was actually prepared to blatantly shove in front of a six-foot-something, leather clad, heavily bearded motorcyclist and carry on the way he currently was. I waited with baited breath for the next act in the performance, and I was not disappointed when he stood up slowly, completely ignored Chloe and me, and addressed his mates.

"What we have here" he assured his appreciative audience "is a bitsa!" They nodded enthusiastically, and he continued, "See? The colour's all wrong for a start, these wuz never that shade of red, oh no, dear me no. And see that carburettor?" He chuckled, as if it was the sorriest thing he had ever clapped eyes on "All wrong, dear me yes, all wrong, should be an SU should that" His mates nodded and grinned, but he was only just getting into his stride apparently because he was off again "Now then, what about this wheel?" he declared, and in doing so he took his life in his hands as he all but shoved me aside and bent down as if to grab it. I'd already had enough of this rivet counting idiot, he'd gone too far and I certainly didn't take kindly to being shoved, or for that matter impeded in my pursuit of pleasure. Putting on my most pedantic voice I leaned forward and addressed the little squirt "If you've quite finished with the bullshit, I'd quite like to leave, and you're in my way"

You'd have thought that I'd just assaulted his granny, judging by the way he reacted. He jumped backwards, almost theatrically, and fired back what I suspected was an often used defensive retort. "There's no need for that! I was only saying!" But he was out of the way, and I couldn't be bothered with any more diatribe so I simply gave him a look that I hoped conveyed my displeasure, straddled Daisy's saddle and prepared for the off. She started on the first kick and I gestured for Chloe to climb aboard, but the gnome managed one last shot as we pulled away "I wuz just pointin' out that you've got the wrong wheels on!" he called after us.

The rest of the ride down towards Cilgerran was enjoyable, although there really was a distinct nip in the air all of a sudden. Threading our way along the coast was just as satisfying as our earlier ride on the periphery of Snowdonia, albeit a deeply contrasting experience. Bowling along past the rocky headlands, lapped by a sea that was so very clear compared to our own local stuff back in Ramsgate, the miles soon disappeared beneath us until it was time to turn inland again at Cardigan Bay and cover the last five to the castle, which was our final target of the day. Another site that in theory should be steeped in history, the ruins of this early thirteenth century fortress actually seem to have very few tales to tell. The family that built the thing had all but died out by the end of the following century, and the place had been left empty as a result. It had stayed that way ever since, slowly crumbling away until all that remained were the few lumps that can still be seen standing today.

The place did, however, offer one superb feature that in its own right makes it worth a visit, and that was the stunning view from its high position above, and at the very edge of, the Teifi Gorge. It was a proper gorge too, was that, complete with a fast running river at the bottom, tumbling crazily along its twisted route, over a stone bed that has been slowly shaped over goodness knows how many centuries. From our vantage point we could see a whole series of white water rapids and we could also see a road following the contours of the far bank. I pointed down at the captivating sight and I suggested to Chloe that we really should try to find that road and follow the river. I didn't need to suggest it twice! We went down to retrieve the maps, before trudging back to our eerie to try and get a fix on the surroundings. We were able to pick out features that could be identified on the map, and eventually we could see what needed to be done in order to connect up with that road. With no further ado we were back down at Daisy and setting off once more, looking forward to what promised to be a fully satisfying trundle.

We were not disappointed either, finding our way easily to the river bank at the bottom of the gorge, and then following the route, with steep rock on one side of us and rushing white-water on the other. Bloody marvellous, and absolutely the best possible way to end what had been a superb day's riding. I found that I had let Daisy slow right down, until we were barely ticking along at twenty, because it seemed almost criminal to pass that experience by any faster than we had to. When we reached the little village of Abercych, the road pulled away from the river a bit but Chloe spotted a sign that promised a ford, and it seemed too good an opportunity to miss. We took the turning back towards the river and pulled up for a rest. Chloe soon ditched helmet and gloves and was paddling about at the waters edge as I wondered what to do next.

I didn't trust the ford, so decided to stay the same side of the river for a short distance, looking to cross further down. I wanted to get to Cenarth, just across the river, in order to find a shop so that we could stock up on provisions for the night's meal and breakfast the next morning. The shop was duly found, provided the necessary stuff, but what we also found in Cenarth was a most enchanting and very well appointed campsite. It was just up the road, close to the lovely little village which also boasted a nice big pub, next to a superb white-water section of the river tumbling past just twenty feet away. Again, I was struck by the sheer closeness of the wild geography; the ability to walk right up, touch it, explore and experience it, with no fences, gates or signs to stop us. And with that little lot literally a minute's walk from the campsite, I reckoned we had found the absolute ideal place to spend the night. Chloe agreed wholeheartedly and we headed straight over to the reception building to check-in.

At first, it seemed as though we were going to be out of luck as we were informed that the place was full. I looked out of the windows at the complete lack of people, cars or any other kind of movement and find that hard to believe, but as my gaze took in the plush drive, the nearest (very up-market) caravans, the swimming pool and the plush-looking clubhouse I realize that this was not about space, but image. The particular image that they don't want to be seen, loitering about in their manicured park, is that of a leather clad motorcyclist and his almost certainly tear-away daughter. OK, I could understand that to an extent, but equally I had mentally switched into 'stopped for the night' mode and really didn't want to leave that rather ideal spot. I decided to try a bit of sleight-of-hand and I went outside again, told Chloe what was going on and after explaining my thoughts we hatched a fiendish plan.

What the eye don't see, the chef gets away with. I was taught that rather useful piece of information years ago, and it can be true in so many ways. I could see no reason why we shouldn't test the theory out, by the simple means of removing from sight anything that might distress the campsite receptionist, and claiming our slot by stealth instead. We would achieve this remarkable feat by simply going away until the reception shut, returning in the dark, sneaking Daisy into the very spacious and strangely unpopulated tent area, and obeying the very clear sign, which I had noted by the entrance, which helpfully suggested that 'Late arrivals - if reception closed please report and pay in clubhouse'. I was banking that the staff would different, or would have changed by then and I wouldn't be recognised for the 'orrible leathery motorcyclist who had the gall to try and get in earlier.

It didn't occur to me to consider a plan 'B' as we retired to the pub down the road to wait things out, so sure was I that it would all be fine. In the event that turned out to be an even finer plan than I had thought possible, as we spent a happy hour by the rushing river, me supping a fine ale and Chloe climbing around in the rocks that made up the rapids. But eventually, with the onset of darkness, the time came when we really needed to sort out our spot for the night, get the tent up and sort out some food. The first niggling pangs of hunger had reminded me that we had the ingredients for a big old stew. I finished the beer, summoned Chloe, and we hunkered down to discuss the commando-style insertion that we were about to execute on the campsite.

It was a masterful operation, I enthused to Chloe, as we sat comfortably in the corner of the club house some time later. I had sauntered up the road to do a recce and finding the reception office firmly closed up as expected, we had put our plan into action without delay. We had managed to slide into the place undetected, pushing Daisy into the entrance, up the short drive and into the well kept tent area where there was just enough light left to get the tent sorted out before total darkness had engulfed us. We had the pick of the field, because far from being full, as we'd been informed, there were but three other tents in residence. Chloe soon had the stew on the go and after dinner we showered and dressed appropriately for an evening at the clubhouse, with the only giveaway potentially being my boots. I managed to do them up tight at the top and force my jeans down over the top of them, so they were not too obviously the footwear of Beelzebub himself.

The formality of checking in late was completed without a hitch, making us legitimate residents with a ticket to prove it, and we could then enjoy an evening of unusual comfort. I made the progress call to Chris at home, talking him through the day's high spots before Chloe took the telephone and burbled about mountains, rivers, castles and the drama with the petrol. It was a full twenty minutes before I got the chance to talk to Diane and give my own account of what had been a highly satisfactory day. We'd picked off six Landmarks on top of the previous day's two, and there were only three to go for the full fifty. Surely, nothing could stop us now?

12. The Final Frontier

Six o'clock. That's the middle of the night in terms of my normal routine at home, or at least it may as well have been, but for us that day it was time to get up and get going. There are certain things that must not be hurried however, and a camp breakfast is one of them. Sitting by the tent in the early chill, watching the world slowly emerge into colour from the grey dawn, whilst scrambled eggs, bacon and tea were prepared was a ritual that I was coming to love. It's a moment and an experience that cannot be reproduced at home, and it had become special for that very reason. To be out in the open air, in the misty Welsh countryside, just after dawn, was simply fantastic and as on numerous other occasions during the challenge, where we had done exactly that same thing, I felt a deep stirring in my soul and had never felt so alive.

For Chloe, the magic was different but every bit as satisfying, and I watched her as she played out her own now familiar ritual of stalking bunnies. As before, she returned with the same happy glow on her face and planted the by now expected kiss. I couldn't think of a better way to start a day. As we polished off the grub, we talked through the day's ride ahead and although there were only three remaining Landmarks they were well spread out. We'd have to put a solid two hundred and eighty miles behind us if we were to complete the challenge that day. Easy, if we weren't deep in the wilds of Wales, but we were, so I reckoned this would be quite a challenge in itself.

Once Daisy was all packed up, we pushed her out onto the road to avoid waking the entire site, and thereby reinforcing whatever prejudices they already had. After allowing her to warm up we were off on what promised to be a superb ride down to Carmarthen. But as we reach the rapids down the road, where we had spent the early evening, I was left almost breathless by the utterly captivating sight before us. The gorge at this point runs directly east/west, and the steep rocky sides had captured the early mist between them like a funnel, with the sun rising directly behind it. The effect was entirely magical, creating an eerie glow as the morning light struggled to break through the thick white swirls. We simply had to stop to get a photograph of Daisy in front of rapids at the bottom and our timing was perfect, for by the time I had captured the scene and re-packed the cameras, the moment had gone. The day had arrived.

Off we went again, straight across country, heading southeast and following the river all the way down. There was no traffic on the road at that early hour and we could allow Daisy to lope along at a steady fifty-five through a magnificent twenty miles of sweeping bends, with woodland on one side and the tumbling white-water cascade on the other. Occasionally a lodge or a Hansel and Gretel type cottage flashed by, peeking from the trees, but for the most part it was a long downhill canter through entirely unspoiled countryside. We stopped at several places to enjoy the scenery, because it really was that good, but eventually we bottomed out and left the tumbling green miles behind us. The landscape changed to wide open arable farmland and gentle rolling hills, all the way to the distant coast.

The open fields gave way to the first signs of human habitation as we approached Carmarthan, and we finally reached the point where we must turn east again, for a leg that was going to be as uninspiring as the river valley was exhilarating. We were forced to join the M4 motorway, heading for Cardiff, where our first landmark awaited our attention. I wanted to put that forty mile stretch behind us as quickly as possible and slowly wound on the throttle until Daisy settled at a steady seventy. At least, I was guessing that it was seventy, because her speedometer had reached the limit of it's tolerance yet again and the needle started its wild jumping between ten and ninety mph. A small detail, and anyway it seemed no time at all before we were turning off and heading south towards the coast, a few miles short of Cardiff. The first of the day's trials emerged then, as we coasted to the first roundabout.

I was jolted awake by the first signs of what would become a major setback to the day's travels. A harsh metallic ringing sound suddenly issued forth from somewhere below, making a sharp, insistent 'ching-ching-ching' noise that matched the beat of the exhaust. It was startling enough to make me pull over urgently and stop the engine. Chloe had heard it too, and climbing off she had a concerned look on her face as she asked "What's happened, what was that noise?" What indeed. I had no idea, but it was scary enough that we would have to investigate before going any further. My mind was churning as I crouched down to start prodding around, but the main thought that was pressing itself to the front was "Don't do this to us Daisy, not this close to the finish!" Whatever it was, it was matched to revs, that much but not much else was immediately apparent as we coasted to a halt.

I checked the obvious things first; a loose chain can bounce around quite alarmingly, making contact with chainguard or casings, but a quick feel around showed that both secondary and primary were well within adjustment. Further investigation failed to show up anything hanging loose that could rattle against spokes or wheels and I couldn't find anything obvious that would make that noise. I started Daisy but as she ticked over sedately the noise had mysteriously disappeared again. I cursed silently. Not another bloody evasive problem surely? I'd nearly gone insane with the sprung hub the previous week, and I certainly didn't need to be playing hide and seek with another problem like that, not here, not now.

I grabbed the throttle and gave it a blip, but as Daisy's engine responded willingly, ching-ching noises remained conspicuous by their total absence. I sat back and considered things, but it was obvious that we were just wasting time and in spite of the fact that I was a little uneasy about both the suddenness and evasive source of the now silent noise I decided that we'd just have to press on and keep an ear out for any further occurrences. Next time I'd keep the engine running and hopefully identify the cause. We continued on our way, heading for the coast at Penarth and the first of that final day's landmarks, a medieval village. Finding it was no great chore, but neither Chloe nor I had the inclination to go into the place, settling instead for the all important photographs and another quick poke around Daisy in an effort to banish my paranoia that something cataclysmic and awful was about to befall us. I could still find nothing out of place, and I told myself to chill a bit. That didn't work, because my inner soul was convinced that Daisy's bottom end was about to fall apart.

I suddenly remembered that Chris would be dying to know of progress today, so before we set out for an appointment with the Brecon Beacons, or at least a particular spot nestling somewhere amongst them, we checked in and updated him. But this merely led to more stress, because as I pulled the mobile from it's resting place inside our tankbag, I couldn't help but notice that it was showing eight missed calls. There had been none showing earlier. My heart gave a little jump – it was that feeling one gets when the 'phone at home bursts out in the middle of the night; you just know nothing good will come from the other end. Eight missed calls in such a short time could only mean that either I'd suddenly become remarkably popular or that someone was having a drama and wanted to spoil my day with it. My immediate concern, of course, was that something had happened at home and I fiddled urgently with the buttons in order to list the time and source of the calls.

When the list appeared it was a mixture of relief in the first part because none of the calls were from home and then irritation, as I recognised the number at the office where I had been working recently. For them to have called so many times in such a short space of time could only mean one thing I was sure - captain cock-up had paid a visit in my absence. I decided to ignore it. There were people there that could handle supplier problems, and I knew from hard experience that if I made the call I'd just get dragged into whatever it was that was going on and would probably end up having to spend the next hour making 'phone calls and getting royally peeved in the process. I made the progress call to Chris at home instead, only to find that he'd also fielded a call from the office and had already told them that I was in Wales. Perhaps they'd have taken the hint, I found myself hoping.

Our woes increased immediately when we finally set off again into the busy traffic. The ring-a-ching noise was back with vengeance, and I now knew where it was coming from because it was so very obvious all of a sudden that in fact I was amazed that I didn't make the connection earlier. It was the clutch, ringing out a warning of impending grief, every time it was disengaged. I experimented whilst hopping around in the stopstart traffic, proving beyond doubt that with each action of the clutch lever, the jarring metal ring could be heard, matching the rhythm of the engine with it's own percussion style backing track. We continued with the flow, me with my head canted at a silly angle as I looked down at the chaincase. My mind was already busy furnishing my paranoia with mental images of a host of nasty scenarios, all of which involved a sudden disastrous cessation of forward motion to the accompaniment of a loud and serious metallic clang - which would be the almost inevitable result if I didn't do something about the problem.

I had good cause to be paranoid in that instance, having once suffered a serious incident from a very similar set of circumstances back in the days when, as a young and inexperienced rider I had not had the sense to understand or heed the warning signs. The memory of that incident was urgently tapping at the back of my skull right at that moment, as if had occurred only last week. It was back in the late seventies, my first ever rally on my hard working little Tiger Cub. I had set forth to attend an all British Isle of Wight gathering over the Easter bank holiday weekend that year, and with no previous experience it had seemed like an impossibly long way away. The world seemed to have shrunk since those tender teenage years of mine, because later on in life I would consider such a run to be a walk in the local park, but back then it was a grand adventure that would take me further from home than I had ever been under my own steam. Things like breakdown cover were simply extravagances to the likes of me and even if I had considered the idea, which I hadn't if truth were told, I wouldn't have been able to afford it anyway. Mobile 'phones didn't exist either, so that was a proper unsupported adventure, with the only concession to survival being a real and bulky canvas tent and precious little else.

I had just come off the ferry from Poole and was riding the last few miles to the site. I was feeling like a million dollars because I had made it, but Lady Fate decided to teach me a harsh lesson in why you should never ignore an unexpected noise. To be fair, that little bike made so many strange and eccentric noises anyway, it would have been hard to detect a new and particularly worrying one, but on that occasion the noise I had happily been ignoring in my youthful innocence was that of the clutch slowly coming off. It reached the critical point of no return exactly one mile from the rally site, having finally edged far enough to allow the roller bearings to burst free, dropping the entire clutch drum from it's hitherto solid mounting and the entire drive chain jammed solid. The back wheel had locked up at fifty of the Queen's miles per hour, and we had cavorted out of control straight across the long sweeping bend I had just begun to lean into, coming to a sudden, heart stopping, but extremely lucky halt courtesy of a large privet hedge.

As is often the way of things, that first frightening brush with death had not only served to teach me a harsh and important lesson that I would never forget, but also introduced me to a phenomenon that until that incident I had no previous knowledge or experience of; the mutual support and camaraderie of other motorcyclists. Within minutes of the incident I was being scraped from the bush by a tough looking guy with arms like tree trunks, and by the time we had untangled the Cub there were no fewer than five bikes parked up along the road, with me the centre of a jocular group of riders, who, after initial enquiries had ascertained that I was in one piece, set about a critical but good humoured examination of my rather sorry situation. Questions were fired at me in quick succession, as several of the group prodded around and before long the diagnosis of chain case or gearbox problem was pronounced. By that time, someone had called the cavalry and an open backed pick-up truck had appeared, with four or five big guys in the back. They promptly jumped out and joined the happy throng clustered around the sorry little machine, and within minutes they had hoisted it into the back of their truck and invited me to climb up. We arrived at the rally site with an escort of five or six bikes riding all around us.

By the end of that afternoon, having ascertained that this inexperienced teenager had no clue what to do next, they had pulled the chaincase apart, exposed my frightful lack of maintenance, shown me how to put it back together and shamed me into buying a round of beer for their trouble. They also left me with a lasting appreciation of the motorcyclists' creed and I had understood there and then that we may be a minority, but we stick together and riding a bike means that wherever we may wander, we're never truly on our own. All good and heart warming then, but the important bit of that memory, the bit that was tapping the hardest, was the bit about the wheel locking and cavorting into a hedge. With a twelve year old on the pillion, not to mention the small detail that I'm just too damned old to be doing stuff like that, it was clear that I must investigate things further and do it sooner rather than later.

We pulled over at the first sensible place and as we stopped my spirits took another dent. The 'phone was ringing insistently from it's hideaway inside the tank bag. I ignored it. We pushed Daisy onto a wide grass border by the road, and whilst removing helmet, gloves and jacket I explained the situation to Chloe. The ringing from the tank continued unabated, and was becoming irritating to say the least so I told Chloe that as soon as it stopped I'd turn the bloody thing off. She was far more concerned with the possibility of an imminent, premature curtailing of our adventure however, a fact that was confirmed by her questions; "Can you fix it then?" I mumbled something along the lines of bloody well hoping so. "What happens if you can't?" A good question and 'Hello Mr. Recovery' was the likely option. "How long will it take?" A lot longer if we didn't get on with it was the obvious answer to that one.

Chloe was always game, and not the least bit reticent to get stuck in when it was necessary. She helped me unpack the gear so that we could get to the panniers, and then, once I had pulled out the paltry excuse for a toolkit she was eager to help with the messy bit. As we set to work, she wanted to know what the chaincase kept hidden within it's confines, so I found myself explaining the whole principal of engine, gearbox, and the vital role of the clutch in that relationship. She was hanging on my every word, peering at the gearbox as I explained its function and asking reasonably astute questions. But before we could get to the heart of the matter, the left footrest had to come off, followed by the left hand exhaust pipe and silencer. Chloe helped, holding the spanner on one side while I undid the nut on the other and I was amazed that amidst this potentially challenge-crushing set back, far from being down hearted she looked as happy as ever. I found that her upbeat demeanour lifted my own spirits considerably. In fact, we were actually having fun it seemed, however unlikely that may sound.

A few minutes later we were attacking the allen-screws that hold the chain case cover in place as I enthusiastically declared my love for the simplicity of these old engines. I freely admit that it's a double edged sword, after all if this was a much more modern machine, it's highly unlikely that the problem we were currently investigating would have occurred at all, and we would not have found ourselves having to fiddle about with the thing, but for all that there was a perverse pleasure to be had from the fact that we could, and probably would, fix it. The cover came free, and the case gave up its half pint of oil on the grass, making me feel instantly guilty. But I shared a giggle with Chloe as we studied our now black hands, before turning my attention to the primary drive arrangement, by then exposed in all its glory. At first, it seemed that we were barking up the wrong tree, because it all looked as it should.

Chloe voiced the opinion that it didn't *look* broken, but even as she said it my eyes settled on the four clutch spring retaining screws, and I drew her attention to the shiny marks on their brass heads. There, I explained to her, was the source of the 'ching-ching' noise – those screw heads had been rubbing against the cover. I picked the thing up off the grass, and using some Kleenex from the tank-bag I cleaned the inside of the clutch dome to reveal a perfectly curved groove, about an inch long, worn into the metal. I explained to Chloe that it was not just one of the screws that had maybe come undone, because all four were showing signs of contact, therefore we had to assume that the whole lot had moved, and I could only think of one thing that would cause that. I grabbed hold of the outer clutch drum, or chain wheel as it's often called, and we needed to look no further for our problem. The whole lot was as loose as an MP's morals and was about to do exactly what the little Tiger Cub had done all those years ago. In short, it was about to fall off, but we had caught it in the nick of time!

"So can you fix it?" For the first time since starting the job, Chloe's face showed signs of concern. "Absolutely we can" I assured her, and added that in fact I was mightily relieved that it was that simple. There could be any number of reasons for sudden noises, and although this particular one could have been disastrous if not rectified in time, the process of doing so couldn't be simpler. I talked Chloe through things as I worked: undo and take out the four clutch spring retainers, remove the springs and the cups, lift off the pressure plate, and voila, the locking nut would be exposed. There was a special washer fitted to that nut, which had a small tab that locates into a hole in the clutch centre, whilst it's outer edge bends over one of the flats on the nut itself. This remarkably simple design was supposed to prevent the very event that we were fixing however. It was plain to see why it had failed though - the tab had broken off and was therefore no longer holding the nut in place. It had simply become a bent washer instead. I couldn't do anything about the tab but I could do the nut back up as tight as possible and hope it got us home, I explained all this to Chloe before realizing that in fact it was not going to be that simple.

The nut was buried in a recess deep inside the clutch, in a round hole requiring a socket wrench to tighten it. The only type of spanners I had with us were the normal open-ended type. I tried to marry one up, but there was absolutely no way it was going to fit. I cursed mightily and sat back, staring at the thing and wondering what on earth we could do. The conclusion didn't take long – there was no way out of the conundrum that didn't involve the right tool, so it was clear that we must find the right tool or call those nice recovery people and hope that they carry standard socket sets on their vans. That likelyhood was fairly certain, but I didn't fancy the hour or so wait, so after thinking for a few minutes, I explained a cunning plan to Chloe.

Ten minutes later, we looked a right pair of Charlies I suspect. I was riding Daisy slowly back towards town, with only one footrest, no chaincase cover and a loose exhaust pipe. Chloe was sitting on the back and cradled in her arms was the missing cover, containing nuts, bolts and the other footrest. We were looking for the first place that looked like could lend or sell us the socket-that-fits and luckily we didn't have to search for long before we found, like an oasis in the desert, an old-fashioned type tool and hardware shop. It was probably called Arkwright's or some such, but that wasn't important right then for regardless of name it was just what the doctor ordered. We bumped up the pavement to park Daisy unceremoniously outside the place.

Before we could sort ourselves out and go into the place, the proprietor appeared at the door and it was a relief to find that rather than lambaste us for cluttering up his shop-front, he was far more interested in Daisy. I fact, he had that enthusiast's glint in his eyes. Those eyes took in the obvious in a jiffy, and I found myself describing the events that had led up to our arrival at his shop with a partially dismantled motorcycle. Two minutes later, we were leaning on his little counter where he had insisted that we should join him in a cup of tea, whilst he scrabbled about in the rear of his storeroom looking for something. A little exclamation of delight preceded his reappearance, and in his hand he was clutching a real gem of a find. "I knew I had this somewhere," he said as he proffered the object towards me "and I reckon it's just the job don't you?" What I was now holding was indeed a superb find. It was a little metal carrier, six or seven inches long, and in it was a neat row of five sockets, held in place by a little tommy-bar that acted as a securing strap and handle. More to the point, the sockets were Whitworth and the largest one looked like the exact size we needed.

We were on the road again within half an hour and our spirits were high once more. Our encounter with the little shop and its proprietor had been one of those heart warming experiences that left us one in no doubt that human nature can be the noblest of things. The socket had fitted perfectly and the nut had a stout star washer in place behind it that would hopefully help prevent a repeat of the near disaster. The old boy had insisted that the little set of sockets should stay with Daisy, and would accept no payment for them or the washer. He had been delighted to help, he assured us, and he was strangely pleased that he had 'found an appropriate home for the socket set that he had possessed for more years than he could remember. He made a mean mug of tea too, it has to be said. When we were ready to go, I had in fact felt a bit churlish to be hurrying off after such generosity and had found myself struggling for the right way of saying that we really had to go. Our saviour assured us that he fully understood, having had chapter and verse from Chloe about our adventures while I had worked on the clutch, and brushing off my final attempt to pay at least something for his kindness, he had all but shooed us away from the place telling us that we "had no time lose – get going!"

We were soon out of the built up area and back on the open road. The Brecon Beacons beckoned us darkly on the horizon. Our next Landmark was literally on the very edge of the range and it was another one that we had simply not been able to identify in advance. The plan was the same as all the others; we'd just have to get there and hope that in front of us there was something obvious. It was Chloe who pointed out to me that we'd had mixed success with this strategy, but this time I was fairly confident because our target was in a place where there was very little else, so it should stand out a mile. She was not convinced. We got as far as Caerphilly on a fairly main 'A' road, but then we branched off and into the smaller roads that meandered across the glorious Welsh countryside and Daisy was back in her element once more.

Stone walls flashed past us on either side for miles as we made a leisurely progress, but as we got closer to the map reference there was less and less evidence of population or civilisation and the landscape was opening up before us to display miles of rolling fields, and not a lot else. But after the morning's trials and stresses it was just wonderful to be roaming free once more and I even managed to forget about all those missed calls, with their promise of trouble and yet another opportunity to get frustrated and murderous. The ride from Penarth had been very pleasant, but as we skirted Myrthyr Tydfil from the south things began to get far more interesting. The geography and roads became very much less predictable, with the edge of the Beacons just to the north, and we find ourselves climbing steadily into the foothills, skirting ridges and dipping into the folds, to rise up the other side again amidst a panorama of a rich landscape, mostly green pasture, but dotted with the odd patch of thick woodland and everywhere the scattered evidence of the rocky plateau beneath.

Daisy was having to work hard and I knew now, with all the clutch work, that if we hadn't stopped to rectify that loose nut we would have run into serious trouble hereabouts and no mistake. The scenery was so captivating I eased off the juice somewhat and allowed the old girl to proceed at an easier pace. Soon we had reached the higher point of that area and the road had flattened out, disappearing off into the distance, surrounded by a sparse and hostile looking plain. Sheep were suddenly the dominant feature, dotting the field of vision as far as the eye could see, and the only other notable sights were the dark bulk of the Beacons , still to the north and the long straight row of telegraph poles stretching ahead of us to the horizon. We follow the very straight road directly east with Daisy cantering with ease below us, and soon we were on the last five miles or so to our unknown landmark. In fact, 'unknown landmark' proved to be a very apt description we decided, after turning off to the little village of Trefil and finding almost nothing there.

The computer maps indicated that we were looking for a spot some quarter of a mile out the other side of the village, but this seemed unlikely to say the least when we discovered that the road stopped at the edge of the place. There was a looping track that went up and over a nearby hill peak, but all that was up there was an old stone outbuilding, unremarkable in every respect and currently serving as home to a few sheep. We trundled back into the village, the centre of which was marked by precious little except for a very small shop, where we stopped to check out the clue and seek some more of that priceless 'local knowledge'. The place looked remarkably like a frontier town in a spaghetti western, with it's few huddled buildings and a single dusty road leading out onto the plain. There was even a little dry bush type thing bowling along gently in the wind to complete the deception.

What there was not, was anything that could be described as a landmark of any sort. I tried the shop, and the lady must have thought I was some kind of raving maniac, waving my strip map around whilst gibbering about temples and lost souls. The clue was exactly that; 'a temple for lost souls' it said, but it didn't make me look any saner for the fact that it's written down. I got absolutely nowhere, but we did buy some cokes and bars of chocolate before exiting despondently. Outside, we saw a man fiddling with a tractor in the yard adjoining the shop and so we tried our luck there. No help at all, nothing, no hint of salvation and no inspirational thoughts whatsoever. Wandering back to Daisy we consoled ourselves with the sugar intake offered by our purchases at the shop and generally discussed our options, which were very few. We then watched in wonder as four sheep, followed by a goose, waddled past us up the middle of the road, heading for the plain.

A little boy appeared, probably no older than five or six years old, all short trousers and scabby knees he was, and after inspecting Daisy he approached us and gave us sudden hope as he asked "Are you finding secret things like the other man yesterday?" That sounded promising. The lad was suddenly the centre of our universe! "We are, yes! Was the other man on a big motorbike like ours?" he was, and the lad banished any doubt in my mind that the mystery man was a fellow landmarker when he pointed at Daisy and added, "The other man had a Trump as well". A Trump? Close enough, but more importantly it confirmed that we must be in the right place, or at least fairly close, even though the 'secret thing', as the lad had described it, was doing a bloody good job staying that way. I was about to ask our potential guide if he saw where the other man stopped, or whether he had seen him taking photographs, when he pre-empted the questions with another marvellous youthful observation. "He was funny!" he offered, and then "He kep' going round and round and round and then he sweared into a telly-fone" with that our spy had a good dig around in his left nostril, and having decided that I was not about to put on a similar show, he lost interest in us and wandered off after the sheep.

The memory was obviously the highlight of the lad's week, but to me it was not good news. Clearly our predecessor had suffered the same problem that we were now faced with, and had engaged in a bad tempered telephone conversation with someone. My guess was that he had called Ken and had clearly not been happy with what he had heard if the boy was to be believed. I was going to have to do the same, so without any further mucking around I dug out the numbers and the mobile. I turned it on but got no signal. Cursing under my breath I wandered around waving the thing in the air, but there was simply no service anywhere within the confines of the village. I cursed some more and looked around for a public 'phone box, but that was just a further waste of time. I decided to walk a little way out and up towards that hill, and luckily, after about fifty yards, a single bar appeared on the signal indicator, but walking further it disappeared again so I returned to the spot and it came back. One bar was all we were going to get it seemed, and that only if I stood right there in that exact spot. Itwas enough to have a bad quality conversation so I dialed the number and waited in anticipation.

Mrs Ken answered the summons, recognized my voice almost immediately and after I explained which clue we'd failed to solve this time she delivered the answer without any hesitation. It was almost immediately apparent that this wasn't going to help us however, because the thing we were seek was apparently a Naval Church and I found it highly unlikely that such a place would be buried amidst the foothills of the Brecon Beacons. We compared some of my observations with her notes, and in short order it transpired that we were nowhere near the landmark at all. In fact, we

worked out between us that I was currently some thirty-five miles off course, and should in fact be down on the coast at Port Talbot!

A pregnant silence would best describe my response to that revelation, but as I stood there trying to work out how I could have got it so wrong I suddenly remembered the young lad in the village with his observations from yesterday. Mrs Ken had been very helpful and good natured in my few dealings with her during the challenge so far, and I picked my words with care as I tentatively enquired as to whether any other landmarkers had reported trouble with this one, and suddenly a penny dropped. "Now you mention it, Ken had a call yesterday from a very rude chap who hadn't read the updates to the ……. Oh! … Hang on ….. You've gone to the reference that was misprinted haven't you?" Aha, now we were getting somewhere. "Have I?" I responded innocently. "Don't you read the club magazine?" she scolded me good-naturedly "We printed a correction last month!" Marvellous. I explained that we had been mostly out on the road, doing the challenge in fact, and as such she was quite right, I hadn't yet read last month's club magazine. I appealed for a compromise - I really didn't want to add a round trip of seventy odd miles of back-tracking to that day's already troublesome journey. Port Talbot is back near Swansea, in the direction that we'd come from that morning.

No wonder matey boy the previous day had been upset as he 'sweared in the telly-fone' but I chose an altogether different tack, and played the Daisy card to great effect. Surely they were not going to make me go all the way back, loose clutch and all, were they? They were not. Mrs Ken told me to take a photograph of something in the village where I were, and be sure to make a note for Ken when I submitted my entry. After all, it wasn't really my fault was it, and I *was* at the spot originally published. I thanked her once again for her help, and indeed for understanding, hung up and turned to look for Chloe. She was kicking stones around by the edge of the village, so I strode back to her and updated her on the situation. She reminded me that there was a very clear sign with the village name on it, on the road in and we agreed to get our photograph there on the way out. Five minutes later I was positioning Daisy just so and as I took the photographs I noticed Chloe had wandered back down the road a bit and was giggling.

I look over to where her own gaze was fixed to find a little group of sheep, ears cocked high, examining us from just across the road. Three of them were youngsters, one was a wily old ewe and in a moment of silliness for Chloe's benefit I piped up with a loud "Baaa!" The response was startling. All three lambs immediately responded in kind, and one of them took several springy steps towards us before uncertainty, and possibly with a dim instinct for survival, it stopped again. Chloe spontaneously burst out laughing and I tried the same thing again, only louder and longer "Baaaaaaa!" That time all three took steps towards us and replied in a high pitched bawl. The old ewe was not impressed, and didn't budge, but her youngsters were more than happy to continue what, for all I knew, was a deeply philosophical discussion in Sheep-ese with this pair of two legged strangers. I call Chloe back, but as we get prepared for the road once more we continued our conversation with our new found, if highly improbable friends. Things changed dramatically when I started Daisy. within seconds we found ourselves alone once more, watching the rapidly retreating sheep waddle in their comical way back towards the village. Complete and unadulterated silliness, so it was, but a light moment in the troublesome day for all that.

Twenty minutes later, we were sitting on top of a steep rise, just outside the village of Crucorney in the southeast corner of the Beacons National Park, looking out over a fantastic sweeping view. The last ten miles or so had taken us along one of the best motorcycling roads on that leg so far. Amidst the late summer splendour of rolling green hills and distant dark peaks, we'd stopped for a last long look back before we finally rejoined bigger roads that would take us through Hereford and on up into Shropshire for the penultimate stop of the whole challenge. We could still take our time too, because despite the setbacks we had actually made better overall progress than I had thought possible and we would easily be able to reach the last landmark that day as long as no more time was lost in any incidents like those of the morning, firstly in Penarth with Daisy's clutch, secondly at Trefil and the cock-up with the map reference. We still had some sixty miles to cover to the Shropshire target and from there another eighty to our final spot, but with the time only just past one o'clock I couldn't see us not achieving it.

I realized that I was feeling totally confident about things, due, in no small part, to the fact that Daisy felt more settled and more solid than she ever had. That revelation had come to me on the long sweeping roads through the Beacons, because as we cruised along at fifty-five or so she had felt so uncannily smooth and untroubled that I had suddenly realised that something quite definite had changed since Penarth. My mind had lazily tried to pinpoint what exactly, and it came to me in the end - the vibration had gone! I remembered being bothered by the sudden appearance of a vibration when we were on the first stage of the Scottish leg with Chris. I had fiddled about and checked nuts and bolts but hadn't got to the bottom of it and as the adventure had progressed I had simply got used to it. It had become part of Daisy's general mannerisms. Clearly, if ignoring a sudden noise is asking for trouble, the same logic should be applied to an unexpected vibration because there was now no doubt whatsoever in my mind that the slowly loosening clutch centre had been the cause, and I should have taken it more seriously back then.

We live and we learn, but as I continued my mental cogitation along those lines another interesting thought occurred to me. With enough miles under the wheels of the same machine, one gets used to its little foibles and those little character traits, and it can be too easy to become used to its particular behaviour, rightly or wrongly. To suddenly find and rectify even a small thing can dramatically change the feel or manners of the machine in question, and in this case the change was remarkable enough to be extremely pleasing. If Daisy had been a reasonable pleasure to ride through most of the challenge, she was now nothing short of delightful. I found myself lamenting the fact that I hadn't discovered that before now, because all those long days would have been that much more enjoyable.

What I could do however, was enjoy it from then on, and with the open road waiting patiently for us, stretching away into the wilds of Herefordshire and Shropshire, I prodded Chloe from her dreamy contemplation of the horizon, stood up and indicated that it was time to go and enjoy ourselves once more. It was rather strange, but I became awre of that run down you get, that feeling that sets in at a certain point in any enjoyable experience, such as a holiday. Time seems to step up a gear and it all goes past too quickly with the inevitable return to the hum-drum of our normal existence seeming to accelerate like an express train. The mind begins to re-focus and adjust to the imminent return to banality. An added burden is that we will almost certainly face a mountain of rubbish to catch up on. This is the price for daring to go away in the first place.

It's often said that the thing to do is to save the best experiences of a holiday until last, and this makes infinite sense, but I found myself wondering what that would have been in our case. Scotland was certainly breathtakingly good motorcycling, and maybe that should have been our last foray, but then again Snowdonia and the rest of Wales had been just as satisfying, but in a different way. Devon and Cornwall? Simply marvellous, and what about all those shorter forays into Norfolk, Wiltshire and of course our own back yard in Kent? Well, they'd been equally good, but for very different reasons. No, I decided, it mattered not and it was not over yet, because we may have been leaving the mountains and valleys of Wales behind us, but we were swapping them for the lush green, and very quaint countryside of middle England. Daisy was eager, we were relaxed but more than anything else we were approaching the final hurdles, beyond which was the finish line, the moment of completion, achievement and, when all was said and done satisfaction.

So we'd better get on with it, I reckoned, and firing Daisy up once more, I waited for Chloe to clamber onto her little perch, selected first gear, gave a tweak on the throttle, let the clutch out and we were off, passing through the last few miles of National Park and setting our sites firmly on Hereford. More sweeping roads, rising and dipping as we went, and the barracks town appeared in no time at all. Once again we were embroiled in a long line of choking traffic snaking it's way slowly into the centre.and we found it nigh on impossible to filter through because there were simply too many trucks and vans going both ways. Before long I was fighting to keep Daisy ticking over as she began to overheat and I knew it was time to give her a rest when a slight hint of oil smoke began to drift up from under her tank, leaving a sharp tangy smell in my nostrils. I could also feel the intense heat radiating off her engine leaving a distinct burning sensation on my calves. We saw a big pub up on the left, and although it could only be a hundred or so yards away, it took nearly five minutes to work our way up to it, but finally we are able to pull off and allow Daisy to cool off.

I didn't need to kill the engine as we came to halt, the intense heat had effectively stifled her idler jet, vaporizing any fuel long before it could be sucked into the combustion chambers, and she sputtered to stop all on her own, letting out a loud 'Phshuth' from the carburettor as she did so. I examined the source of the smoke, which was drifting in little wisps across the car-park now she was completely stationary but decided it was no big thing; a small amount of oil had seeped from her rocker spindle and where it had dribbled down onto the cylinder head it was bubbling away to atmosphere as if it was in a frying pan. The heat on my face was fearsome as I peered under the tank, so I reckoned we'd better stop for a while and suggested to Chloe that we should maybe get some lunch in the pub. She never needs asking twice when it comes to food and we managed to grab one of the outside tables where we could keep an eye on Daisy. We sat down and I point out the ripples in the air around Daisy's engine, a real heat shimmer. Chloe was already eyeing up the menu though, which for her was far more interesting.

A relaxed lunch followed, as the garden filled up all around us, and after a while the shimmer was hardly discernable at all. I nipped over to check by placing a tentative finger on one of the rocker boxes, and although it was still too hot to keep in contact for long, it was no longer the furnace-like intensity it had been only twenty minutes earlier. I wondered idly why she had chosen today to overheat quite so dramatically, because we had suffered many a traffic bottleneck before now, and although she had certainly let her displeasure show by way of a bit of lumpy, uneven running she had never been this bad before. I hoped it wasn't a sign of things to come. Wandering back to our table, I noticed that the endless queue of traffic hadn't abated at all and as I was not sure how much further we would have to sit in it before we could break out onto open roads again, it seemed to be a good idea to wait for a while longer and allow Daisy to get properly cool.

I sat back down and chatted to Chloe, finding out that the highlights of her day so far had been the sheep and surprisingly, the fettling of the clutch. She'd had fun helping apparently, and had enjoyed our encounter with the old boy at the shop. No mention of the ride through the Beacons and all that spectacular scenery at all. Strange girl. What was certain though, was the building sense of anticipation, and that was a feeling we both shared. Chloe was eager to know how many miles were left so I sent her off to retrieve the maps and we then sat there happily plotting the final stages. We reckoned it was a hundred and twenty miles, give or take a few and with the realisation that we were so close, we suddenly wanted to get at it once more.

Shropshire has one rather endearing feature, other than some of the best riding to be had anywhere, and that is the place names. It had become a favourite pastime during the challenge, noting the various quaint, eccentric or just damned funny names on the signposts, and the border lands of Herefordshire and Shropshire are easily equal to anywhere else we'd travelled in that respect. As we continued our trek north, we were delighted by Moreton on Lugg, giggled at Weobley and positively guffawed when Hope-under-Dinmore slid past on the signs. It constantly fascinates me to this day where these names came from in the first place, but it certainly made our meandering progress more pleasurable and the time fairly flew by until we found ourselves able to turn off the A49 to complete the last ten miles via Stanton Lacy and Diddlebury (snigger) to arrive relaxed and happy at the equally wonderfully named Much Wenlock, wherein resided our landmark.

Shipton Hall is a sixteenth century manor house, and if we were inclined to go inside we found that we couldn't because it was closed. But we decided that we would take ten minutes out, because the place was set in the most delightfully rustic little village, absolutely typical of the English rural scene. It was also unbelievably peaceful, with the only noise coming from birds scrabbling about in the big tree under which we currently stood. But soon the urge to get on once more became too much, for this was it, the very last leg of the challenge. Eighty miles, one landmark and success would be ours! We'd better telephone Chris at home, I suggested, and I let Chloe do the honours. She looked at the 'phone and with concern on her face she held it up to show me that the missed call count had by then reached twelve! I assured her that we were not going to play that game, not until we had completed what we came to do, because I had an increasingly niggling suspicion that someone wanted to really spoil my day. If I allowed that to happen it would take the shine right off our pending success. It could wait, whatever it was.

Laughably, Chris seemed to be even more full of anticipation than we were. He wanted to know how long the last leg would take, what time would we be calling and wanted absolute assurances that we would 'phone as *soon* as we were there. He got all the answers I was able to give, but I had to stress that the estimated time of arrival was obviously just that, an estimate. I had used our previously agreed method of assuming an average speed of thirty odd miles per hour after the odd rest and the fuel stop that we'd have to make before too long, and that gave us an expected arrival sometime around six thirty in the evening. That was if Daisy had no final surprises for us, of course, but I assured Chris that she had never felt better and that reminded me to tell him that we had found the source of the vibration that had started when he was riding pillion on the Scottish leg. He was far more interested in me shutting up and getting back on the road though, and told me in no uncertain terms to get going without any further delay.

It's strange, but I suddenly felt under pressure to perform, and it was the most peculiar feeling heightened I suppose by my own anticipation of the great moment. Chris was right, the best thing to do right at that moment was to get going once more, because every mile would edge us closer to victory and after all that we'd been through, the highs, the lows and the odd, occasionally near-terminal setbacks, it would be a moment that had been well earned. By all of us. I remembered the very first exclamation that Chloe had used at the start of this last foray, and I couldn't resist using it myself on Chris just before I hung up. I said it loud enough for Chloe to hear; "Right, OK then we're on our way ... To infinity and beyond!" With that, we got going on the very last leg.

It became pretty clear almost immediately that an average of thirty miles per hour may have been wishful thinking. The road we found ourselves on was fairly narrow, which in itself was fine, but coupled with the fact that it was twisty with high banks or a thick hedgerow on either side, effectively killing any forward vision, cautious riding was necessary. But the real problem was the seemingly suicidal drivers that were hurtling in both directions, giving very little consideration to the blind bends and the potential for meeting an equally mad lemming coming the other way. In fact I was appalled at the total absence of road craft on display as we threaded our way through the lanes and before long I was seriously looking forward to getting out onto bigger roads. That was what I think people call a 'rat run' – a local shortcut between two popular destinations, known only *to* the locals, and it was scary. Despite the lunacy, we managed to stay in one piece, finally breaking out of the boonies and onto the A458 just west of Bridgenorth. We were in desperate need of a fuel stop by that time, so I took the first turning into the town in order to hunt down a petrol station. I was glad that I did, too, because hiding along the road was a delightful little town centre and in fact we stopped for a short break whilst we had a little poke around the place. Whilst getting fuel it also occurred to me that I hadn't put any oil in the clutch casing, after splitting the thing earlier. I had thought that the clutch seemed a bit recalcitrant back in the Hereford traffic and it is now clear to me why that had been.

Back on the main route, the plan was to skirt around the west and south peripheries of Birmingham, then cut across country to Royal Leamington Spa, and from there it was only fifteen miles or so to the grand finale. It was no kind of hard work either, as I noted once again how close to the City one could be whilst enjoying some of the best scenery and nicest roads going. Those roads had opened up a bit by then. We seemed to have lost the rat-run syndrome, our final goal was firmly in sight and because Daisy was feeling better than ever I decided that it was time to let her off the leash a bit. Sweeping along towards Kidderminster I slowly twisted the throttle until the burbling exhaust note had climbed to a most satisfactory roaring howl. We passed the seventy mark, indicated by the simple fact that the speedo needle was doing it's wild gyrating dance again, and the wind force on my upper body and face told me that it was time to grin. I grinned, probably enough to scare the locals should any look my way, but it was impossible not to really. Thus did things go for a while.

It was bloody annoying when we reached Kidderminster and had to negotiate a series of roundabouts, but once the other side, we could open up once more and I went for the full compliment of flies in my teeth once again. That all came to a halt with the arrival of Bromsgrove, and then we were threading through the southern brown belt which is a strange mixture of urban built up, a bit of open country, more urban built up, culminating in us getting right royally lost and ending up in solid urban city. I had no idea how I had done it, but we were thoroughly embedded in what seemed to be largely a collection of little communities all rolled into one bigger one. There were a myriad of what I can only describe as separate little high streets, with their own row of shops and amenities, then more residential streets followed by another little high street. And so it went. We have clearly lost the ring road and with no obvious direction to take we were going round in circles in suburbia.

For some reason, the overwhelming tang of curry spices seemed to hang in the air wherever we went. A not unpleasant aroma by any means, but I had never been in a built up area that possessed such a potent and pervasive signature as right there. We were still lost though, so eventually we had to stop and hunt down someone who might help us out of the place. That turns out to be a mistake, because we immediately attracted the attention of a local drunk. As he weaved his way unsteadily straight towards us (well, if not straight then at least firmly crookedly), an unknown purpose clear in his face, I eyed him warily and took a step forwards to put myself between him and Chloe. I knew from experience that these situations can be extremely unpredictable, but I needn't have worried because this was a happy, if somewhat befuddled, drunkard and he was coming over to be mates with us.

"Whoooaaa lookit you on this booty!" was his opening introduction and I relaxed a little bit. He didn't seem to be holding a baseball bat or anything, and seemed to be fairly good natured, but I quietly advised Chloe not to engage the guy in conversation. He finally reached us, via most of the available pavement and a bit of the road. "Issa Bourneville ainnit?" he declared, confusing plain chocolate with one of Meriden's finest, and as he stopped to sway gently before us he seemed to have a revelation inside his head, because his face lit up and he raises a finger in the air. I waited for the next Einsteinian proclamation, but instead he scrabbled about in his pockets to produce a tin of Special Brew, which he promptly thrust in my direction. "'ave a drink!" he said, beaming mightily and displaying a truly scary set of teeth in the process. I cursed silently and tried to think of the best way of escaping from our new chum without upsetting him, but before I could articulate a response he upped the stakes considerably "Gotta flat jus' there" he said, pointing across the road to a dismal looking boarded up basement "You can stay if y'like 'cos blokes like you is al'as welcome in my flat an' I got more o' this!" he waved the tin about in the air.

Bugger. Things were getting awkward and time was ticking by steadily, but I couldn't think of an easy way to extricate us from the situation without running the risk of upsetting our admirer. A happy drunk can become a very aggressive drunk in the blink of an eye if handled incorrectly and with Chloe there I had no intention of risking that kind of a scene. But the decision was taken out of my hands when matey's dazed eyes focused on Chloe, still half hidden behind me, and he leaned round a bit and tried his persuasion on her. "You wanna stay in my flat?" he asked. That set things on a rather sticky path, because the unfortunate thing about youngsters, when faced with a situation that horrifies them, is that they tend not to think diplomatically or look for the careful response that a more mature person would probably adopt. Chloe recoiled from the sudden attention and said basically what was on her mind. "No way!" she exclaimed, and then finished the obvious rebuff off superbly with "Urrgh!"

Just in case that message hadn't been clear enough she retreated behind me and mumbled, in an unfortunately audible way "Can we go now Dad?" That little lot stopped chummy in his tracks, and he looked confused. He was clearly, in his own mind, being gregarious, generous and indeed charitable. He was obviously somewhat taken aback by the less than enthusiastic, ungrateful response to his offer. I needed to take control of the conversation quickly, before he had time to become affronted, and the best way to do that was to lie through my teeth. "Hey, that'd be great!" I enthused, and just to make sure he was is no doubt that we were now best buddies, I took the still proffered tin of Special Brew, opened it and took a swig. While I did that I was making signals behind my back with a wagging finger, hopefully indicating to Chloe that she should not add any more helpful contributions at this stage. I then played my cards in the hope of a clean exit, adopting a conspiratorial tone, and pressing right on. "That's good beer!" I enthused "But I tell you what, if we are going to stop here with you we'll have to go and get a lock for this bike! Can't leave it out here unlocked, so I'd better nip off and get one." He seemed to be buying it so I continued, resisting the urge to babble "Can you hold this 'till we get back, we'll only be a couple of minutes" I held out the beer, hoping to God he'd swallow this rather feeble reasoning, and amazingly he did. In fact he leaned forward, adopting a conspiratorial tone of his own, looking surreptitiously around as he spoke. "Yeah, s'right. Nick anyfing round 'ere they will an' issa nice bike… gotta lock up a nice bike like that 'un." Marvellous.

I signalled Chloe that she should get ready for a quick getaway, before chummy could go off on any tangents. I had Daisy started in a jiffy and with Chloe barely seated I pulled away with a nod and the assurance "we'll see you back here in a minute!" A few streets away, I pulled up once more and looked round at Chloe "Bloody hell, was he one of *your* mates?" I asked her, and was rewarded with "Yeah – right!" and a smack on the back of the helmet. We sniggered for a while, partially in relief that we'd escaped, partially because it was an amusing encounter in retrospect, but we needed to focus back on the fact that we were still no closer to finding our way out of that bloody place. I went for the compass option once more. We needed to be heading east, or southeast and so that's what we'd try to do until hopefully we found a bigger road and some signs. It took us nearly twenty minutes of constant stopstart riding from junction, to traffic lights, to junction and as we struggled with the traffic I couldn't help but feel that this was not how our big finale was meant to be.

I had imagined the last triumphant leg would be a glorious ride through open countryside on a road of sweeping bends until finally, there before us would be Draycote Water, the last landmark, where we would pull up at some idyllic viewing point, call Chris, crack open the bottles and declare ourselves victorious. I had not imagined this uninspiring and progressively tedious experience at all, and it was irksome to say the least. Surely we would break out of it soon, I thought desperately as we choked on the black fumes of yet another bus. Then, just to douse our spirits even further Daisy began to overheat and muck about once again. What a complete anti-climax that was turning out to be. Finally, we found a sign to Warwick and Leamington. "Hurrah! About bloody time too!" I yelled over my shoulder at Chloe, and she responded with a little cheer of her own.

As we left the built-up sprawl behind us, I was amazed to see a sign that informed me that the borough of Solihull thanks me for driving carefully. Solihull? Good grief, that was way off course and I couldn't imagine how on earth we had ended up going so badly wrong. But it mattered not, for we had signs that promised us that Leamington was a mere thirteen miles away, which meant that we were only twenty five miles or so from glory. Daisy, however, was not going to let us finish that easily. She obstinately refused to settle down after the snarled-up congestion of the last hour, and had developed a constant misfire that wouldn't go away. I let her lope along at a very relaxed speed, hoping that she'd cool quickly enough, but after a few miles it was clear that something else was bothering the old girl. We pull up in a lay-by and I checked to see how hot her engine was, but there was none of the bubbling and smoke that we had witnessed earlier and the heat didn't seem to be particularly fierce. I decide to wait for ten minutes or so and allow her to cool off a bit more in the evening air.

It was nearly seven o'clock by that time, and I was beginning to fret a little, remembering that we had no lights and it was becoming increasingly clear that we had better start looking out for camping before long lest we get stranded. The thought of not reaching the final landmark that day was galling, after all we'd been through, but then again it would still be there in the morning, so what the hell. It would mean another night of suspense for young Chris, and Chloe too, but I told myself that staying alive was probably more important. Any doubts regarding the early retirement plan were soon dismissed when we came to set off once more. I was so used to Daisy starting immediately with one kick when she's warm that I was a bit surprised when she didn't. I tried again, with same result, but the third attempt earned me a shock as she backfired violently and her engine juddered to a halt with a loud 'phitt' from the carburettor. Bloody marvellous – less than twenty miles to go and we had this.

I prodded around checking leads and connections, but in the back of my mind I just knew that the bodged points inside the magneto had finally given out once more and I did a passable Victor Meldrew impression, muttering "I don't believe it" as the realisation dawned that it could be quite serious if it was broken points. I tried one more kick, having fiddled about, just on the off chance that I had disturbed something enough to make it all work, but the result was the same. Chloe piped up with the inevitable; "What's wrong *this* time Dad?" but her face showed genuine interest rather than blind panic or disappointment and I found myself explaining the woeful tale of my stupidity and lack of preventative planning.

We huddled down and removed that dreaded cap once more, as I explained my misgivings about delving around inside the thing again. I couldn't shake the niggling feeling that this might *not* actually be the cause of Daisy's current sulking, but by prodding around I could easily break the bloody thing again, just like I had last time. The cap came free and we peered inside, but just like before everything looked fine. I could see both contacts in place, where they should be, and the one that I had bodge repaired was still attached in its proper place. I nervously poked a finger in there and gave the whole assembly a prod, and it wobbles around alarmingly under hardly any pressure at all. Could it be that simple? I dared to believe that it might well be. It looked like the little pillar bolt that retains everything (the same little bolt that I had lost the washer for in Scotland) had come loose again. Any doubt was soon killed when I grasped the thing between thumb and forefinger and wiggled it around, because the entire assembly came off in my hand! That time, I was ready for the little washer and I saw it make its break for freedom amongst the long grass. I managed to retrieve it, and a few minutes of re-assembly, followed by the ministrations of the pliers had it all done up tight once more. Confidence was high, and a test kick before replacing the cap confirmed that all was fine once more. Daisy roared her approval and settled to a steady beat. "Thank Christ for that" I exclaimed, but Chloe was even more pleased with the result and issued a little "Yeeeah!" of appreciation. I wondered what else would go wrong, what could possibly happen in the last twenty miles to stop us, and irrationally I had an overwhelming urge to just get there so that I knew that we had. But a more pressing concern overshadowed those thoughts – we were rapidly running out of light once more! We manage to get through Leamington but as we headed out on the A445 all thoughts of the last landmark were banished as we raced against the sunset, hunting feverishly for a place to camp. We seemed to be in a general farming area once more and I couldn't see any obvious place to scuttle for shelter. We decided to dive off into the lanes in the darkening evening. Eventually, I had to accept that we had been caught out good and proper and, coming across a large pub standing off the road, I pulled in and turned off Daisy's engine. We wouldn't be riding any further that night.

The pub had looked inviting in the late dusk, and I had suggested to Chloe that hopefully, they'd be able to help with some ideas as to where we might stay the night. Inside however, the news wasn't good. There were no camp sites anywhere near, neither were there any B&B's. We couldn't stop where we were because the pub had no land to speak of, just the car park, and the landlord wasn't too keen anyway. We got ourselves drinks and headed outside to consider our options. We didn't seem to have any and I cursed the fact that our adventure should end like that, in disarray. Captain cock-up had truly staked his claim on us, and no mistake. Thinking hard I could only come up with three options, and in the spirit of our adventure I decided to run them by both Chris and Chloe to see what they thought we should do. At least that way a small bonus could be salvaged from the situation because both of the kids would feel that they'd indeed been involved in high adventure.

We made the call, and were soon having a three-way debate. "Right, the options are these. One, we call recovery and get them to take us to a hotel or B&B somewhere. The downside of that is that we'll have to wait quite a while for the man, and we may not be able to get into the first places he takes us. It could be a long and painful evening, and we also have to worry about Daisy's security overnight." They took this onboard, and prompted me for the next option. "Two then, is that we have a walk along this road and try to find a spot where we can put the tent up. The downside of this one, is that we haven't any facilities if we do that, and we might just get moved on by police or somebody." That one sunk in and I pressed on with number three. "Three, we don't bother with the tent, we stay here at the pub until chucking out time, and we simply bunker down at the first spot where we can fit two sleeping bags side by side. The downside to this one is obvious" I leave them contemplating the options and went back inside to get some more beer.

I was depressed and peeved that our last day had come to such a shambolic end, but accepted that there was nothing that I could reasonably do about it and I supposed that it was all part of the adventure really. We'd just have to get over it. I got the beer and strode back outside with a new purpose. "We should call the breakdown people," Chloe declared on my return "That's if we can't fix it," she added. That stopped me in my tracks. Fix it? Bloody hell, why hadn't I actually thought of that? I had made no attempt to carry out even the most rudimentary investigation, and it wasn't as if I hadn't had the time over the past few evenings. The problem really could be as simple as a broken wire or dirty pick-ups, and it wouldn't take long to check the obvious. I felt a bit stupid as I placed my pint on the ground, and it was only right to give Chloe some credit. "Why didn't I think of that?"

First things first then, I undid the antiquated strap that holds Daisy's battery, checked all the wires out and, finding nothing amiss in there, shoved it back on again. Next up were the wires from the dynamo itself but these too looked fine, as far as I could physically follow them. They disappeared under the tank though, and I was not about to try and get that off, what with it's nightmare panel and the spaghetti hiding within. I'm an old enough hand to know that sometimes, just by prodding and fiddling with ancient wiring, the desired result could be stumbled across, so before taking the dynamo cap off I started Daisy, peered hopefully at the ammeter and gave the throttle a few blips. The needle stayed obstinately still. Off with the dynamo cap then, and straight away it was obvious what the problem was when about a quarter of a pint of oily water pours out of the thing!

"Is it meant to do that?" asked Chloe, as she lent over my shoulder and peered at the still dribbling dynamo in the barely useful light from the pub's big sign. "No it's not!" I was surprised that the thing could have collected so much, and kept it sealed inside the lid, but I could see how it had happened. The wires that run from under the tank come down the front frame section and connect to a little block at the top of the dynamo. They enter the cap via a slot which is supposed to have a rubber seal but the rubber had long since perished and it was clear that all that rain in Scotland had found the weakness, funnelled down inside and collected amongst the vital gubbins. Chloe got the Kleenex from the tank bag as I pulled out the little spring-loaded carbon brushes to expose the all important copper commutator ring. We gazed at the emulsified oily mess that was covering everything and then set about cleaning it up. It took a good ten minutes of dabbing, rubbing and then I needed to start Daisy once more to get the dynamo core spinning so that I could press down on the commutator to clean it's entire circumference.

It certainly all looked better than when I had started, but the general impression was still one of dampness. Using my lighter carefully, I played it's flame back and forth across the carbon brushes, and once they were good and warm, therefore in theory dry, I slotted them back in place and stood up to start the old girl once more. I blipped the throttle, but at first nothing happened but then, miraculously, I saw the first blue sparks appear on the brushes and suddenly the ammeter needle gave a jerk. Bloody marvellous! The lights on these old machines are rarely very good, and with a battery that was as dead as Daisy's there was no ready juice on tap to activate them. But once the dynamo was turning fast enough an amount of the vital tingle-juice could get through the system to kick the glow-worms into life. I experiment by turning the things on, and note that at tickover the things barely glowed at all, but a hefty twist on the throttle had them flaring up immediately. As long as I could keep the revs up then, we would have lights, and that meant we could go hunt down a campsite again, or even continue to the next landmark and look for camping nearby.

Either way we were back in the game and we could be pleased with ourselves for not needing to wimp-out on a recovery truck. I congratulated Chloe again for the simple observation that had led me to do what I should have done days ago, and she beamed at me with obvious happiness as she mock-scolded me in response "I dunno Dad, what would you do without me?" she teased. "I'd be a lot richer!" I shot back, and with that she giggled and reached for her helmet and gloves once more. We were ready to go again, but a thought struck me. If we had managed to get lost in broad daylight out in these lanes, finding our way in the dark would be so much less certain. Who cared, I told myself, we were, after all, very nearly there.

It took us half an hour of blundering around in the inky darkness to decide that our quest was hopeless. We stopped at a smallish junction and after a short while of peering at the maps which failed to offer any insight, in the dim glow of Daisy's headlight, I declared that the game was up and we'd simply have to camp at the first bit of flat ground we could find. Chloe looked far from impressed with this latest turn of events, and I tried to keep her spirits up by gibbering something about adventuring, how that was all part of it and what the hell, Chris and I had camped in far more remote conditions up in Cumbria. She wasn't buying, and soon it became clear why, as she bashfully mumbled that she needed the toilet soon for a 'number two' and no way was she doing that out in the open. I quite agreed, not least because it would be a fairly antisocial thing to do, but I didn't have a ready solution to the dilemma either. I stared at the maps again seeking any kind of inspiration. Then an obvious answer to our problems dawned on me, because right down in the corner of my map I noticed Newport Pagnell and in a flash of rare inspiration I suddenly know exactly what we should do. I just needed to work out where we were exactly, plot a course out of these lanes, do a bit of motorway riding and salvation would be on hand. I checked my watch; got a shock to find that it was gone nine o'clock, but decided that it was fine because hopefully within the hour we'd be ensconced in a comfortable, familiar (at

least to me) bar. Time to fill Chloe in on the plan then.

I told her of the many, many times during my working life that I had stopped for the night at the Newport Pagnell services, which possessed one of the very few lodge type motorway hotels with its own bar and restaurant. It was about thirty-five miles I reckoned, but if we could find the big roads, the M45 and the M1, we could be there in maybe forty minutes or so. She looked immensely relieved, said "cool" and simply grabbed her helmet and gloves expectantly. Right, unanimous decision then, and we set off north in search of Stretton-on-Dunsmore, the nearest town according to the signs and very close to the sought after big roads. Five minutes later we were well on our way, with Daisy galloping along at somewhere above the seventy mark, and it was a matter of only twenty-five minutes or so to reach the promised oasis. We checked in with no trouble, I waved goodbye to forty-five quid, but it was absolutely worth it after what had been a long, eventful and at times challenging day.

The next problem was how to secure Daisy. I had no lock with me, choosing to leave the thing at home for this leg as I had been absolutely sure that we would be camping the whole way. These places have no secure parking, and I chided myself for not thinking about that before we went there. I couldn't just leave her unsecured outside. My only hope was to persuade one of the businesses based there at the services to allow me to park her in the secure areas that they always have round the back, but first I agreed to let Chloe into our room so that she could get a bath or a shower on the go. We looked for our room, and found that it was one of the 'outside' rooms, with doors opening straight out onto the car park. As we entered, it struck me that the door was quite wide. Would it be possible, I wondered, to squeeze Daisy through the thing and park her in the hallway? It certainly looked that way to me, and although the management may take a dim view it seemed like a perfect answer to our dilemma.

After unpacking her and chucking the stuff in our room, I set off to the nearby services to look for newspapers, and in short order I was back, laying the content of two of them out to protect the carpet from any unsightly marks. Next I

grabbed some Kleenex from the bag and knelt down outside to give Daisy's underside a thorough wipe. Now for the moment of truth, but there were a few people walking around and as I didn't really want to be caught in the act of what I was about to do, I loitered around until the coast looked clear. Right – go! I grabbed the handlebars, shoved her up to the door, which was a tight squeeze, jinked the 'bars a bit to get past the frame, but she was in! I had to breathe in and do the vertical limbo to get past her, into the room, but we could relax properly now and that thought reminded me that the bar was still open and should be visited without delay. Luckily Chloe hadn't actually finished running the bath yet and I suggested that she postponed the event until after a drink or two. She readily agreed, as she always does when offered free food or drink, and without any further mucking about we limbo'd back past Daisy and headed off for a well-deserved nightcap.

Chloe put in a call to Chris in order to update him, and we all agreed that we'd be in no rush in the morning, looking to reach our final, fiftieth landmark any time after nine o'clock. It seemed ironic after all the anticipation, to have ended up riding past the thing and then have to double back in the morning, but that's the way it was and that's what we'd have to do. It was only twenty-five miles anyway. Victory this time, *surely*, was guaranteed! Chris assured us he'd be waiting by the telephone from nine O'clock onwards, and after that had all been agreed he handed over the 'phone to his mum so that I could update her and have a short chat, during which I promised that we'd be home tomorrow, even if it's on a breakdown truck! We stayed in the little bar until booting out time, after which dinner came courtesy of a fast food joint. We settled for chicken, chips, beans and wedges of some description and having collected that lot we headed off for the luxury of a good hot bath, a spot of TV and a comfortable bed. It wasn't how I had envisaged our last night, but from Chloe's perspective it is just wonderful. She spent an impossibly long time in the bath, and was deeply impressed that there was free shampoo, bubble bath and soap for her to use. There was no point telling her that it's all in the price and therefore not really free and I made do with reminding her that there needed to be some left for me!

Later on in the darkness, laying in a comfortable bed each, we recounted the events of the entire day and all the things that had occurred that seemed to have been sent by fate to stop us. But instead of dwelling on those we ended up sniggering at the memory of the happy drunk. Shortly afterwards I found that I was talking to myself – Chloe was fast asleep. I turned over and drifted into a doze, my last thoughts being that despite the setbacks, all in all it had been one of the most enjoyable days of the whole challenge so far, and more to the point, it had all but delivered us to our final destination.

I woke up to an overpowering smell of petrol and had a mild panic. I had entirely forgotten that Daisy's rather antiquated carburettor design tends to be mildly incontinent, and in the enclosed space, with virtually no ventilation, the fumes had nowhere to go. I dressed as quickly as I could, and opened the large window as far as it would allow, before similarly opening the door to the room. Next thing was to get Daisy out, and I discovered that manoeuvring her out of the narrow opening backwards was a lot harder than getting her in. The next ten minutes was spent clearing up the newspapers, and then spraying the room with deodorant in a desperate attempt to rid the place of the awful smell. Chloe managed to remain oblivious to all of that frenetic activity, snoring gently, quite undisturbed. I took a shower, leaving the front door partially open still, and by the time I emerged again Chloe was stirring from her slumbers. She came fully awake, I waved at her, she pulled a face and by way of a morning greeting she pronounced "Urrgh, what's that smell?" While she showered, I spent the time flapping a towel round the room in an effort to move the air around, but even by the time we were ready to leave there was still a distinct tang to the air. We sprayed a bit more of the smelly stuff around, but there was nothing more that could be done and we took the last of our stuff out to Daisy feeling slightly guilty.

What I should have done the previous evening was run Daisy's engine with the petrol turned off, until the large float bowl standing proud and upright next to the carburettor had emptied. I am of course stupid, so I hadn't taken this simple step. Hadn't even thought about it. I knew that the smell would disappear, with any luck before the next guest stayed, but I found myself hoping that the cleaners didn't go in there before we'd breakfasted and made our escape. I needn't have worried. The cleaners were far too busy having a fag and discussing the latest terrible events to be dreamed up by the script writers of last night's soap operas, and didn't look like they were in any danger of doing any work for a while. We scuttled into the restaurant, but I couldn't help feeling slightly guilty about our dark secret, so breakfast was a rushed affair. Chloe was eager to up and get at it too, and it was only fifteen minutes later that we were heading for the door. The cleaners hadn't moved but it was a relief to be outside and away, and as Daisy warmed up in the morning chill we turned our attention to the last leg of the challenge and hopefully the great moment of success.

We both agreed that we didn't want any truck with the motorway. It was absolutely heaving with the morning ratrace of commuters and no fun was going to be had fighting with that lot. No, we'd go cross-country and as there was a little service exit we'd take that and see where it led before sorting out a proper route to Draycote Water. We climbed aboard, and set off into the misty lanes once more. An hour later, having got ourselves tangled up in the peripheries of Milton Keynes for twenty minutes, we were picking our way through the very last few miles of lanes, searching for our final, much anticipated landmark. For the last ten miles, my mind had been feeding the hungry wolf of paranoia again, nourishing it with visions of potential disaster, a last minute problem to stop us in our tracks so tantalisingly close to our goal. Another puncture perhaps, those points could finally break or a seizure would do it for sure. Irrationally my mind turned every little sound from Daisy's engine into the fear of a sudden cessation of forward momentum.

So convinced was I that imminent disaster was going to strike that I even found myself idly wondering whether we could persuade a breakdown driver to take us the few remaining miles, just for the photographs, before the shameful trek south riding shotgun in a pickup truck. Of course I had no grounds whatsoever to really believe any of this, and it was ridiculous to be thinking that way at all, but even though deep down I knew I was just being daft, I couldn't shake off the feeling. Then suddenly Chloe jerked me out of my morass of misgivings. She'd spotted the lake and the anticipation within her was released in a spontaneous, explosive outburst. "Yeeehaa!" I nearly die of heart failure, because the exclamation was delivered directly into my left ear, which has been keenly straining to pick up any sudden noises from Daisy, but I recovered magnificently as I saw her pointed finger and realised that we had finally made it. "Yeeehaa" indeed!

We parked up by the entrance to the place, and as I dismounted I am almost immediately bowled over by Chloe as she flings her arms around me. "We've done it Dad......we've *done* it!" she exclaimed. I was amazed at the sheer exuberance and joy coming off her in palpable waves as she barely paused for breath. "Where's the 'phone, we've got to call Chris!" I dug the thing out, handed it over, and as she dialed the number with barely contained excitement I relaxed and gazed across at the lake. We really had done it, and I switched my gaze to Daisy, sitting there quietly without fuss, just the odd 'tinc' or 'ping' sounding as her engine and exhausts cool off. I felt a sudden pride swelling in me as I looked at her, and I considered that as far as I was concerned she had earned respect. In fact, I decided, she could blow up now, have as many punctures as she pleased and divest herself of magneto parts at leisure and I wouldn't hold it against her. Yes, *she* had done it and that was that. These thoughts were interrupted as Chloe, face flushed with happiness and pride, shoved the 'phone at me and I turned my attention to sharing the moment with her and Chris. In normal circumstances beer at nine-thirty in the morning would be an abhorrent prospect, but Chris had already opened his and well, why not just this once? We celebrated our achievement in fitting style and just before hanging up the 'phone I call for a toast "To Daisy - and all who sail in her!"

I had mixed emotions on the ride back to our base camp in Cambridge. On the one hand, it had been a great adventure and I had, without any doubt, spent more time with the kids than I probably had in the whole of the previous two years, so wrapped up had I been in the business and my professional life. And not just time together, but real personal time. Talking, planning, laughing, almost crying at times, yarn-telling and most importantly sharing the experiences of the open road. We had certainly come through some challenging times, had overcome many setbacks, suffered exposure to appalling weather, enjoyed the opposite experience of long days in the sun, and we had seen and done things that would stay in the memory for ever. But these happy positive thoughts were tempered by less pleasing ones. What happens now that it's over? What does life have to bring for the next few months, years and God forbid decades? It starts next week, with the kids back at school, my obligation to see a project through that will take me to the other side of the world before the year is out, but what comes after that? I decided that all such thoughts could wait. Right there, right then, I simply wanted to get home, see my wife, Chris, the dog and I owed Daisy a few hours of attention with a bucket of soapy water and a session with the spanners. I just hoped the bloody car would start this time!

Epilogue

October, and as Timmy the RAF Tri-Star made his final descent into Brize Norton, on the return leg from the Falkland Islands, I found myself replaying the events of the summer in my mind's eye, and I liked what I saw. I was loath to let go of the freedom that had been discovered out there on the open roads, and I wanted more than anything else to continue what I'd started with the kids. It was clear to me right there, that I must resist at all costs the pressures, which were considerable, to be sucked back into my former existence. I determined at that moment that this trip would be the last such diversion.

Every story should have an ending, or so I'm told, but that's only true if the end of the story has in fact been reached. For Daisy, the kids and me the landmark challenge was only the beginning. There were other challenges waiting for us, many more roads out there waiting to be explored, the story was set to continue and perhaps the best way to finish this particular chapter is to look back to where it all started, and compare that to where we are now.

Take a peek into *this* garage then. The air may be heavy, but no longer is it due to neglect, that particular atmosphere of neglect that comes from years of inactivity. Peering into the darkness, the shape and outline of an old machine can still be discerned, but this time it's a proud one waiting not for eternity, but simply, patiently, for its next appointment with the open road, wiling away the short time since its last canter and ready to put miles beneath its wheels once more. The dust has had no time to settle, the once-dulled edges are bright and shiny and the slick oil waits, not to become thick and useless, but to be warmed once more by an engine that is ready and willing to work. Shards of lazy yellow light may still stab through the murk, leaking around the door and through the odd crack, and they may still highlight the dust motes, swirling gently around in the dark interior.

But now they cannot settle for this proud example of one of Britain's finest will not rest long enough to allow it. Daisy is a working motorcycle once more, and while her owner is seeking the next challenge, the next adventure, right now she merely dozes.

No, the overwhelming sensation now is one of anticipation.

Printed in Poland
by Amazon Fulfillment
Poland Sp. z o.o., Wrocław